LEROY ROBERTSON

MUSIC GIANT FROM THE ROCKIES

Transitory trials are nothing to the life of the soul.
Leroy Robertson, USC Class Notes, 1946

Leroy Robertson

Music Giant from the Rockies

Marian Robertson Wilson

Blue Ribbon Publications
Salt Lake City

Blue Ribbon Publications is an imprint of Freethinker Press.

Copyright © Freethinker Press, 1996

∞ *Leroy Robertson : Music Giant from the Rockies* was printed on acid-free paper, and meets the permanence of paper requirements of the American National Standard for Information Sciences.

This book was composed, printed, and bound in the United States.

99 98 97 96   6 5 4 3 2 1

———————————

Library of Congress Cataloging-in-Publication Data

Wilson, Marian Robertson, 1926-
    Leroy Robertson, music giant from the Rockies / Marian Robertson Wilson.
        p.   cm.
    Includes bibliographical references (p.   ) and index.
    ISBN 0-9634732-2-0 (alk. paper)
    1. Robertson, Leroy J. 2. Composers—Utah—Biography. I. Title.
ML410.R6245W55 1996
780′.92—dc20
[B]   96-1123
                                        CIP
                                      MN

In memory of my father
Leroy Robertson
who lived the life and made the music
of which I write

CONTENTS

LIST OF ILLUSTRATIONS

Frontispiece, Leroy Robertson, 1947
    Epigraph by Leroy Robertson, "USC Class Notes," 1946.
    Author's Collection

INTRODUCTION

NESTLED in a shallow valley not far east of San Diego and the nearby Southern California town of El Cajon lies "Singing Hills," a popular resort named for the cry of the coyote. It was such a cry that was among the myriad sounds absorbed in the creative mind of Leroy Robertson while he herded sheep as a youth in his "singing hills" of Utah's Sanpete County. The songs are always there, but only the true listener enfolds them.

Much has been made by musicians and writers, including the meaningful reference by the author of this lovingly assembled biography, of that tender boyhood period in Robertson's life. Stored at that time within the youth were the sounds of mountain grandeur, of the meadows, the rivers, the rills, the wildlife and the elements. The collection was enhanced during the young musician's prep school days in Pleasant Grove at the foot of Mount Timpanogos and on the doorstep of Brigham Young University, later to be a long-time home for teaching. Long before Oscar Hammerstein put the words into a most popular Broadway musical, Leroy Robertson was well aware that "the hills are alive with the sound of music."

This early developed background became a natural foundation on which Robertson achieved greatness as a truly American composer. Boris Kremenliev, once chairman of the Composers Council at the University of California at Los Angeles, looked upon Robertson as a "native Westerner who has always looked to his beloved mountains and majestic surroundings for his inspiration," and in an early 1952 issue of *Music of the West Magazine* declared him to be "one of the few truly American composers."

Writing of Robertson's prizewinning *Trilogy* on its premier in 1947, Russell MacLaughlin of the *Detroit News* hailed the work as "a constant blooming . . . fresh and free and altogether American." A

Detroit Free Press critic added that "there are climaxes as moving as the snowy peaks of the West that gave it birth; there is a gusty sort of humor that springs only from the American soil."

As innate with this American composer as his attachment to music was his integrity, his modesty, a deep humility, and his incredible penchant for learning. His greatest desire, the bringing to life of the music he nurtured within, was charged with learning, expectancy, excitement, and wonder. He hungered for knowledge and found it with such greats as George Whitefield Chadwick, Ernest Bloch, Ernst Toch, Hugo Leichtentritt, and Arnold Schoenberg. Even after his success with *Trilogy* he continued his schooling, receiving his doctorate at the University of Southern California nearly seven years after receiving the Reichhold prize. The degree was granted January 27, 1954; the dissertation was *Oratorio from the Book of Mormon*.

Some two months earlier Robertson was presented at neighboring UCLA in two seminars and a public lecture. On the front of a program he sent to me were two significant notations:

"Book of Mormon recordings made a deep impression here."

"World's leading composers on this series—I was followed by Villa Lobos of Brazil."

So it was that Leroy Robertson found himself among his peers, enjoying a spot in the sun as he brought to a climax his feast of knowledge. What he did with that learning in a life devoted to creating the music that occupied his being is faithfully related in the pages to come. He was a complete musician, his creative talent unmatched among Utah musicians. He gave his beloved homeland a musician to be counted with the greatest of his day.

Conrad B. Harrison

PREFACE

JUST after my twenty-first birthday, father asked if I would one day write his biography. Having already achieved both national and international renown as a composer, he felt his story might interest others. He explained that he was, and would continue to be, too busy with more pressing projects to take on the task. Somewhat awed by his request, I answered, "Yes." Inevitably tinged by the multitudinous memories of a daughter and appearing 100 years after his birth, this book now stands as a fulfillment of that promise made so long ago.

Because throughout his lifetime Leroy Robertson was very actively and intimately involved with many phases of music in Utah and the surrounding states, I have endeavored to tell not only of his life and compositions, but also portray what the musical scene was—and wasn't—in the Intermountain West, how it changed during the twentieth century, and how this resolute man contributed to its astonishing development.

Over the years, father helpfully supplied me with significant documents. I, in turn, sought out supplementary information from everywhere imaginable. As a painstaking research scholar, I tried to leave no stone unturned in my efforts to base the biography on material with as wide a scope as possible. The selected bibliography indicates the extent and variety of the sources consulted.

Apart from this published text, there is a companion manuscript which, while having the same narrative, contains documentation much more complete than that given here. In this lengthier manuscript, virtually every sentence has at least one reference number; the chapters usually have more pages of extensive endnotes than narrative; and there are eleven appendices that provide useful, additional information. But printing such a big work would have proved impractical. Therefore, for those wishing this supplemental material, copies of the companion manuscript have been placed in the Manuscripts Division of Special Collections at the University of Utah Marriott Library, in the Special Collections and Manuscripts of the Brigham Young University Lee Library, and in the Archives of the Historical Department of the Church of Jesus Christ of Latter-day Saints (the Mormon Church).

For titles of compositions, I have followed the format established by Eric Fenby in *Delius as I Knew Him* (New York: Dover Publications Inc., 1936 and 1981). Titles of larger works are italicized, while those of shorter works (songs, anthems, etc.) are placed within quotation marks. In order to write a narrative both vivid and well paced, I have woven some quotations into this text without indicating any source. For all citations, full credit as to persons, places, and dates can be found in the endnotes of the aforementioned companion manuscript. Except for the policy just noted regarding titles of compositions, the original orthography of all citations has been scrupulously maintained.

So many people helped along the way that it is impossible for me to name each one individually. However, I would like to acknowledge and thank the staff in the LDS Church Archives Historical Department, who quickly and readily provided specific data otherwise unobtainable; the staff in the Special Collections and Manuscripts at the BYU Lee Library, who generously made available to me all their materials concerning Leroy Robertson; the staff in the Manuscripts Division of Special Collections at the University of Utah Marriott Library, who freely gave me full access to the Leroy Robertson Collection; father's numerous colleagues and students, who enthusiastically related their own personal experiences with him; and his brothers and sisters, who happily reminisced with me about "their" Leroy. In addition, I would like to thank my mother, the late Naomi N. Robertson, who recounted many rich anecdotes; good friend Conrad B. Harrison, who wrote the beautiful introduction; Michelle L. Whitesides, who patiently and meticulously typed the large companion manuscript; and Stan Larson, who supervised the bibliography, compiled the index, and who as editor skillfully guided the entire publication. Finally, I offer a very heartfelt thanks to my late husband, W. Keith Wilson, whose unstinting and unselfish support in every way truly made this book possible.

And now, to this biography, long labor of love, I say "Godspeed."

Marian Robertson Wilson

PART I

FROM THE HIGH MOUNTAINS OF UTAH

PROLOGUE

In 1923 Utah had a high school named North Cache, and it was located just south of the Idaho border at Richmond, a small rural community in the fertile Cache Valley. North Cache students were by and large farm kids, children of the land who worked hard helping tend the crops and animals from which their families made a living. They were big, strong, high-spirited, prone to pranks and high jinks. One of their favorite pastimes—which indeed had almost become a tradition—was to gang up on the school music teacher and make life extremely miserable for him (or her) by turning music class into general bedlam. In fact, due to their well-organized disrespect, the students had been so successful the previous year that two or three hapless musicians had come and gone, and already, just three weeks into this new school year, yet another had left in discouragement. They were now turning their sights on the new replacement recently come to town, wondering how long "this one" would last and confidently anticipating another abrupt departure.

The new teacher did appear to be an easy mark. A young man himself, standing taller than six feet though a bit stoop-shouldered, and barely tipping the scales at 130 pounds, he certainly could not compete in brawn and muscle with the Cache Valley teenage boys. Bespectacled and clean-shaven, he kept his fine, black hair meticulously slicked straight back, and nearly always wore a dark well-pressed suit complete with white shirt, stiff collar, and bow tie. Just graduated from the New England Conservatory of Music in faraway Boston, he showed a refinement and dignity not often seen by these down-to-earth Mountain West youngsters. Furthermore, his credentials described him as a composer and violinist. Truly, this latest music teacher, this quiet Leroy Robertson, would make a good target for their high school shenanigans. Little did they realize that he had arrived forewarned and forearmed with a combat plan of his own. Even less could they ever have imagined how stubbornly committed this man was to making good music wherever he found himself.

At the designated hour of his first class, most of the entire student body tumbled into the music room. And what a bare room it was, with only a piano in a far corner and a chalkboard on the front wall. There were no instruments, no music stands, no music, not even a single song book.

As the bell sounded to signal the beginning of class, the door opened and into the brewing mayhem stepped Leroy Robertson. Without so much as a glance either to the right or left, he strode directly to the piano and with all his might struck one note as loud as he could. Catching everyone quite off guard by this sudden sound, he startled the students into momentary silence, and at once began peppering them with questions: "What is the name of the note you just heard?" "Who can come and write it on the board?"

These were new and strange ideas. Never before had the students considered naming notes or transcribing music. Deftly, Robertson drew a staff and clef on the board, quickly wrote the note, announced that it was "middle C," and then commanded, "Sing it. . . . Everyone together now. . . . Listen, get it in tune, listen to each other, sing together. . . . Sing. . . ."

Somehow, with all the attention focused on this quick-thinking teacher, the incipient troublemakers lost their following. Robertson, always just one step ahead, kept everything going so fast that no one could think of anything except learning music. Directing the students to sing as he wrote, he methodically proceeded from one note to another, carefully constructing a series of simple chords. The youthful voices responded. The sounds were rich. The youngsters liked what they were hearing. Already a chorus was in the making.

As the hour progressed, Robertson challenged different members of the class to step to the board and try their skills at musical notation. Not wishing to appear cowardly before their classmates, they shrugged and grinned as they came forward to try their luck at this novel task. Before they knew it, class ended, and the enthusiastically conceived plans for rebellion never materialized. Robertson had clearly won the "Battle of the First Day."

During the days and weeks that followed, this new music teacher continued the work of that first crucial hour. Because they had no instruments, he taught his students to sing. Because they had no music books, he simultaneously taught them how to create their own songs. First came the words written by the class under Robertson's guidance, and then came the music, especially composed by the teacher right on the spot before quizzical eyes and ears. Soon these farm kids were regularly bringing in simple poems about what they knew and loved: the land, the fields and animals, their homes, their town, their school. And every day as they trooped into class with their latest contributions, they could hardly wait for Robertson to take these words and set them to melodies made almost as if by magic just for them. No one else had tunes quite like these, and the boys and girls of North Cache learned to sing "their songs" with pride.

One day when a big red-headed lad—one of the chief pranksters and a prime mover in the old revolt—timidly brought in a paean he had written about his prize heifer, Robertson immediately put it to music and taught the class to sing it. Thereafter this boy was one of Robertson's staunchest champions. And again, when this adroit music teacher took the four main ringleaders aside and organized them into a male quartet that was soon ready to perform before classmates and parents, he scored yet another victory. Teenage defiance turned into respect. In no time at all, Robertson emerged triumphant. The longstanding "War Against the Music Teacher" finally and definitively ended.

Whatever had brought such a musician from urbane Boston to the beautiful but remote Cache Valley? That story has its beginnings nearly twenty-seven years earlier in another high valley of the Utah Mountain West.

Chapter One

PIONEERS AND INDIANS

LEROY Jasper Robertson[1] was born just a few days before Christmas, December 21, 1896, to Jasper Heber and Alice Almyra Adams Robertson in Fountain Green, Sanpete County, Utah. There are no records to tell whether it was a clear or stormy day, but one can be certain that it was very, very cold, for this little Mormon community is nestled low on the eastern slope of Mount Nebo—one of Utah's highest peaks—in a narrow Alpine valley where in winter the temperature often used to drop to forty degrees below zero. Surely, on this, the shortest day of the year, the snow had drifted high and deep.

Leroy descended from persevering pioneers who settled themselves literally on the cutting-edge of the raw western frontiers of Central Utah.

His maternal great-grandfather, Matthew Caldwell, as a member of the Mormon Battalion, had made the 2,000 mile U.S. Army march from Fort Leavenworth to San Diego, while three of Leroy's grandparents crossed the plains with subsequent groups of Mormon immigrants to Zion.

Many stories of their adventures remained as part of the family tradition for generations. There were tales of how Battalion-member Matthew became ill from marching in the desert sun and gulping

---

[1]In various LDS Church records Robertson's first name is listed as both "Le Roy" and "LeRoy," and for many years he signed his name "LeRoy J. Robertson." However, during the last half of his life, he adopted the shorter and simpler form, "Leroy Robertson." This latter form will henceforth be used throughout the biography.

brackish water from small isolated water holes as he tried in vain to cool his parched body; and there were tales of how Matthew was among the first army troops to discover and bury the remains of the ill-fated Donner-Reed party. "The most awful sight that my eyes were ever to behold," he wrote later.

There was also the story of the young girl with long red hair, driven mad by the torture of the daily trek, who always had to have two men from the company walk at her side to guide and restrain her. One day as they all trod the plains, an Indian brave on horseback suddenly appeared on the near horizon. With the men momentarily distracted by him, the young girl wrested herself free and ran towards the Indian, who swiftly swept her up onto his pony and galloped away. The last thing anyone saw of the girl was her long red hair flying in the wind.

Leroy's Grandmother Robertson, Hanna (Johanna)—pregnant and disowned by her parents for becoming a Mormon—left her native Sweden to seek refuge in Zion. On her twentieth birthday, far from home and family, she bore her first child on the prairies of Nebraska en route to the Salt Lake Valley. Leroy's grandfather, Edwin Robertson, walked with his brothers and crippled mother from Illinois to Utah, where he met Hanna, fell in love, soon married her and adopted her infant daughter as his own.

Leroy's maternal grandmother, Melissa (Matthew's daughter), was the first white child born in Utah Valley, and this in a shallow cave hollowed out from the side of a ditch bank on a bitter day of early spring. At age two, Leroy's maternal grandfather, Will Adams, sailed with his parents nine weary long weeks from Dover to America, and within the year made the long trek with them from Iowa to Utah. Some twenty years later he met and married Melissa before she turned eighteen, and took her away from her parents to make a home in the remote Fountain Green Valley.

Indeed, both Edwin and Hanna Robertson, and Will and Melissa Adams were among the earliest settlers of this region, which soon had the town of Fountain Green as its center. The Adams took up farming while the Robertsons went into the sheep business.

The Robertsons made their home in the north end of town, and a good home it was, complete with parlor, summer kitchen, and big front porch. Here they reared a family of eleven children, with Leroy's father, Jasper, being their first son to survive infancy.

The Adams at first resided on a farm several miles south of town, but after some dozen years, Will built a fine red brick house in Fountain Green not far from the Robertsons. Will and Melissa reared a family of eight children, with Leroy's mother, Alice, being their second child.

During their years on the land south of town, the Adams had a number of frightening experiences with the Indians, who would often come in tribes to their little home, threatening and demanding food or land. Melissa frequently recounted how one day when she was home alone caring for her first-born, a tall Indian buck came right into her kitchen. Seeing no one else around, he braced his back against one side of the open door, blocked her exit by extending his arm across to the doorjamb opposite and began to utter threats against her. Fearing for herself and her baby—but not betraying her feelings to the Indian—she quietly took the child into her arms, and then, abruptly ducking under the brave's outstretched arm, she dashed from the house like a streak of lightning and went running towards the fields where the menfolk were working. The surprised Indian did not give chase.

On another occasion some years later, when Melissa and Will had to go into town to exchange eggs and butter for cloth and other supplies, they left ten-year-old Alice with her younger brother and sister to take care of things. A tribe of Indians rode up, tied their horses to the rail outside, and approached the house. The children, scared to death, turned white as sheets. Alice, remembering her parents' instructions, immediately put the two little ones to bed; then when the Indians came to the door asking for the "White Squaw," she replied that the squaw was "sick, very sick," and pointing to her pale brother and sister in the bed, she continued, "And the children are very sick too." Thereupon, the Indians, who were greatly afraid of the white men's diseases (diphtheria, typhoid fever, small pox), departed at once, leaving the trembling children unharmed.

Fountain Green eventually became a town of about 1,500

people, and at one time it was numbered among the richest communities in Utah thanks to its many well-to-do sheepmen. Early on, the good citizens somehow classified themselves into three distinct social groups. There were the sedate "Lower-enders" of the southern or downtown area, who were acknowledged by all as the city's aristocrats; and there were the "West-enders," descended from a large family of Indians intermarried with non-Indians, who played mandolins and guitars, danced hoedowns all night long during the winter, and in general seemed to have more fun than anyone else; and lastly, there were the "Zion's Hillers," that indefatigable middle class, ensconced on Zion's Hill at the north end of town. Here the Robertsons and Adams were to become prominent citizens.

Fountain Green was also visited from time to time by colorful gypsies, who would camp near Zion's Hill with three or four wagons trailing six or seven horses. Keeping to themselves, they only came into town to trade a horse for a cow, or beads, or anything else, but their exotic costumes and ways added an aura of excitement to the routine of the town. Another kind of excitement stirred the inhabitants of Fountain Green when roaming Indians would descend upon the town and boldly stop at many homes to ask for a handout. Partly in fear and partly in sympathy, the housewives always gave them a loaf of bread, a pound of butter, or some such item from their larders.

Although each section of town was clearly identified, the people were not segregated. They all went to the same school, the same church, and the same weekly dances, which were truly the highlight of Fountain Green's social life. Here all the folk in the valley—from the venerable elders to the tiniest infant—congregated every Saturday to dance in the Amusement Hall, with its one room heated by two big round stoves at each end and lined with benches that were practically filled with young babes wrapped snugly and left to sleep while their parents cavorted to the tunes of the fiddler.

Such was the place where Leroy's parents were born, and such were the people among whom they lived. As a young man, Jasper Robertson worked with his father and brothers in the sheep business. He herded sheep, and when they camped on the mountain west of Fountain Green (West Mountain), he regularly walked the many miles from the herd into town to fetch supplies. Later, he was able to afford two herders and a camp-mover. Jasper also acquired some farmland north of town where he raised alfalfa and grain. He was such an efficient farmer that during haying season, he eventually kept three teams of horses and eight or ten men busy hauling hay.

For her part, Alice Adams learned the skills of a frontier farm woman. Like her sisters and brothers, she had a beautiful voice and could sing extraordinarily well in tune. She was a member of the ward choir and was a faithful soloist in the Relief Society. Alice often heard about her paternal grandmother, Martha Jennings Adams, who, as a young girl in England, had been a leading soprano soloist in one of London's great cathedrals.

Jasper and Alice were married June 28, 1893, in the Latter-day Saint Temple at nearby Manti, and Jasper took his bride to a small brick home that he himself had built on Zion's Hill within short walking distance of both their parents' homes. Three and one-half years later, their first child, Leroy Jasper, was born.

Chapter Two

THISTLE ROOT INSTEAD OF CAVIAR

LEROY'S birth was a big event for the Robertsons. Not only was he the first son and eldest child of Jasper and Alice, but also the first grandson to carry on the Robertson family name. Arriving as he did just a few days before Christmas, this little boy must have been a most welcome holiday gift.

He was a very high-strung baby, uncommonly alert and curious. From the beginning, music had an extraordinary hold upon him. Many years later, he wrote of himself:

> I was a howling baby. My parents said the only sure way they could hush me up was to hold me near the fiddler at the town dances. Then I was enraptured.

Jasper and Alice were loving parents. Alice cared for her son "just as if he were the only thing in the world, watching over his welfare day and night, talking about him, praying for him, ever doing those things which only a fond mother can do for her child." Leroy was truly the center of attention for the entire family: his parents, grandparents, and the many uncles and aunts living on Zion's Hill.

One day, when he was but a toddler, Jasper and Alice took Leroy to a gala picnic held by the townspeople on the "green," and somehow in the excitement, the little fellow wandered away from his family. Frantic at missing their infant son, Jasper and Alice cried out, and soon had everyone looking for the child, shouting his name in all directions. As time went by and the search yielded no Leroy, his distraught parents feared the worst. Had he wandered out into the road or a nearby barnyard? Had he fallen into the stream or headed towards the mountains? After what seemed an eternity, an uncle finally spotted Leroy close by, right on the "green." There he was, standing on the bandstand motionless in front of the town band, tiny hands clasped behind his back, intently watching and listening to the players. He had heard the music, and following his ear, had made his way to it. So enchanted was he by the sights and sounds of the performers that he was oblivious to all else.

At about this same time, along with his compelling love for listening to music, Leroy also showed a striking talent for making it. He could play any tune he heard on the family organ, i.e., he could play if someone would oblige him by pumping the pedals since his legs were far too short to reach them. He quickly became the only grandchild with ready access to the secluded parlor where the organ stood, a room customarily opened only to special guests. Here the small child would amuse himself for hours, more often than not devising melodies of his own.

Leroy became a particular favorite of Edwin, his "Grandpaw Robertson," and between the two there developed a very close bond. Edwin would hold the boy on his lap, feed him forbidden goodies, and amuse him by telling fantastic stories, usually of his own invention. Edwin always wore an enormous gold pocket watch, so precious that no one save him was allowed to touch it. But he readily made an exception with Leroy, who had become enamored of the shiny round object. The doting grandfather would often let his inquisitive grandson hold it and listen to it ticking. On one occasion, Edwin even permitted the wondering child to dismantle this intriguing timepiece just because Leroy wanted to see if he could put it back together. Of course the small boy couldn't, but Grandpaw didn't seem to mind.

As soon as Leroy was big enough, Edwin used to take him along every day to help herd the cows up on the Divide in the canyon northwest of Fountain Green. The two made quite a picture as they tramped together towards the mountains, the little grandson holding fast to his grandfather's large, protecting hand, trotting rapidly along in order to keep up with the older man's broad and steady stride. During these hikes Edwin showed Leroy firsthand how to live with nature. He taught the boy how to gather berries, how to whittle, and how to strip bark from thistle root so as to eat its succulent, though bitter fibers. He taught Leroy passages from the Bible, quoted to him from the Declaration of Independence, spoke to him of justice and truth, and all the while spun out remarkable stories of his own adventures, both real and imagined. Many years later, Leroy would soberly state that if he possessed any greatness at all, it was because he was "raised on thistle root instead of caviar."

Leroy was also greatly influenced by his parents, who were strong and good people, "all wool and a yard wide," as the saying goes. Throughout his life many of their characteristics would appear in him.

From his father, a strong and courageous man, he inherited a spirit of honest perseverance. Jasper, described by his peers as the most decent of men, never cheated anyone out of a penny. Indeed, every man who ever worked for him attested to his integrity. As soon as a man had finished his job, Jasper paid him in full, something quite different from some of the wealthier Fountain Green sheepmen, who would keep their herders—young boys for the most part—hanging without pay for weeks on end. But, on the other hand, neither would Jasper tolerate a shirker. He expected a full day's work for a full day's pay. Once, when he found a man whom he had hired sleeping under a tree, Jasper upbraided the idler in a sharp, even devastating way. But the man's brother said he deserved such a tongue-lashing.

Furthermore, Jasper had high standards for everyone, constantly repeating that "if things were to be done at all, they were to be done well." And for this man of rock-ribbed honor, his word was truly his bond. He taught his children over and over: "Your word is the greatest asset you can have. When you lose your word, you've lost everything."

He not only spoke, but lived that principle, and each child admiringly remembered and recounted many anecdotes about how their father kept his word. As adults, if any of Jasper's children ever wondered about following through on a promise, they were quietly reminded, "You know what our father would say, don't you."

Jasper also possessed a certain raw courage. Fountain Greeners long repeated the story of how he stopped a runaway team that was hitched to a carriage in which a little girl had been left alone. For some unknown reason, the horses bolted, and Jasper, racing towards them, managed to jump on one of the singletrees, grab the reins, and pull everything to a halt—as much from the force of his willpower as from the strength of his body. Needless to say, he saved the little girl's life.

This man provided well for his family. Their furniture was not fancy, but was solid and of the best quality. The big black kitchen stove, with its broad cooking surface, ovens, warming ovens, and reservoir to hold and heat five gallons of water, would have been a luxury item in any household of that day. As the family grew, he added new rooms to the house, and eventually a second floor to provide more bedrooms and storage space.

In the barn Jasper kept a beautiful team of white horses, "Prince" and "Mag," which were his pride and joy; and the two-seated buggy they pulled was considered the "Rolls Royce" among carriages of the day. It was black, had curtains on each side that could be fastened up for protection against storms, and two large kerosene lamps on the front to light the way after dark (but Jasper never used the buggy at night so the lamps were never lit).

Nonetheless, although Jasper always bought the best equipment possible, he was a frugal person. Both he and Alice were "very particular" with their means, and took very good care of whatever they had. Alice made everything "go the full mile, and never wasted anything, for she never had anything to waste."

This lady was a good companion for Jasper. Like him, she was extremely well organized. Later described by Leroy as "beautiful and highly artistic," she had to have everything "just in order," and kept her home and yard immaculate. She sewed all the clothes for the family, at first by hand, then later with a grand treadle machine. Along with the work inside, she had regular chores outside the house as well, such as feeding chickens, gathering eggs, and sometimes milking the two cows.

At haying time her work was especially heavy, for Jasper insisted that all who labored with him in the fields dine at his table, and Alice did all the cooking. Her pies were unmatched. And to insure a supply of food throughout the long winters—both for the family at home and the men away at the sheepherd—she bottled meat (freshly slaughtered mutton and pork), vegetables, and fruit (never less than three or four hundred quarts). At pig-killing time, all the bacon and hams had to be cured, and the lard rendered out for soap and other things.

When Leroy was nearly four years old, a little sister, Ora, was born, and by the time he was nearing his thirteenth birthday, there were two more sisters and a brother in this close-knit family: Wanda, Macel, and Joe.

Leroy began his schooling just before age six in Fountain Green's only school, which had but eight grades. He was extremely eager to learn, and it soon became apparent that nothing ever thrilled him quite so much as becoming acquainted with new facts and ideas. He excelled in mathematics, and often would aver during the last years of his life that if he "had it to do over again," he would have majored in mathematics along with music. He did love to read, but aside from his textbooks, he had only the standard reading material common to every Fountain Green home: an imposing family Bible, which he readily devoured, and regular issues of the *Farmer's Almanac*. How fervently he longed for something more to study. On the lighter side of his school days, it should be noted that Leroy—tall, never husky, and of wiry build—was a natural sprinter, and early on, he became a most valued runner and southpaw pitcher for the school baseball team.

When not in school, Leroy worked and played with his brother and sisters and the other children of Zion's Hill. They all spent a lot of time together on "the knoll," a hillock completely covered with sagebrush and juniper just behind the Robertson home. While the girls played at gentler games, the boys went "hunting Indians," the "Indians" being tumbleweeds scattered and hidden about. They formulated elaborate strategies for capturing "the enemy," "guarding the flank," and bringing back the dreaded foe. But when they returned from these grand forays, they usually found Leroy seated under some juniper, exactly where they had left him, intently working out some new tune that had just come to his mind, or else whittling out a fiddle.

However, Leroy did join in teasing the girls. Nor were Leroy and his chums above stealing apples from the orchard of a certain good "Zion's Hiller." Indeed, so deft were they that the only time they ever got caught was when a boy from the Lower End came up to help them.

Within the Robertson household, Leroy somehow naturally became the leader for his brother and sisters, and as the big brother, he really felt more concerned for other members of the family than for himself. Jasper and Alice had carefully drilled into their children, "If you have something, and the other one needs it more, share it." For example, occasionally when the family would get one or two bananas—a truly exceptional treat—it was Leroy who would meticulously slice the fruit, then count and distribute to each child one slice apiece until everyone received exactly the same amount of the precious delicacy.

When the family dog, "Old Shep," died, it was Leroy who enlisted Wanda to go with him to perform the burial rites. With great solemnity and ceremony, the two heartsick children carried their old friend up to the rocky ridge in the fields above their home, placed him in a grave, said a few sincere words of prayer, and then set up a tombstone upon which they carved the dog's name and date of death.

By nature very inventive, Leroy once rigged up a merry-go-round for all the neighborhood kids from an abandoned pair of wagon wheels. First he securely buried one wheel deep in the ground, leaving the other above the turf to revolve freely on the axle that joined them. Next, he found some wooden boxes which he nailed around the rim of the revolving wheel as seats for the riders. Then, loading the eager children into their "seats," he would push the wheel, making it whirl, giving everyone on board a very fast ride. Later, for a bit more excitement, he extended boards outwards from the wheel, and fastened the "seats" to them. Now, when the wheel turned, the riders went so much faster and so wildly that Alice, fearing for their safety, would rush out of the house to slow things down. The merry-go-round remained a fixture on the Robertson lot for years and years.

Furthermore, Leroy was also largely responsible for writing and staging plays in the barn, where the hayloft above the granary made an ideal stage. But such plays could occur only in the springtime after the barn had been emptied of hay, for as soon as the loft was filled, the stage disappeared. Leroy and sister Ora were the main producers of these spectaculars. They hung a curtain from the pole that traversed the barn, constructed furniture from wooden boxes (of which there was always a good supply), and made themselves costumes, the most memorable one being a pair of red and white checkered pants worn by Leroy, which his mother had sewn from a table cloth.

When all was ready, the Robertson kids rounded up every other child on Zion's Hill to come and see the great performances. With sisters Wanda and Macel collecting a straight pin for general admission and a safety pin for the reserved seats nearest the stage, and with the audience thus duly seated on the hay, the play would begin. These dramas usually consisted of some loudly spoken dramatic dialogue and a bit of singing. Eventually all the Zion's Hill children were involved in the action, and the plays became a tradition for many years.

In wintertime, Fountain Green turned into an arctic world. Everything would freeze solid, and the snow was so deep that the children could literally walk over the fences on their way to and from school. But the frigid air did not keep them from playing outdoors. Sleigh rides in the big horse-drawn sleigh were a family affair with Jasper driving the sleigh, children all wrapped in hats, mittens, and blankets, and sleigh bells ringing as they sped along. At other times, Leroy would often bundle his little sisters onto a hand-drawn sled, and out on Zion's Hill—the best spot in the valley for such sport—he devised a game wherein he would pull the sled very fast, then suddenly whirl around to make the girls tip off into the soft snow, all of which they loved. He also helped them build great snowmen.

Christmas in Fountain Green was a thrilling time. Every Christmas Eve, it was Leroy's job to go out on the knoll and bring back a tree, one not too big but well shaped. With the tree set up in the kitchen, the family would then line up their chairs and prepare to light the candles. Standing on either side of the tree, Leroy and Ora would each hold three candles, which would then be gravely lit and carefully placed on the tree. Leroy and Ora also had the additional responsibility of staying on the alert to protect against any hint of fire.

Christmas gifts at the Robertsons were largely handmade. Nothing was ever purchased, and Leroy, who was very creative with his hands, could always find inexpensive materials from which to fashion something for his sisters and brother. No matter what, he always gave them something.

However, wonder of wonders, one fine Christmas, Jasper and Alice were able to buy a game as a surprise for the family. They had it secretly stored at the neighbor's home till Christmas Eve, and then stealthily put on the porch to be kept hidden until the children had gone to bed. For some reason, Leroy and Wanda stepped outside beforehand and saw the wonderful gift. Because such a fantastic store-bought present was so extraordinary, and not wishing to spoil the surprise, brother and sister solemnly vowed to keep their discovery secret, and never, never tell the others what they had found. Nor did they.

All the children were taught to help in the regular house and farm work, and when Jasper was away with the sheep—as he often had to be—the load was very great, especially for Alice. Leroy, as the eldest child and son, shouldered much responsibility. One of his daily chores was to draw water from the well north of the house for all the horses and other animals, as well as for all household use since there was no indoor plumbing at the time.

Drawing the water was a particularly big task on Saturday when everyone in the family took a weekly bath. For the occasion, a "Number Two" tub would be brought in, set in a corner by the kitchen stove, and chairs draped with sheets then placed around the tub to insure privacy for the bather. So that each person in turn would have some warm water, the stove's five-gallon reservoir had to be kept full, a duty that invariably fell to Leroy.

He also milked the two family cows, but had a tendency to turn this job into a game. Taking Wanda with him, he would have her stand to the side, lean forward with her jaws as wide open as possible, then aim the milk directly from the cow into her gaping mouth. More milk usually ended up on Wanda than in the bucket.

In the fields above the house Jasper kept a small herd of sheep which had to be taken out of their corrals twice a day to feed along the knoll, and Leroy was assigned this chore as well. But truth to tell, with Leroy as "Chief Herder" and little brother Joe as "Tag-along," the two boys spent more time chasing wild rabbits than watching over the sheep.

On the farm Leroy was always inventing some tool or other to lighten the workload. However, he could not work very long in the hay or grain due to a severe allergy. Out in the fields, he was able to cut and mow, but was unable to "put up" the crop into the barn. Once, before anyone realized how serious his problem was, he was stationed inside the barn where he was supposed to distribute the hay evenly over the area as it was being unloaded. But as more and more hay dust filled the air, Leroy felt his nasal passages and throat swell shut. Choking and smothering, his lungs afire, the poor boy wondered if he would live through the hour. Fortunately, someone saw his plight in time, and got him out of the barn into the open air. He did recover, but forevermore, was excused from working in the hay.

At about age ten Leroy's unwavering love for the violin grew so strong that he was no longer content with merely listening to its enchanting tones. For years, he had yearned for such an instrument to play and create the sounds he could hear only in his head. Ultimately, since there was none to be purchased anywhere nearby, he determined to make one. Somewhere he found a cigar box that would be the proper size for his youthful hands, then patiently set out to adapt it to his needs. But this was no easy task. With only his observations to guide him, he laboriously carved some "F holes," affixed a strange little fingerboard, and somehow carved a bridge, scroll, and pegs. Next he had to find something that could serve as violin strings. He had discovered that thread stretched taut would make a sound if plucked, and so he talked his mother into giving him a few strands of her precious embroidery "silkateen." According to some accounts, he also experimented with thin wire taken from the screen door. Next, he whittled out a stick for a bow, and haired it with hair cut by Jasper straight from the tail of his favorite mare.

For young Leroy this project became a long labor of love born of burning need. Whether at home or on the mountains with his Grandpaw Robertson, or even with his friends at play on the knoll, he spent hours every day diligently carving out his violin and bow. Finally, after many, many weeks, the crude little instrument lay before him, beautiful and ready for his eager hands. Placing it beneath his chin just as he had seen the town fiddler do, he tuned the violin in his own way, and carefully drew the bow across the strings. There was no sound, nothing that he had imagined and hoped for. What disappointment.

But then someone told him if he would put rosin on the bow, this would improve the tone greatly. Immediately he hied himself to "the Merc," Fountain Green's general dry-goods and hardware store. Here, he purchased a big bag of powdered rosin for five cents —more than enough to last any violinist a lifetime. Liberally coating the bow, he again tried out his little fiddle, sure that he would now reproduce the tones he kept hearing in his mind. Sad to say, there was scant improvement. No more than a faint squeaking sound came forth, but until he could somehow get a real store-bought violin, he would have to make do with this one. And indeed, he was able to play many simple melodies, some original, some not. As the weeks went by, he even whittled out other violins for his neighborhood pals who became interested. He would later write: "We strung them up, and with virgin hair from the old mare's tail played familiar melodies on them."

According to some accounts, many of the herders and farmers round about regarded Leroy's constant musical activities as rather frivolous and not worth the time spent on them. However, in later years, he would enjoy telling how he won over these people by his playing of a difficult violin solo during an outdoor community gathering; and how, one by one, the noisy talkative group turned from their visiting to become a spellbound audience, captured by the beautiful violin sounds produced by this youngster. Thereafter, whether they understood his passion for music or not, the community always took pride in his talent and no longer questioned his need for music-making.

Nonetheless, Leroy still felt thwarted and dissatisfied. On his uncle's "Talking Machine," he kept playing over and over a recording of Schumann's "Träumerei" as arranged for 'cello solo, and oh, how he longed and longed for a better instrument and the chance to create such tone.

Finally, when Leroy was in the seventh grade, his dreams seemed about to be realized. Jasper had taken the sheep to sell in Omaha, and upon his return, he presented Leroy with a shiny new violin and bow purchased for twelve dollars directly from Sears Roebuck. It had probably been Alice's idea to get this violin for Leroy, and Jasper, wishing to please his wife and be good to his son, had parted with some very hard-earned money for this surprise.

Heart pounding in anticipation, Leroy took the gorgeous new instrument in hand, placed it beneath his chin, and drew a few sounds with the bow. He played a little bit, paced across the kitchen floor, played a bit more, and then sobbed and sobbed and sobbed. Tears of frustration and heartache ran down his cheeks as he tried and tried, once again in vain, to produce the tone he so desperately wanted, a tone always heard in his mind that not even this glossy new violin could give.

It was a double tragedy. Leroy could not hide his bitter disappointment, and frugal, practical sheepman Jasper simply could not understand what more his son needed.

However, now armed with this new violin, Leroy did at last begin some formal violin study. His first teacher was E. G. Edmunds, who had charge of the eighth grade and was also principal of the Fountain Green school. After but one year, Edmunds left Fountain Green, so Leroy then turned to Ben Williams, a young LDS convert from London whose main livelihood came from working on the railroad then being constructed down the Spanish Fork Canyon. He had taught himself violin by studying a "Violin Method" book selected from the Sears Roebuck Catalogue.

Mr. Williams lived at the extreme south end of Fountain Green, at least three miles distant from the Robertson home on Zion's Hill. Once a week, in all kinds of weather, Leroy faithfully and eagerly trotted with his fiddle to and from these lessons, lessons which cost his parents twenty-five cents each, an exorbitant price for the time. He was a conscientious student, practiced diligently, and remembered what his teacher told him. In later years Williams would recall:

> Leroy always had his lesson . . . , never had to be prodded . . . , was sure of himself. Never when appearing in public did he lack self-control. He knew where he was going. He charted his course and sailed onward.

Leroy also had another violin teacher, Warren Allred, who taught him not only in Fountain Green, but subsequently in both Pleasant Grove and Provo.

Soon after beginning his violin lessons, Leroy was emboldened to organize a little orchestra with his school chums, a venture he would later describe:

> We ordered some music from a mail-order house in Chicago and arranged the rest ourselves. This orchestra became so noted that it attracted the attention of the school board. They promptly hired a "professional" musician to coach us. That was the end of the orchestra.

It was at this time that he taught himself how to notate music and began to write down his early compositions. Encouraged by his family, and anxious to have his work evaluated, he shyly turned to the local "professional" for advice. Here is Leroy's account of the event:

> A bandmaster came to our home town who had quite a reputation as a composer because the choir sang one of his hymns and the band played a march he had dedicated to the sheepherders. I finally gained enough courage to ask him if I might show him some of my compositions. He asked me if I had ever studied "harmony and theory." I told him I had never heard of such things. He then replied that no one had any business to compose without first knowing "harmony and theory." Long afterward I came across these early childhood compositions. They were simple but correct.

Indeed, from the beginning Leroy likely taught himself most of what he learned. He always seemed to have an inborn sense of what was right—not only technically but musically as well—an inborn feeling for the sound, the phrasing and meaning. Furthermore, he worked assiduously, and his friends could not remember a time "when he was not doing something with music, and doing it very well."

At every holiday program, Leroy was on stage performing for the people, sometimes with a composition of his own. Wherever he was, he had but one ambition—to make music.

In the spring of 1910 Leroy finished his primary schooling of eight grades, and since he was now thirteen years old, Jasper felt his son was old enough to learn more about the family business of sheep-raising. Therefore, Leroy began to work for his father as a sheep-herder.

Work at the herd went round the year. But for young Leroy it would usually begin in early May when the sheep returned to Fountain Green after wintering in the West Desert, the ewes heavy with unborn lambs. Here, in the large shed on the farm set aside for the "lambing out," the herders would help the ewes give birth. Then, with the ewes and lambs properly cared for, and the weather sufficiently warm, they would take the herd on foot to the Robertson summer range located to the east of Fountain Green, high in the mountains above Fairview, in an area known as the Big East. Much of it was rough country with lots of oak, but the "Bottoms" had "big beautiful streams of water—icy cold—pines and quaking asps, and all kinds of berries. . . ." With only two herders on the job, this became a lonely life, "so lonely a boy would almost want to cry when it came time to leave town and go to the herd," one lad would later recount.

The herders' day started early, for they had to be up at first light —long before sunup—so as to be with the sheep before they awakened and "broke bed-ground." Otherwise, the sheep, without the herders, would scatter on their own, and then be lost for the day. It was the herders' task to start the sheep down the side of a hill so that the animals could work their way down to the "Bottoms," where they would then "shade up" till mid-afternoon. After getting all the sheep headed in the right direction, the herders could go back to camp for breakfast. After an unvarying meal of sourdough bread, fried eggs and hot coffee, they would go back to watch over the sheep for the rest of the day.

During these hours, the sheep could pretty much take care of themselves, leaving the herders free to do as they wished. Leroy, who didn't really like fishing or any other such sport, used this time for reading, writing, and composing. He would find a shady spot at the foot of a tree, generally where there was some soft moss to sit on, then plant his back against the tree, pull out some manuscript paper, place it on his knee, and be absorbed in writing music for the next three or four hours.

Thus passed the days on the mountain. At summer's end, Leroy then helped take the herd out to the West Desert for the winter. This was no "featherbed life" for a young teenager, and the lad gladly returned home before the winter snows set in.

That same year in the early fall, a crucial period set in for the Robertson family. Jasper was called to be a missionary for the LDS Church in their Central States Mission. This meant that he would be gone from home for two years and that the care of his family and business would have to be left to others. One may wonder how this prudent man, who was always so concerned about the well-being of those whom he shepherded, could have brought himself to go so far away and for such a long time. But, devout man that he was, he never thought of refusing this call. The same raw courage that had impelled him to stop the runaway team and save the little girl's life gave him the strength to go forth as a "Minister of the Gospel."

Jasper went into the mission field November 29, 1910, just one month before Leroy was to turn fourteen, and just twenty-six days before Christmas. With his father gone, Leroy resolved to make this holiday especially memorable for everyone. He began spending hour upon hour out in the barn—a barn so cold that even the manure was frozen—and from simple materials that he had collected and stored in the loft, he carefully prepared his humble, yet glorious surprises. With fingers no doubt chilled to the bone, he fashioned a matchbox for his mother; a cradle for Macel's doll; a three-foot high cupboard made from an old orange crate to hold Wanda's and Ora's doll dishes.

Across the top, amidst fancy carved leaves and other decorations, he inscribed in ornate letters "Wanda" on one side, and "Ora" on the other. Among the gifts he received there was an autograph book which he kept throughout his life.

With Jasper gone, the daily work load grew even heavier than usual. True, Jasper's parents and brothers likely helped out as did Alice's family. Nonetheless, a great deal fell upon Leroy, who was now the "man about the house." There were the two cows to milk every morning shortly after daylight. Then, after breakfast, when the younger ones had departed for school, there were the forty or fifty head of sheep to be fed in the fields above town. Either Alice or Leroy, or both, would trudge up to feed the animals through the snow, sometimes in raging blizzards. Once arrived they would have to dig the hay out from the frozen haystacks, throw it over the fence, scatter it with a rake, then somehow carry it to the feed mangers. This was pioneer living, and it was bitter. But everyone accepted and took it in stride.

There is little detailed information available about Jasper's mission. Some months after his departure, he did receive photos of his children. Posing on the front porch of their home, Leroy, Ora, and Wanda stand very straight and tall, while Macel and little Joe sit on the railing. Dressed in their Sunday-best clothes—all sewn by Alice no doubt—the children have very solemn, earnest, even sad expressions. A wistful half-smile plays upon Leroy's lips.

Then suddenly about two months ahead of schedule, Jasper's mission came to an unexpected halt when he learned that nine-year-old Wanda was acutely ill with a ruptured appendix. Without waiting for official authorization to leave the mission field, the dismayed father rushed home to find his little girl in the hospital, her life hanging in the balance. Alice was spending day and night with Wanda. The two youngest, Joe and Macel, were staying at the home of their Uncle Jim, while Leroy and Ora were left at home trying to keep everything in order. After several weeks, Wanda did recover, and with their father home once again, family life returned to normal.

However, for quite some time, Jasper and Alice must have been wondering whether or not to send Leroy away from Fountain Green to continue his education. In the whole area there was no schooling to be had beyond eighth grade, and this oldest son had always been very anxious to learn. His ever-growing need for more skillful music teachers had doubtless been apparent for a long, long time.

With Alice's parents, Will and Melissa Adams, now moved from their home in Sanpete and settled in Pleasant Grove, Utah County, Leroy's good parents saw an ideal opportunity to help their son. Pleasant Grove had a high school that offered not only more advanced courses in basic subjects such as English and Mathematics, but also Music. Here, Leroy could get the help he had been craving for so many years, and at the same time, he could live with his grandparents and not be completely isolated from his family—an important consideration since the boy was still a young teenager who had always been particularly close to his loved ones. After much discussion among those concerned, it was agreed that Leroy should go live with his grandparents and pursue his schooling in Pleasant Grove.

His beloved autograph book holds messages written to him from family and friends which indicate their expectations and wishes as they contemplate his departure. Their simple wisdom and love must have gone straight to his heart.

His mother, in a careful, explicit hand, penned:

> To Leroy—
> While far away from mother's care you roam,
> Remember all her precepts you have heard;
> Encourage lofty thoughts; do noble deeds,
> And from your tongue let fall no evil word.
> Your Mama

With that graceful penmanship, then so highly prized and cultivated, his teacher, J. N. Dorius wrote:

> Dear Leroy. Character is what we are; reputation is what people think we are.

One of his best friends, Irvin Oldroyd, advised:

Mr. Leroy Robertson—Dear Friend:
> May your life be like a snowflake,
> Leave a mark,
> But not a stain.

In the corner Irvin added, "Across your path may sunbeams play."

Family members also wrote. Sister Ora, in deliberate pencil strokes, inscribed:

Dear Leroy—
> When the golden sun is sinking,
> And your mind from care is free;
> When of others you are thinking
> will you sometimes think of me.

Sister Wanda expressed somewhat more sobering thoughts:

Dear brother:
> When the golden sun is setting
> And you sleep beneath the sod:
> May your name in gold be written
> in the autograph of God.

In the fall of 1912 Leroy enrolled as a full-time student at Pleasant Grove High School. Thus, in a sense, he left home at age fifteen, for never again did he live in Fountain Green except as a long- or short-term visitor.

Chapter Three

LEMON PIE ON SATURDAY

WHEN Leroy moved from Fountain Green to Pleasant Grove, he exchanged his home at the foot of high Mount Nebo for another in the shadows of high Mount Timpanogos. Will and Melissa Adams's farm, lying close to this great Utah County landmark, was not unlike a Garden of Eden, with its land watered by natural artesian wells and its cottage built by Will among tall trees and tall grasses. Down a small hill behind the little house there were fruit trees —mainly apple and plum—and Will kept beehives so there was always a supply of fresh honey.

These good grandparents welcomed Leroy, gave him time and a place to study, and like his Robertson grandparents in Fountain Green, they opened their parlor especially to him so he could play the family organ at his pleasure, much to his and their delight. Of the many children born to Will and Melissa, one son, Burton Henry, was still at home. He and Leroy became fast friends, and this brought the bond between grandson and grandparents even closer. For the next eight years, their home would indeed be his home too.

Leroy enrolled at once as a freshman in Pleasant Grove High School, and quickly settled into his studies. This was a most unusual class, always in trouble, and Leroy—who had observed in Fountain Green that a lot of rough stuff often resulted when a new boy, or "stray" as they called him, came into a rural community—met his classmates with some trepidation. "A timid, little knee-pants kid who could run but couldn't fight," Leroy did, however, find some good understanding friends who would fight in his behalf. So, all in all, he got along all right. Here he met A. Ray Olpin, who became a loyal, lifelong friend.

During these first high school years, Leroy, of course, took classes in such basics as English, History, and Algebra. To these studies he added Bookkeeping (likely as a practical gesture), German (a harbinger of things to come), and much music—his first and ever-present love. As in Fountain Green, he loved to learn and was later remembered as an outstanding student. It has been told that Leroy and A. Ray took all the academic honors in the school, much to everyone else's discomfiture. In any event, whenever Leroy would later reminisce about these years, he took his greatest happiness not so much in his musical accomplishments as in the fact that he had bested A. Ray in Algebra!

His two music teachers, Warren Allred and Arthur Overlade, gave Leroy much encouragement. He became a prominent member of the school orchestra, and a star performer on every program. Soon, as he had done in Sanpete, the young violinist was performing at various functions not only in Pleasant Grove but throughout Utah County. Many years later, A. Ray would write:

> You were known only by your first name among your schoolmates . . . but most of us could detect that you were destined to become a leader in the field of music. We listened to the soft tones of your violin and received inspiration.

Grandmother Melissa used to delight in recounting how Leroy had been asked to play a violin solo at a program in Pleasant Grove, and how his number was listed just before another violin solo to be performed by an honored guest, a professor from Brigham Young University. Leroy played as scheduled, but when the BYU professor came to play his solo, the good gentleman simply arose and said, "The young man has just played the number I had prepared so I will not perform," whereupon Leroy naïvely and sincerely replied, "I'm very sorry. I have another number I could have played."

In fact, during these years, Leroy made such remarkable progress as a violinist that he soon became convinced that he was destined to become a virtuoso on this instrument. He also began rudimentary training in Music Theory, and thus was at last introduced to "Harmony and Theory."

It was during these same years that Leroy often heard Melissa sing many old pioneer ballads which she herself had learned from her parents: tunes from England, Scotland, Ireland, and even Italy. These songs remained with him for life, and he would later incorporate some of them into his own compositions, such as the haunting "Winter Song," whose poignant melody would eventually serve as the basis for the slow movement of his *String Quartet No. 1*. Its text is a vivid expression of early pioneer sufferings and sympathies:

> Old winter is coming and cold is the breeze,
> All the leaves are fast falling from trees.
> Fair nature seems touched with the finger of death,
> For all things are beginning to freeze—
> When poor robin redbreast lies close to her cot
> And icicles hang 'round your door—
> And your bowl steams with something reviving and hot,
> That's the time to remember the poor.

Because he devoted so much time to his studies and violin-practicing, Leroy had little social life, but all in all, he was a happy teenager. Nonetheless, he did miss his family to whom he was ever deeply devoted and saw only rarely. At this time, the journey between Fountain Green and Pleasant Grove (about eighty miles) was made by horse and buggy over dirt roads, and required two days with a camp-out overnight under the stars at Spring Lake, the halfway point. As a result, Leroy was no longer able to spend much time with his younger siblings. Indeed, his youngest brother, Doyle, who was born about a year after Leroy started school in Pleasant Grove, has little memory of Leroy during these years.

However, Leroy always did come back to Fountain Green for Christmas, for lambing-time in the spring, and for his summer vacations. Whenever he arrived home, his brothers and sisters eagerly helped him unpack his trunk, for tucked away in some corner or other there was inevitably a little present for each one.

During these visits he easily resumed his accustomed role of "Special Brother and Leader." In the long evenings, especially at Christmas time, he would sit with the family around the kitchen table near the warm stove, often helping young Joe with his arithmetic, painstakingly teaching the little fellow how to line up the numbers, one precisely under another so as to make absolutely straight columns of figures. Since Leroy was by nature extremely meticulous, Joe had to "do it 1000 times over if it wasn't exactly perfect."

Once, while home in the summertime, Leroy perfected a death-defying trick with his favorite horse, "Old Dick," which came to amuse his brothers for years to come. He would jump on the horse, urge it to a gallop, and then as if on cue, the animal would suddenly stop dead in his tracks, sending Leroy straight over its head to land on the ground unhurt. "The horse stopped, but Leroy kept right on going," was Joe's description. While everyone applauded Old Dick for being so clever as to fool its rider time after time, no one ever seemed to perceive the joy that Leroy unfailingly took in performing this stunt so deftly planned for his innocent audience.

After two years in Pleasant Grove, Leroy transferred to Brigham Young University High School in Provo, popularly called BY High. Here, he finished his last two years of high school, continuing his record as an excellent student. While he studied required subjects such as English and Biology and even managed to take a class in Agriculture, he placed by far the greatest emphasis on music, with more courses in Harmony, Music History, Solfeggio, Orchestra, and Violin. Though but a high school student, he was permitted to enroll in the music classes taught at the university, where his violin teacher was Mose S. Gudmensen and his theory teacher, Anthony C. Lund, soon to become director of the Salt Lake Mormon Tabernacle Choir.

All this time Leroy helped himself along financially by playing in dance orchestras and by giving private string instrument lessons in the towns round about Utah County. In short order he had organized many community "orchestras" with his students, and because these ensembles were of varied instrumentation, he was obliged to arrange most of their music. This he did for love and enthusiasm, with never a thought of asking the school boards to recompense him for his service.

After graduating from high school in 1916, Leroy again felt "the old urge for creative work which had for some time lain dormant."

This same year he wrote his first composition for orchestra, a "Minuet" of considerable charm and invention. In addition to the "Minuet," he also composed many songs, for which he often wrote both words and music. A particularly lovely example from this period—one that shows the ardent feelings of a nineteen-year old—is a song entitled "A Lover's Envy":

I envy ev'ry flower that grows
Along the pathway where she goes
And ev'ry bird that sings to her
And ev'ry breeze that brings to her
The fragrance of the rose.

I envy poet's rhyme
That fills her heart at eventime.
I only wish to live for her,
I only wish to give to her
All her heart desires.

At about this time Leroy met George W. Fitzroy, a graduate of the New England Conservatory of Music in Boston, and former student of the eminent American composer, George Whitefield Chadwick. Mr. Fitzroy, who had recently come to teach private music in Provo, introduced the young Utahn to a whole new world of music. He gave Leroy his first intensive training in counterpoint and analysis, having him study, among other things, the *Well Tempered Clavichord* of Bach, and some Schubert songs. Leroy's analyses were of incredible detail, with not only every chord but every note carefully explained as to its harmonic and melodic structure. Mr. Fitzroy also lent Leroy the first orchestra scores he ever saw: Mendelssohn's *Overture to a Midsummer Night's Dream* and the Dvořák *New World Symphony*.

The young Utah musician was intrigued by the sight of the instruments on paper, but he could only imagine the sound, for thus far he had heard but one symphony concert in his entire life, this being at age nineteen when the New York Philharmonic, under the direction of Walter Damrosch, appeared in the Salt Lake Tabernacle. Among other numbers, they played Tchaikowsky's *Pathétique Symphony*, a performance that ever remained one of Leroy's fondest musical memories.

From that moment on, he firmly avowed that sometime, somewhere in the state of Utah there would be others who would have the chance to thrill as had he in hearing a symphony orchestra, and that he would do all he possibly could to help the region have an orchestra, be it a professional group, a school organization, or both.

It should likely be mentioned that for Leroy to have heard but one symphony concert so late in his life was not an unusual circumstance for rural America. After all, in those early years of the twentieth century, there were as yet no radios broadcasting far and wide, and of course no television. Thus, beyond what he created himself or heard performed by other local artists—usually less skilled than he—the only music to which Leroy was exposed was on the primitive recordings owned by his father and uncle.

In addition to his private studies with Mr. Fitzroy and his own composing, Leroy now expanded his private teaching, travelling during the week by interurban train from Lehi on the northernmost end of Utah County to Payson on the south. Saturday was his "day in Payson," and here, after a long day of intensive teaching—not to mention a long week—just before catching the train back to Pleasant Grove he would systematically treat himself to one piece of lemon pie at a local cafe. This "Lemon Pie on Saturday" became his one luxury, a treat that he patiently, and sometimes impatiently, anticipated from one week to the next.

As a result of his teaching, Leroy quickly developed many students who themselves began contributing more and more to the music programs in their own communities. He continued to form local ensembles throughout the area, and thus, by training good performers and by building an audience interested in classical music, he was already laying the ground for the creation and support of a good, local symphony orchestra.

One anecdote illustrates the simple pride and love these fine people took regarding "their" music and music-makers. In one small town, Leroy had a student, Rosco by name, whose violin was well above average insofar as its tone was concerned, but which was an old family instrument with a dull finish that in no way could ever compare in appearance to the bright new store-bought violins owned by most of the other kids. One day, as Rosco came for his lesson and with a big grin took his fiddle from its case, Leroy saw that the old instrument was suddenly shining more brilliantly than any other violin in the entire valley. "What happened to your fiddle?" asked the surprised teacher. The happy boy answered, "Ma was varnishing the furniture and had some varnish left so she touched up my violin." Of course, the tone was ruined, but Rosco's violin did glow in glory.

By this time Leroy's father had acquired a sizeable flock of sheep and needed men to help with the herd. So every spring, with his formal schooling now ended, Leroy regularly had to leave his teaching in Utah County and again go herd sheep, following them from the lambing grounds to the high Big East summer range, then taking them at summer's end out onto the vast West Desert for wintering. Since he usually had a certain amount of time on his hands during the day, he was somewhat free to study the precious orchestra scores lent to him by Mr. Fitzroy, and they became a necessary part of his equipment for several summers. On the mountain, without the aid of any instrument whatsoever, he taught himself to hear each orchestral part simply by looking at the notes. This was also a time for his own composing. Of these days he would later comment:

> One of the great experiences of my life was living in the heart of this marvelous mountain retreat with nature in her most varied and inspiring moods, and a faithful horse and dog as understanding companions.

Then came the fall of 1918, and Leroy was drafted into the United States Army for service in World War I. He reported for duty at Fort Douglas in Salt Lake City, but almost immediately fell victim to the great flu epidemic then raging across the land. Because Fort Douglas did not have adequate facilities to accommodate the hundreds of men struck down by this disease, the commanders decided that any flu victim with someone nearby to care for him should be sent off base to these care givers. Leroy did have relatives in Salt Lake City and was accordingly sent to them. His mother came from Fountain Green to nurse him, for he was desperately ill.

Long before he recovered, armistice was declared thus ending the war. In all the excitement, Leroy was never recalled to duty and simply went home to recuperate. His stint as a soldier in the United States Army had not exactly been heroic. Nor was he ever officially discharged.

After recovering from the flu, Leroy resumed his private teaching in Utah County. One Saturday evening, as he boarded the interurban train at Payson to return to Pleasant Grove, he happened to sit beside Apostle Melvin J. Ballard, a high dignitary in the LDS Church. Apparently intrigued by this earnest young man with his violin and briefcase filled with music, Elder Ballard engaged Leroy in conversation. Upon learning that Leroy aspired to be a serious composer as well as a first-rate violinist, Elder Ballard told him of a wish he himself had long held in his heart that someday some composer would write an oratorio—something in the order of Handel's *Messiah*—based upon scripture found in the Book of Mormon. This whole incident sparked in Leroy an ambition and dream that stayed with him thereafter, but which would achieve reality only some thirty years later with the completion of his *Oratorio from the Book of Mormon*.

It was now 1919, and Leroy knew that he had long since exhausted all the resources for musical training offered in the West. On his own, he had read extensively and had compiled many notebooks filled with carefully detailed information on music history, analyses of form, harmony, and orchestration. His remarks written after studying Mendelssohn's biography reveal a bit of Robertson's own philosophy as a composer:

> While other composers have brooded away their lives over composition alone, Mendelssohn was active as a leader in all the practical possibilities of his art and yet equally prolific in his output of original, perfectly constructed and highly musical creations. . . . One cannot imagine his immense activity, generally self-imposed and directed more than often at unselfish ends, and still be thankless toward him.

Robertson's citation of Mendelssohn's motto, "What is worth doing at all is worth doing well," shows how deeply this same precept learned in childhood from his own father had been ingrained in him.

At about this same time, Robertson took courage and sent some of his violin pieces and songs to the eminent American composer, Charles Wakefield Cadman, asking for criticism and advice. While there is no copy extant of Robertson's letter to Cadman, it must have evidenced a certain trusting sincerity. The manuscripts must have been meticulously ink-drawn copies of works taken from a book of compositions and sketches dating from 1917; and the music itself must have shown enough raw talent to capture Cadman's attention, for even though it was against his policy ever to review the work of anyone not his student, he did respond to Leroy in some detail, offering opinions both positive and frankly negative. Noting that criticism is "only a personal matter, [and that] my views may not be those of another," Cadman concluded, "These are my honest ideas and if they help or discourage that's up to you."

This being Leroy Robertson's first direct contact with any musician of national and international stature, he no doubt pondered Cadman's critique very seriously. Apparently more encouraged than discouraged, the young Utahn at once felt inspired to compose a "Grand Waltz," which, as he later wrote, he "feverishly scored for orchestra." When he had completed it to his satisfaction, he knew that he had reached a plateau in his musical development and must somehow learn to do much more than what his situation in Utah allowed.

George Fitzroy had long been urging Leroy to go back East and attend the New England Conservatory for more study with his own former mentor, George W. Chadwick. Other musicians, well known and highly respected in Utah, had already attended this school so its reputation was well established in the West. And there was no argument that Chadwick was among America's foremost composers, and likely the best. Leroy could not help but agree with Fitzroy that this was where he now had to be.

Of course, he had to convince his parents, especially Jasper, that further education in Boston was a real imperative. Leroy argued that finances would not be an insurmountable problem, for he had been working hard many years and had saved a certain amount both from his private teaching and from his earnings as a sheepherder for his father. And most of all, he desperately needed to be where he could hear more and better music than what surrounded him in Utah. Finally, after much heartfelt discussion, Jasper and Alice acceded to Leroy's wishes, gave their consent and blessing for him to go.

Therefore, in the summer of 1920, Fitzroy wrote Chadwick a letter about Leroy, to which the great composer immediately replied, saying that he would see this young Utahn and look over his work. Leroy at once began preparations to leave for Boston. His friend, Frank W. Asper, happened to have a return-trip train ticket to Boston which he did not intend to use and gladly turned over to Leroy.

In late September, the eager composer-violinist packed his scores, notebooks, theory exercises, analyses, and other compositions along with a few clothes. Then, bidding everyone good-bye, with violin in hand, he boarded the train that was to transport him for the first time to a world far away, clear across the continent, and very different from his "Beautiful Mountain Home" in Utah.

Chapter Four

CHICKEN WINGS ON MONDAY

LEROY Robertson's heart must have been high in his throat as the train sped him towards Boston, that great musical center with its conservatory holding the key to all his dreams and ambitions. Upon the advice of friends, he had purchased an upper berth in the Pullman car, and many years later would confess, with a chuckle, that he was quite concerned when he found the berth to be so close to the roof of the car. "Not until the conductor assured me that I wouldn't have to sit there for the whole trip, but could use a seat during the day, did I feel better." By nature a quiet and nervous person, he likely neither slept nor ate very much due to the excitement and anticipation of what lay ahead for him.

As he watched the plains of Nebraska and Iowa roll by, he must have remembered how his father annually took the sheep to Omaha for sale, and how this was the land where, just ten years before, this good man had lived and labored as a missionary. Wide-open spaces—all so different from the narrow mountain valleys he had known his whole life. Surely he thought of his mother, his five younger brothers and sisters, and of his grandparents. He always missed his family when parted from them, and this first great separation must have been a keen one. But Boston—indeed, the entire music world beyond Utah—was awaiting him.

He truly felt quite prepared to meet whatever challenges the eastern metropolis would present. Financially he felt secure, for he had saved a good sum over the years. Intellectually he was sure of himself, for he had gleaned everything possible from his teachers and had studied a lot on his own, though most of this learning had of necessity been "on the side." His talent was not to be denied. He

knew that his compositions—this fresh new music from the West—
would take Boston by storm.

En route Leroy did stop over in New York for a few hours just
long enough to see a bit of Tin Pan Alley, that part of the city where
musicians gathered to play and hawk their songs. But very soon, he
again boarded the train, an "overnighter" that brought him into
Boston at daybreak. Upon arriving, he proceeded directly to the
apartment of good friend, Bill Lym, an oboist who had himself
studied at the New England Conservatory and had since been residing
in Boston. It was only 6:00 A.M. when the eager Utahn pounded on
Lym's door, rousted him out of bed, and prevailed upon him to get
an appointment with George W. Chadwick that very day. Leroy
simply could not wait one day longer to begin his studies, and
besides, the first term was already in session.

Good-hearted Bill Lym was able to arrange for his impatient
friend to meet Mr. Chadwick later in the day, and went with him at
Leroy's request. Tense, full of hope and excitement, manuscripts in
hand, Leroy was anxious to show this eminent musician all his works,
especially the "Grand Waltz." The young composer was certain that
this masterpiece would bring an immediate Boston Symphony
performance, with him, Leroy Robertson, on the podium conducting
its premiere.

As it turned out, Mr. Chadwick first asked to see Leroy's
exercise books of harmony and analyses, which he scrutinized very
carefully and at great length. Then came the moment when Leroy
finally got a chance to show this Dean of American Composers his
"Grand Waltz." Mr. Chadwick quietly looked it over, and after a few
seconds meditation, commented, "Well, you'll learn more about these
things after you have been here awhile."

Sadly, Chadwick's apparent dismissal of Leroy's most cherished
composition was only the first step in a very rude awakening. During
the next few days as he became acquainted with the other students at
the Conservatory, Leroy was shocked to see that they were all five to
ten years younger than he. At age twenty-three, he had suddenly
become an "oldster." Furthermore, when he heard these "youngsters" perform, he realized at once that they were much more accom-

plished and far better trained as violinists than he. Despite all of his hard work and study, despite his lifelong commitment to training himself as a musician, Leroy Robertson had to face the bitter fact that in technique and repertoire he was far behind his classmates.

As he later wrote:

> . . . I soon found out there was much to be learned. The experience gained in conducting an orchestra of aspens did not help me secure a position in Symphony Hall and my scores which were Masterpieces when I left Utah suddenly became quite worthless.

Elsewhere he continued:

> I was born into a land of natural wonder and among a people of character and integrity but I cannot imagine many composers having a more impoverished musical youth than my own.

Indeed, with a slight twinge of bitterness, he lamented that too much of his life had been wasted in unessential activities when it could have been devoted to acquiring the musical education he had so dearly wanted and needed.

In a frantic, almost frenzied effort to make up for lost time, he drove himself beyond endurance. Driven by "his unquenchable thirst for musical knowledge, he responded almost like a person coming from the desert to a beautiful clear spring—He took in too much too quickly." Relying as always on his compelling innate talent, his extraordinary capacity for hard work, and his indomitable willpower, he simultaneously registered for classes that would lead to Majors in four fields: Composition, Piano, Violin, and Public School Music.

What Leroy did not know—and perhaps never discovered—was that Chadwick, recognizing the talent and dedication of this newly arrived student, immediately had written a letter to Leroy's former teacher, Mr. Fitzroy, expressing his confidence and pleasure in admitting Robertson to the New England Conservatory and congratulating Fitzroy on having prepared him so well.

In any event, Robertson passed the theory requirements by special exam, and with such success that Chadwick placed him directly into his Advanced Composition Class on a provisional basis, a course to which but a few students were admitted each year and which always had a high attrition rate because of its difficulty. This particular year, the class began in the fall with about fifteen students only to end the following June with but two survivors: the eminent Latin-American pianist, Jesús-María Sanroma and Leroy J. Robertson from Fountain Green. Leroy also took classes in Counterpoint, Music History, and English Literature.

Along with the intellectual shock he suffered upon entering the Conservatory, Leroy soon faced another kind of disillusionment, for he discovered almost at once that the funds he had so carefully guarded and built up over the years would not go far in Boston. What had seemed financial wealth in Utah was akin to poverty in urban New England. He found a small room amidst the noise and smoke of Boston's Back Bay District, a "walk-up" on the uppermost floor of a building at 564 Columbus Avenue within walking distance of school. His room stood across the hall from a Jewish couple, Mr. and Mrs. Strauss, and within a short time Leroy was enjoying their friendship. He especially savored his philosophical discussions with Mr. Strauss, who was very well read. He also arranged to take some of his meals with the Strausses, and this must have helped him a great deal in more ways than one.

His carefully kept financial records show that he paid $4.00 per week for board and $3.00 per week for his room. He rented an old upright piano at $6.00 per month, which to many in similar circumstances would have seemed an unaffordable luxury, but which to Leroy was a crucial necessity. To improve his piano technique he spent at least four hours every day practicing scales, etudes, and repertoire, but for the most part, he used the piano for his ongoing work in theory and composition.

Soon after arriving in Boston, he bought himself a new Sunday-best suit and a light raincoat—both for only thirty dollars. For warmth, he had brought from home a fine cardigan sweater, but although this sweater was new and 100% wool, it was not much protection against Boston's humid, bitter winters. With no overcoat, he was often very cold as he walked everywhere on his various errands.

In order to supplement his savings, Leroy found a job playing violin evenings in a high-class Boston restaurant. Here he discovered that on Mondays the restaurant would offer, at a greatly reduced price, the chicken wings that could not be sold to the customers of the previous day. So, as a very special treat—not unlike the "Lemon Pie on Saturday" of his Utah County years—he varied his spartan fare by having "Chicken Wings on Monday." It was his best meal of the week, one that he anticipated with much pleasure and perhaps a bit of nostalgia as he remembered the sumptuous cooking of his mother and grandmother back home.

He was, all in all, very happy to be in the East with its myriad opportunities for his musical development. Somehow, he even found time to go to New York to hawk his music on Tin Pan Alley and make a recording of himself playing the violin. He succeeded in having two popular songs published, the one, an exotic number entitled "My Oriental Dream," and the other, a folksy ballad, "Take Me Back to Dear Old Home."[1]

Nonetheless, he seemed to derive his greatest pleasure from his studies, and his large loose-leaf volumes of detailed notes, meticulously copied in pen and ink, evidence his serious commitment to and excitement for learning.

In addition to classes, Leroy was preparing regular violin and piano lessons, writing out his homework assignments, and ever, ever composing. In order to accomplish all this work he set himself a strict schedule. This brief reminder he wrote to himself in one of his notebooks to "Copy lyrics every two weeks," indicates how organized his life had become.

For Leroy, the highlight of all these activities was to attend the Boston Symphony concerts every Saturday afternoon. As a matter of fact, his very first purchase upon arriving in Boston had been a season ticket to their matinees, which gave him a seat in the upper-

---

[1]It is interesting to note that in these songs, whereas Robertson is named as the author of the words, and while his personal stamp is clearly evident everywhere in the music, for some reason, he did ascribe the music to Leonard Ivory, a dear boyhood friend from Fountain Green.

most—and cheapest—section of the balcony. Such a ticket was yet another item that for others may have been a frill, but which for Robertson was an indispensable requirement. During each performance, he paid careful attention, and took special note of those passages in the music whose sound particularly impressed him. Then immediately after the concert, he would go directly to the Boston Public Library, borrow the scores of the compositions played that day, and hand-copy those passages he had noted so as to study their orchestration in detail. Robertson, whose orchestration technique later became one of his hallmarks, often remarked that this work was the most valuable help and instruction he ever received in orchestration—another evidence of his ingenuity and ability to teach himself.

Obviously, Leroy did not leave himself much time for socializing although he did enjoy walking along Boston's Charles River and the Fenway. While he attended LDS Church services regularly, he was rarely involved in their "socials." But, he did make a few close friends with whom he spent "good times on Bickerstaff Street."

Though Leroy was far from Utah, newsy letters from home kept him in touch with his family. A note from his Grandfather Robertson, sent soon after his arrival in Boston, is typical:

> Leroy Dear Sone,
>   I will answe[r] your ever welcom Letter just received read with Pleasure glad to here you are well an feeling good we are well at home we have had a good rain here it has been quite Stormey here it is fine today your Pa an uncle George has gon to Payson with ther Lambs it is very busey times here moven Sheep to the winter rainge I was talkin to your ma this morning they are all well . . . how is Polateks [politics] in they Bay State they are getting warm here. I guess you have seen quite a bit of the country you must not get home sick I will take a trip up north Soon to Pass the time away I get Lonsom Staying around here.[2] . . .
>   Dear Sone I will close may the Blessing of the Lord bee with you and guid you all the time write again.
>   from Gran Paw

------

[2]Edwin's wife, Hanna, had died the year before.

Leroy did write home often, especially to his mother. For Mother's Day of 1921, from his little room in Boston, he sent her a beautiful card, on which one side pictured a mother and her young son, both dressed in the ancient garb of the Holy Land, and looking out over the rooftops of an age-old village; beneath the picture was the inscription from Psalm 121, "I Will Lift up Mine Eyes Unto the Hills," all reminiscent of his life in Utah. On the reverse side, Leroy had written:

> Dear Mother: This is your day. There could be three-hundred and sixty-five of these days in a year and then not do you justice.
> Your son

Despite the continual interchange of letters, however, Leroy's parents had worried greatly about their son in distant Boston—which to them seemed as far away as the moon. Never completely recovered from the flu of 1918, he had been in poor health when he left for the East, and because he was working so hard, with so much constant mental pressure, he was unwell much of the time. Alice, who seemed to idolize Leroy (as she did all of her children), was always sending him little things to help him in a practical way, and faithfully wrote every few days.

Gradually this year of unremitting study did begin to affect Leroy's health seriously. He became extremely overstrung, grew thinner than ever, and his incessant copying of so much music led to eye troubles that would plague him the rest of his life.

Nevertheless, he completed all of his courses—required and audited—with good success. His final examination grades for the year were all "B's" and "A's," which was, after all, not a bad record for this largely self-taught young man fresh from the high mountains of Utah.

When school ended in June, Leroy returned to Utah, gaunt, stooped, and very worn out, much to his parents' dismay. He again spent the summer with his father's sheep on the mountain range and slowly began to recuperate. But, in the fall, when it was time to resume his work in Boston, he was not yet well, and his parents did not feel that he should go back East ever again. Indeed, his father likely thought that this eldest son had had enough musical training, should "settle down," and at last take up the Robertson tradition of sheep-raising.

Moreover, both of his beloved grandfathers died that fall just about eight weeks apart. These two deaths doubtless affected Leroy deeply, for his grandparents had constantly been his second line of support. Christmas of 1921 must have been a sad time for the Adams and Robertson families. But, stories of Leroy's ever-ready wit and dry humor would indicate that he once again was telling his "Sanpete jokes" and clowning around so as to make life a bit merry.

He had always loved to mimic the older Fountain Green townsfolk with their colorful Scandinavian dialect and manner. One story that unfailingly brought gales of laughter from his listeners was about good old "Bruder Yonson" (Brother Johnson), who got into an argument over the water with "Bruder Yensen" (Brother Jensen) and called him a "Son of a ----," all of which was immediate cause for "Bruder Yonson" to be called into Bishop's Court. Leroy always ended the somewhat drawn-out yarn with the following dialogue:

> Bishop: Bruder Yonson, did yew call Bruder Yensen
> a "Son of a ----"?
> Brother Johnson (head hanging): Vall, yes, I did.
> Bishop: Vall, don't yew tink yew should apoloyize?
> Brother Johnson (scraping his feet, reluctantly): Vall,
> (pause) he don't hef to be it ef he don't vant tew.

As the winter of 1922 wore on, Leroy grew increasingly uneasy. That constant inner urge for more musical training would not let him rest, and he felt compelled to return to Boston to complete the studies he had begun. His parents, ever concerned about their son's health —which, in truth, had not as yet greatly improved—were reluctant to have him leave. However, they realized that his great discontent would never be relieved until he did finish his work in New England, and thus, they sought a possible solution to the dilemma.

Jasper and Alice Robertson had always been religious people, not overly pious but naturally devout, living their Mormon faith as a matter of course. Leroy, too, was profoundly religious, but not in an ostentatious way. Therefore, it was not surprising for Jasper and Alice to feel that if Leroy were to go through a Latter-day Saint

Temple and receive its blessings, his health would be restored. Consequently, in early March, Leroy went with his parents to the Temple in Manti.

With his family thereby reassured, he returned at once to Boston, and immediately resumed composition studies with Mr. Chadwick.

Leroy elected to remain in Boston during the summer, and was called to serve a short-term mission—from mid-July to mid-September—for the LDS Church in the New England States. Here, he used his talents to perform, arrange, and direct music for the Church. Like other missionaries, Leroy was extremely parsimonious, spending but small amounts, and only for necessary items such as a pair of eyeglasses ($11.00), a hat and shirt ($4.61), and board ($3.50 per week).

Upon completing his mission, Leroy went back to his little room on Columbus Avenue, once more arranged to board with Mr. and Mrs. Strauss, and again registered as a full-time student at the conservatory. Along with his work in Violin, Piano, and Theory, he enrolled for classes in Public School Music, including High School Orchestra Conducting, all of which likely indicates that he had now decided the most practical way for him to earn a living as a musician would not be as the great concert violinist or highly acclaimed composer of his early boyhood dreams, but rather as a teacher. The following remarks, taken from one of his class notebooks and written in a large, forceful hand, show his idealism and commitment toward teaching music:

> . . . there is a tremendous opportunity for good, open to every [music] supervisor. His spirit toward the subject should be precisely that of the zealous missionary in preaching the Gospel. He is a bearer of good tidings to all men. His mission is second only to that of the Gospel message. Of both it may be sung with almost equal fitness, "How lovely are the messengers who preach us the gospel of peace." Then "magnify" your office and let your zeal and enthusiasm become contagious. Make your community proud of you and your blessed work.

His concluding comments on the last page of this same notebook emphasize the importance he assigned to this profession and describe the sort of teacher he himself had been and would continue to be:

The role of teaching music in the public schools is really missionary and no one should undertake it, who is not prepared to give
much time, thought and effort over and above that for which he
is paid. Those who do this will find that the work calls for the
best that is in them and that they are building for the future; that
some succeeding supervisor and generation of young people will
reap the fruit of their labor.

Leroy was again working at fever pitch. A number of compositions for piano, violin, and chorus stem from this period, and he was
writing a large overture for orchestra as well. However, he tempered
his arduous schedule with workouts at the YMCA (probably upon
the advice of a physician). And his sense of humor also stood him in
good stead.

Life was going along well. Just after resuming his studies at the
Conservatory, he had received word from the General Music Committee of the LDS Church that two numbers he had submitted to a
previously announced Church competition had won two of the three
prizes awarded. Both were closing hymns. The one, "At Parting,"
had placed first, and the other, entitled simply "Closing Hymn," had
been named "third best." Furthermore, the Committee praised his
work highly and asked him to submit, at his earliest convenience, an
anthem to be considered for publication in a "new book of anthems
[then being planned] by the Church Music Committee." These two
hymns stand as the first in what would become a long list of awards
for Leroy Robertson's compositions.

In early December a letter arrived from his Grandmother Adams
telling him about the people in Pleasant Grove, the family, and men-
tioning his violin recording. His December birthday and Christmas
came and went; and there was another encouraging letter from his
mother saying that, according to his sister Wanda, his recently
published song, "Oriental Dream," was "doing well up north."

Then around New Year's Day, Leroy received yet another letter
from the Church Music Committee, this time from its chairman,
Apostle Melvin J. Ballard. Elder Ballard was writing to remind Leroy
of their request that he submit an anthem to be used in a "collection
of anthems by home composers."

New Year's Day 1923 came and went. The Monday following

Leroy enrolled for the second term at the New England Conservatory, intending to graduate in the spring. Then suddenly, just one week later, a terse and tragic telegram arrived from Jasper in Fountain Green:

Mother very low. Come quick.

Benumbed Leroy checked his accounts, immediately left school —even without informing Chadwick—and caught the very first train for Utah. The trip, which lasted nearly a week, must have seemed interminable. One can only imagine the heartsickness of this most loving son and the anxiety mounting within him as the train chugged endlessly along, mile after mile after mile.

Was his mother really dying?

If so, why?

Was she ill, injured?

Would he get home in time to see her once again?

At last he reached Salt Lake City, then traveled as fast as he could south along the Wasatch Front, then over the Divide into Fountain Green. As he stepped off the train and saw the sobbing faces of his waiting family, he knew he was too late. Alice had died without seeing this beloved son, and her funeral had already been held. Mid-winter, freezing cold, drifting snow, and his mother was buried in that icy ground beneath his feet.

It did not seem quite true that she was gone. Leroy could only picture her "as she stood by the corner of the kitchen range" on that March day he had left for Boston but ten months previous. Heartsick, heartbroken, Leroy wondered what more could he have done, what should he do now?

He was torn. Should he relegate music to a back seat in his life, stay in Utah and at last go into the family sheep business as his father had so long desired? In fact, after his abrupt and unarranged departure from the New England Conservatory, he did not know whether he would even be allowed to continue his work there.

However, a very sympathetic letter from Mr. Chadwick arrived in early February reassuring Leroy that his registration would be extended indefinitely and that his absence for such a necessary cause would not disqualify him for graduation. But, at the same time, Chadwick suggested that he not stay away from school too long. This letter suddenly crystalized Leroy's thinking. More driven than ever to become a first-rate musician, he was forced to admit that he could no longer remain in Fountain Green and would have to complete his studies in New England. Leroy must have departed again for Boston soon thereafter, for by mid-February he was back at the Conservatory, fully immersed in his work.

Within weeks he finished his large *Overture in E minor (Overture Symphonique)*. A *Suite for Violin and Piano*—with a beautiful "Lament" as its central movement—dates from this time; and an extended song for Soprano Solo, Ladies four-part Chorus and Orchestra, was completed in mid-May. Entitled "Under the Walls of Paradise," and based on a poem by Thomas Buchanan Read, this last piece shows Leroy dreaming not only of Italy, but also thinking of his mother as he set these lines to music:

> My soul today
> Is far away
> Sailing the Vesuvian Bay;
> My wingèd boat
> A bird afloat
> Swims round the purple peaks remote.
>
> I heed not if
> My rippling skiff
> Flow swift or slow from cliff to cliff;
> With dreamful eyes
> My spirit lies
> Under the walls of Paradise.
>
> No more, no more
> The worldly shore
> Upbraids me with its loud uproar;
> With dreamful eyes
> My spirit lies
> Under the walls of Paradise!

In June 1923, Leroy Robertson completed all class work and graduated with honors from the New England Conservatory. In two years and two months of study, he had earned diplomas in Violin,

Piano, Composition (his real major), and Public School Music—any one of which would normally require four years to complete.

More important, he won the coveted Endicott Prize in composition—carrying a cash award of $300—for his *Overture in E minor*, which he immediately retitled the *Endicott Overture* in honor of the donor. That Leroy Robertson won this prize was particularly significant, for his overture was in competition with works by students representing the entire Western Hemisphere, who, unlike the Utahn, had had the best and most formal lifelong training.

However, the most important honor for Leroy was that Mr. Chadwick chose him to represent the New England Conservatory in the United States competition for the "Prix de Rome," or "Rome Prize," which would have enabled him to study in Italy for at least two years.[3] Alas, however, a nervous breakdown—brought on by overwork, constant pressure in trying to make up for what he felt were years lost, and the strain of his mother's death—put a temporary halt to all such dreams.

Mr. Chadwick, ever persistent, urged Leroy to go on to New York's Juilliard School of Music and work there for a year, which would have absolutely assured him of this prestigious award:

> They have asked me to pick someone for that prize, and I have told them I'd like you to have it.

But Leroy, completely exhausted in every way, could not write any more music just then. His "eyes had gone back on . . . [him, and he] simply couldn't do much about it."

With a disappointment that haunted him for decades, Leroy had to say "No" to the competition and come home to Utah. Once more he was turning to the mountains for refuge, solace, and peace.

---

[3]What Robertson referred to as the "Prix de Rome" is actually the "Rome Prize," established by the United States in 1920, and whose winner resides at the American Academy in Rome. The "Prix de Rome," an award instituted by the Academy of Fine Arts (Institute of France) in 1803, is limited to French composers.

Chapter Five

PRIX DE ROME IN UTAH

AGAIN in Utah, Leroy found the rest he so badly needed by going back once more to the Big East and herding his father's flocks. The summer range truly was "one of the most restful places ever to be." To help Leroy with the sheep that summer, Jasper sent younger brother Joe, who was now thirteen years old and in Jasper's eyes, old enough to start learning the family business. Thus, again, as when they had both been little boys so many years before, Leroy became "Chief Herder" while Joe followed along as his "Right-hand Helper."

However, for young Joe, life on the mountain was very lonely because after completing the regular morning chores with the sheep, Leroy buried himself in his music, and really left the boy to his own devices for hours. Though Leroy could at times be amusing and fun, once he started writing, he was no company, absolutely no company at all, and Joe, who inevitably tired of fishing by himself and putting his initials on any flat surface available, was soon begging his father, "Send me on the mountain, but not with Leroy. Send me with any-one but Leroy."

Nonetheless, Leroy was not always lost in his music, and indeed was constantly "thinking about ten miles ahead of everyone else" in devising things to make life at the herd safer and more comfortable for him and his brother.

One of his best inventions was a bed. It had long been the custom for all the herders on the mountain simply to spread their bedding over a tarpaulin and sleep directly on the ground. But the area had many rattlesnakes, and Leroy was concerned about him or Joe being bitten as they slept. Therefore, one bright day with Joe's help, Leroy rigged up a bed from aspen branches, which held their bedding well up off the ground, and if the brothers happened to be in an area of pines, they would take pine boughs, knead them in, and make a wonderfully soft, sweet-smelling mattress as well. As other herders heard of this bed, they, too, copied the idea, and it soon became a popular item on the mountain.

About midsummer, one anxious day suddenly broke the calm sheepherding routine, a terrible day whose memory stayed with Leroy the rest of his life. He and Joe had run out of flour and bacon. So early in the morning, Leroy—knowing that the sheep could not be left unattended—reluctantly sent Joe alone down the mountain to the nearest town to fetch these needed supplies. Since Joe had their two horses—one for riding and the other for carrying provisions—and since he had ridden the trail many, many times and knew it well, Leroy expected his brother to be back in camp by mid-afternoon at the latest. But Joe did not return when expected, and Leroy, fearing the worst, began to hunt for the missing boy. He hiked far down the mountain, shouting Joe's name every few seconds, but to no avail. By sundown, Leroy's fear had become dread—heartsickening dread that Joe might have had an accident with the horses, that he was lost, or that he had met with some angry wild animal. As darkness set in, Leroy was near panic. He didn't know what more to do, where else to go to find his brother.

Finally, about two hours after dark, Joe rode nonchalantly into camp, unharmed and happy, for he was bringing not only the flour and bacon he had been sent to fetch, but was also proudly carrying a packsaddle full of fresh vegetables he had stopped to pick from the garden of a family friend whom he had met during his journey. Thirteen-year-old Joe, excited at the prospect of having new carrots and peas to supplement the rather monotonous herders' diet of mutton and sourdough bread, had never given a thought as to whether his older brother might be concerned, and had merely taken his own slow time going along the trail he really did know by heart. As Joe tells it, "Leroy was fit to be tied," but embraced his brother in warm relief and happiness at his safe return. Thereafter, Leroy always made sure to keep plenty of supplies on hand.

During this summer of 1923, Leroy was working on his first

symphony, subtitled *Desert Symphony*. Also, as a diversion from the demands of this large orchestral work, in late summer within three weeks, he composed his *Suite No. 2 for Violin and Piano*, a virtuoso setting of three Mormon hymns: "Beautiful Mountain Home," "O My Father," and "All is Well" (better known as "Come, Come, Ye Saints").

At summer's end, Leroy left the herd, and with his health improving, he went to North Cache High School to begin his first year as an "official" teacher, a year he sometimes referred to as his "Prix de Rome at North Cache."

Never again did he watch over his father's flocks.

Many years later a professional sheepman would write about Leroy's contributions to the world as a sheepherder. After comparing the composer to David of old who also made music while tending his father's flocks, the writer continued:

> While his [Robertson's] early days herding sheep . . . are insignificant to the history of the sheep industry, the music which was inspired by his experience there at the herd will remain a vivid picture in sound of blue skies, mountains, green grass and grazing sheep. Such is the spirit of his creations.

Leroy Robertson's entry into Richmond and North Cache was awaited by curious and very lively students, whom, as has been seen, he deftly won over. Upon his arrival in town, he found lodging at the home of one of the Merrill families, whose daughter, Audine, was a student in nearby Logan at the Utah State Agricultural College, generally known as the "AC." After Leroy had been at the Merrills for a few weeks, Audine invited a college chum, Naomi Nelson, to come and spend the weekend with her and her family in Richmond. On Sunday morning as the two young coeds returned from Church, they found Leroy seated at the table writing music. Audine introduced her friend to the "new boarder," whereupon Leroy immediately arose from the table to show his respect (as was his lifelong custom whenever a woman entered the room), smiled and said a very few words in response. In all truth, his crooked-toothed smile and figure, whose extreme thinness was accentuated by a tight blue pullover sweater, did not really impress Naomi favorably, but the dignity and politeness of his greeting she never forgot. For his part, Leroy, after briefly acknowledging the introduction, returned at once to his work, never suspecting that he had just met someone who would one day become the most important person in his life. Nor did she give him another thought at the time.

Whereas his chief concern of recent years had been for himself and his own development as a musician, Robertson now began to focus his attention on the challenge of bringing truly great music to the people of the Intermountain West. He wanted somehow to create for them a musical environment far better than what he had known during his early years. To be sure, his work at North Cache would be a modest start, but never did he lower his standards, ever maintaining his innate refinement of spirit and never-ending tenacity for setting high goals.

Along with his Music classes, Leroy was also assigned to teach a class of World History, a subject which really taxed his teaching skill. For although he loved history, he had never before taught a straight lecture course, and the daily class hour seemed to drag on endlessly. In the first three weeks of school, he took his history students through an entire textbook designed to last all year long. As a result he had to figure out how to write, devise, and review history lessons for the remainder of the year. Somehow he did it.

As always wherever he was, Leroy played his violin in many programs around the region, and often performed at the AC for their special programs, sometimes as a soloist, sometimes as a member of their musical organizations. On one such occasion, Apostle Melvin J. Ballard, who was visiting the campus as a member of the College's Board of Trustees, spotted Leroy seated among the performers, and remarked to AC President E. G. Peterson, "There is a coming great musician."

Of course, Leroy was ever composing, mainly violin pieces and rather intricate songs, usually scored for voice, piano, and violin obbligato. One song in particular, "The Dawning Morrow," for which he wrote both words and music, attests to his own deep search for some consolation to the unhappy events of the previous year:

Verse I
Shadows of eventide grow long o'er the meadow,
While out beneath the West the day descends,
With her beauty, with her glory and her majesty departing.
O bright and radiant day,
Farewell we cannot say
But wait for you and greet your coming on the morrow!

Refrain
Evening brings peace and rest, a soothing tenderness,
For all the air breathes forth a stillness sweet and holy;
Night's forces murmur low,
From out the dark we know
That light will come and sadness only do we borrow.
Evening brings peace and rest,
For we look with joy to greet the dawning morrow!

Verse II
Shadows of doubt and fear cloud heavy around me,
The way looks dark and drear, for all lies dead.
Even hope seems gone, Oh, what can be remaining?
Those happy days of yore,
I dream them o'er and o'er,
In memory I live, and hope returns to bless me!

Refrain
Yes, there is peace and rest, a soothing tenderness,
The very air breathes forth a stillness sweet and holy;
Night's forces gather near,
Yet from the gloom I hear
A cry ring out that joy will conquer sorrow.
Trusting in peace and rest,
I look beyond the night to greet a dawning morrow!

In Cache County, winter meant basketball. But the basketball games between North Cache High School and its arch-foe, South Cache, were particularly dreaded by the administrations of both schools. This rivalry had grown so fierce that there was a real danger when the students met for their traditional basketball games, two per season being the rule. While the teams were actually playing, everyone was tense and rough, but more or less under control. However, at half time, when the floor emptied, the students of both schools would form lines opposite each other in the bleachers, then wildly "snake dance" onto the court. Here they would meet, exchange cheers, jeers, and vicious blows. The tumult would become so great that the game often had to be delayed, and there were always injuries, some very grave. In light of this violence, the authorities were seriously considering canceling all future games between these long-standing opponents, but after much discussion pro and con, they finally decided to take one more chance. Quiet Leroy Robertson had proposed to them a plan that just might save the day.

After convincing the school officials, he then presented his idea to the students, and at once they enthusiastically joined in. The kids worked in great secret, revealing nothing of their scheme to anyone —not even to their parents—for they had a big surprise in store.

On the night of the scheduled game, the students assembled in the bleachers, each school facing the other as usual. The game began and proceeded with its customary roughness. With half time approaching, familiar rumblings already were beginning on the South Cache side in preparation for the anticipated snake dance. But this time, North Cache did not respond. Excited, alert, and intently watching for a command from their music teacher, they paid little attention to the antics rising from the other side of the gymnasium.

The whistle blew signaling the half, and simultaneously Robertson cued the North Cache students, who immediately stood up as one and broke into song. They sang the songs they had been writing all year long: songs about their school, its greatness, and their love for North Cache, songs they had been learning in secret for this game and for this unlikely audience. On and on they sang, going from one melody to another without stop.

The South Cache students, bewildered by this unexpected turn of events, gradually stopped their snake dance. With no one to oppose them, without their old enemies to fight, they found no point in continuing. Indeed, they were so confused by their rivals' strange behavior that they could only stand in wonderment and listen.

Thus half time continued, the North Cache students in chorus, lustily singing their hearts out, following their teacher's rapid-fire direction, holding all the spectators spellbound from shock if nothing else. Before anyone realized it, the half ended, the game resumed, and there had been no trouble.

At the next scheduled basketball game, the North Cache students were again prepared to sing. They came with new words, new tunes, new praises, all composed and learned in their Music class. However, this time, South Cache was prepared as well. Taking a tip from their adversaries, they, too, had learned some songs, and so both schools took turns chorusing loud and fervently. The rafters literally rang, first from one side of the court, then the other. Another half time came and went, and the old snake-dance fighting did not occur. It had been definitively replaced by a spirited singing contest that vented everyone's energies and harmed no one.

This happy solution to what had seemed a hopeless dilemma earned Robertson even more admiration from the community than what he had already achieved. The school board asked him to take over as music supervisor for the Cache District. However, he politely and thoughtfully refused. He had also been offered the positions of both music supervisor for the Alpine School District and music teacher at his old alma mater, Pleasant Grove High School.

Wishing to be nearer to his family and his friends at Brigham Young University, he decided to return to Utah County.

Chapter Six

"BONNIE"

DURING the summer of 1924, before going on to begin the school year at Pleasant Grove, Leroy did much composing. Among other things he wrote two grand waltzes, or *Valses Brillantes*, for two pianos (four hands), and also made an excellent four-hand piano reduction of his prizewinning *Endicott Overture*, which perhaps would give it more possibility for immediate local performance.

Returning to Pleasant Grove in late August or early September, he once more lived at the home of his Grandmother Adams, now in her seventies and alone. Her unfaltering pride and love for this grandson-musician strengthened him, and he was good company for her.

Just before school started, the administration had scheduled an institute for the faculty of the entire district, and to set a festive mood, they held it in beautiful American Fork Canyon. As the teachers from Pleasant Grove met at the high school to depart for the canyon, Leroy was on hand, driving a new Model T Ford coupe and ready to take any extra teachers who might need a ride to the institute. He already had one passenger, a friend whom he knew from his days at BY High. But when he spied the lovely new home economics teacher standing alone and in need of transportation, he quickly asked his friend to move over so as to make room for this newcomer. Together all three rode to the meeting.

As part of the program, Leroy, who was introduced as the new district music supervisor and teacher from Pleasant Grove, played a violin solo. C. W. Reid, one of the top pianists of the state, travelled from Salt Lake City to accompany him. The two played so beautifully that they were obliged to play an encore, Fritz Kreisler's "Schön

Rosmarin." The new home economics teacher found this to be "the first really good violin playing she had ever heard." Deeply impressed, she would later describe it as "the sweetest experience."

The following day, at the first faculty meeting for the teachers of Pleasant Grove High School, it became Leroy's turn for a "sweet experience." As he walked into the faculty room, his glance fell upon this new home economics teacher, and although he had chauffeured her to the institute just twenty-four hours before, at this moment there was something about her that made him look twice. For the first time in his life he really noticed a girl. Until then, he had been so preoccupied with his music-making and with his other serious studies that no female had ever succeeded in catching his fancy (though many had tried to do so). However, this pretty new teacher was different. She sat quietly, neatly dressed, soft brown hair curling across her forehead, gorgeous big blue eyes opened wide, and a friendly smile upon her lips. Leroy could not take his eyes away from her. Then and there he decided that she was "the one and only girl" for him and determined to have her as his wife.

This lady was none other than Naomi Nelson, the coed whom he had briefly met the year previous at the Merrill home in Richmond, but, truth to tell, neither Naomi nor Leroy recognized each other. Only years later did Naomi remember him as that tall, thin man who had so politely stood up from his writing to greet her and her friend, Audine, as they came into the room.

Leroy's method of courting Naomi was perhaps somewhat unusual, but typical for him. He simply set out to attract her by his qualities as a musician. All year long he played his violin, in solo and in groups, with many of the compositions likely being his own. As music supervisor, he gave private lessons to students from all over the county, and organized small ensembles in all the schools throughout the district. At Pleasant Grove, he formed a "crackerjack" band that played and marched with unusual precision in every school and town parade. With his string and band students, he developed a fine, if somewhat small orchestra, and as at North Cache, the chorus under his direction thrilled everyone. He seemed to know how to help all these young people perform better than they ever had before.

He even conceived the idea of having the students put on an opera, a very ambitious undertaking that involved the entire school. He chose to present von Flotow's *Martha*, complete with costumes, scenery, staging, and, most important, a full-fledged orchestra. The project was a big success, and when the tenor hit the high notes in his famous solo, "Ah, So Pure," it stopped the show every night.

The preparation of this opera did help Leroy's courtship of Naomi slightly, for as home economics teacher, she was appointed to be costume mistress. This gave Leroy more opportunity to be with her and become better acquainted, for, otherwise, he only seemed to see her at faculty meetings. Indeed, a less willful swain might have become discouraged. During that whole year, whenever he gave a performance and turned around to acknowledge the audience's applause, or whenever he walked alongside his carefully prepared, smartly parading band, he did see Naomi standing at the sidelines cheering or sitting in the theater applauding, but always in the company of some other man (since her early teens, Naomi had been very, very popular, and never ever lacked for a beau).

Actually, from Naomi's point of view, she had no idea that Leroy was trying to win her favor. Nonetheless, she could not help but notice that he was forever gazing at her and seemed to be unusually earnest in his demeanor towards her. For that reason, when Leroy began to invite her to go out with him, whether it be a concert in Salt Lake City, a movie in Provo, or a school dance, she would always arrange to have one of her girl friends accompany them so that they would never be alone with each other. She did indeed like this man, but simply was not ready to settle down with anyone just yet.

Meanwhile, Leroy, ever seeking a wider audience for his compositions, undertook to publish five pieces written the year previous at North Cache (perhaps he also regarded this as another tack to try in his courtship of Naomi). He had already inquired about the costs of such an enterprise, and now, having saved sufficient money, he contracted with a Chicago company to print these compositions under the rubric: Intermountain Music Publishing

Company. He himself took charge of the distribution and sales, a venture that proved to be both costly and time-consuming. He diligently sold a great many copies, but never again did he attempt such large-scale publication on his own.

Ever hoping to impress Naomi and wishing to give her something special—something that he alone could offer and that was for him the best he had to give—he dedicated one of these pieces to her and another to the Glee Club of the AC, her alma mater. The latter, with both words and music written by him, was a romantic love song whose message to his ladylove must certainly have been clear.

However, it was only when school ended in the spring that Naomi finally agreed to go on a date with her persistent suitor. Leroy had been wanting to go meet her family in Milton, Morgan County, but she proposed instead that they drive to Ogden for a visit with her older sister, Zetta (Rozetta) Wilson. Zetta liked Leroy the first time she saw him, as did another sister, Minnie Evalyn, who happened to be at the Wilsons when Naomi and Leroy arrived. One at a time, each sister took Naomi aside to impress upon her that here was an extraordinarily good man.

After this visit, Naomi went on to spend the summer in Milton. Leroy came to see her once or twice, and then in mid-June invited her to go with him on a short trip to the scenic national parks in southern Utah and the Grand Canyon, with sister Zetta as chaperone. Naomi consented.

Zetta, who had to leave her own family to make this journey, had already agreed with Leroy to go, for she wished to encourage the romance; and knowing that Leroy's music was his most eloquent voice, she insisted that he bring his violin. Then, along the way whenever they stopped to rest, Zetta would ask Leroy to play, ever requesting popular love songs of the day, such as "Let Me Call You Sweetheart." Leroy was only too glad to oblige, for he realized that clever Zetta was giving him a chance to express his feelings.

Once arrived at the Grand Canyon, Zetta insisted that she needed a nap, whereupon Leroy immediately suggested that just he and Naomi take a stroll together to see the mountains. He led her to a beautiful, grassy spot beneath a tree overlooking the vast canyon.

Here they sat down, and Leroy, on his knees, poured out his heart. All his emotion, so long pent-up and now centering on her, welled forth as if a dam had burst, and he asked her to marry him.

Naomi did not answer "Yes," but neither did she say "No." She could not immediately decide what to do. She had signed a teaching contract for the next year and wanted to continue her work, which she liked very much. Moreover, she had accepted another man's fraternity pin. However, Leroy's deep ardor, his sincerity, and his unquestionable devotion did succeed in penetrating her heart. After a few weeks she accepted his proposal and equally returned his love.

The summer of 1925 was indeed a pivotal time in Leroy's life. In addition to winning Naomi's hand, he had secured a contract to teach in the Music Department at Brigham Young University and was to begin his work immediately. It has been related that when he had come to be interviewed for this position, Robertson neither paraded his achievements (which by then were many and already well known), nor did he lay out any elaborate agenda for improving music at BYU. Nor did he express any concern about his salary. Rather, he stated only that what he wanted was an opportunity to work and the chance to build a musical organization around which he could center his efforts and through which he could express himself. "That is all he wanted, that is all he needed, and that is all he got," BYU President Franklin S. Harris would later remark. Thus began Leroy Robertson's long career as a respected faculty member at this venerable Church institution.

That summer, with Leroy teaching full time in Provo and Naomi living at her family home in Milton, the pair kept in touch by writing to each other every day. Also, Leroy took his fiancée to meet his own family, some of whom were in Fountain Green and some at the summer range high on the Big East. Here they camped and rode horses, this time with sister Wanda as chaperone. Leroy's adoration for his "Bonnie"—a term of endearment that he reserved for her throughout the rest of his life—was obvious to everyone. It was a beautiful summer.

But the course of true love never runs smooth. When Naomi informed her Alpine School District Superintendent of the forthcoming wedding, adding that she planned to commute from Provo to Pleasant Grove to fulfill her teaching duties, he would not accept this arrangement, and demanded that she choose between her job and marriage. Though disappointed with the thought of giving up her teaching career, love won out, and she did finally opt for marriage.

The wedding took place September 1, 1925, at the Nelson home in Milton with all members from both the Nelson and Robertson families present.[1] Immediately after the ceremony, Naomi's younger brother Leslie created some unexpected anxiety for Leroy when he and some buddies noisily snatched the new bride away from her groom, tossed her on the back of a waiting car, and drove her around the county for a brief, rural "shivaree." However, after a short while she returned unharmed, all ended well, and the following day, the newlyweds departed for Provo to begin their life together.

---

[1]The marriage was later solemnized in the Salt Lake LDS Temple.

PART II

AT THE FOOT OF MOUNT TIMPANOGOS

Chapter Seven

NEW PROFESSOR ON CAMPUS

JUST three days elapsed between Leroy's and Naomi's wedding and the beginning of the new school year at BYU, days which the newlyweds spent settling into their new home. At first, they lived in a small bungalow near the Provo Railroad Depot, but after a few months, they moved to a more comfortable duplex closer to the university. As their only furniture, the bride brought an upright piano, while the groom contributed two original oil paintings. This apparent preoccupation with such "impractical" items did arouse some concern in Naomi's pioneer mother, but she need not have worried. The young couple, steeped in the spartan, hard-work ethic of their forebears, were satisfied to add merely a stove, table, and bed to complete their "necessities." "Use it up, wear it out, make it do, or do without" became their motto for years to come.

Naomi's homemaking skills stood them in good stead. A fine seamstress, she fashioned curtains, bedding, and other household items; and as a cook, she concocted truly good meals from very little, meals that she always served on a clean linen tablecloth, with linen napkins in napkin rings at the side of each plate. Indeed, through all the years of their marriage, she managed the home so well that Leroy never had to worry about household matters. As Naomi later remarked, "We didn't have an awfully lot, but what we had was of very good quality. We never knew how poor we were."

However, despite their frugal life-style, and even with his full-time faculty appointment, Leroy realized that he would need a second job to supplement his meager BYU salary. Therefore, he moonlighted as a violinist in a small movie-house orchestra that provided background music for the silent films just beginning to prosper at this time. Playing two shows each night seven days a week, he directed the other musicians as he kept one eye on the film and the other on the music. He used to recall—with a small smile, for he also arranged the music—how the players, who had the various themes "numbered and thumbtacked all over their music stands," would jump from one number to another at his cue. The only theater in the area to have such a unique group of instrumentalists, this small movie house soon became the most popular entertainment spot for miles around.

In the BYU Music Department, Leroy had a basically threefold assignment: to expand the theory curriculum, build up the string program, and direct the university orchestra. To be more specific, this meant that Leroy taught most of the theory courses, tutored private students in violin and viola, and organized many string ensembles, with, however, his most challenging responsibility being the orchestra. His studio was in the old College Building on the school's "Lower Campus," which also housed College Hall, the main auditorium where all orchestra rehearsals and most of the concerts were held.[1]

Leroy was, in a way, just continuing on a larger and more advanced scale the work he had begun so many years before, when, as a mere high school student himself, he had traveled throughout the county giving violin lessons and organizing small instrumental groups among the students. But now, fifteen years older, and enlightened by his studies in Boston and recent experiences at North Cache and Pleasant Grove, he enjoyed the more secure backing of a university as well as having more advanced students. He himself saw no limit to what he could accomplish in bettering music in the region. Indeed, throughout his life, the restrictions imposed by his physical strength would prove to be the only thing that ever slowed him down.

But he did not proceed without some faculty opposition. Not everyone readily welcomed this energetic new arrival with his high

---

[1]At this time BYU had two campuses, of which the "Lower," subsequently called Academy Square, faced University Avenue. This property no longer belongs to BYU.

aspirations and constant challenges to their established ways and musical taste. In fact, even his most loyal colleagues would sometimes get upset by his uncompromising nature. But whenever they passed by his studio and heard the beautiful music he was making, they could only shake their heads in wonder and let their anger melt away. Despite the prolonged turf battle that inevitably developed between Robertson and some of the old guard as to who should teach what, by his third year at BYU he had already risen from instructor to associate professor. "Somehow, there was never any doubt that he was sort of the master," President Harris averred.

As to the theory courses, from the beginning of his BYU tenure, Robertson worked very hard to build up the enrollment and interest in this subject, which had hitherto been undervalued and seen as only an adjunct to performance. Robertson, to the contrary, always maintained that a sound knowledge of music theory was essential for all good musicians—composers and performers alike. Comparing a composer's score to an architect's plans, and the performer to a construction engineer, he reasoned that just as the construction engineer must understand the architect's plans in order to construct an edifice that will stand, so must the performer understand the composer's score in order to communicate in an accurate and meaningful manner what has been written.

As a result of his efforts, he attracted growing numbers of students to these heretofore neglected and unpopular classes. In fact, he even brought in a few high school youths, in whom he recognized a special musical talent, and whom he taught with the same diligence as he did his university students. One of these young recruits, a tenth-grader who took the First Year Harmony course twice—first as an auditor, then once again for credit and to really grasp it—reports that whereas this demanding professor was kind to him the first time around, during his second try, Robertson "really clamped down [on him] and never let up after."

This same boy would also learn that as a teacher, Robertson "had a very objective way of looking at things, factual, not given to embroidery, and [he] could get to the heart of the situation, see what was needed, then design a program for the benefit of each student.

He taught the student rather than just the course." Although he might have thought out a few basic outlines for his classes, he constantly varied the materials from one year to the next. One could attend the same course many, many times, and always be learning something new.

During his classes, Robertson often illustrated his ideas by punctuating the instruction with laconic comments laced with a dry sense of humor. One day when a Second Year Harmony student had given the alto but one note to sing throughout his entire composition, Robertson—thinking of his own lanky, non-curvaceous body—softly observed, "That alto-line has a shape just like mine." And again, upon perusing the very complicated beginning of a class member's new composition, he tersely challenged, "Just be sure you don't have a tiger by the tail." On yet another occasion, when a student submitted a page blackened with needless notes, Robertson calmly remarked, "You know, a composer's most important tool is his eraser."

But then in every case, he promptly proceeded to show the students an easier, more beautiful way to solve the problem at hand. A man of economy, he taught them how to make the finest music with the least means, whether in performance or composition. Everything he taught was related to music as a means of deep expression, and if this note or that note, even though correct, made poor music, then Robertson struck it down and a found a better way.

To his students, Leroy Robertson was "much more than just a teacher of theory. . . . He had a knack of teaching ideals, . . . of teaching what was good—why Bach was Bach and why Beethoven was Beethoven. . . . He got beyond the rules to teach music, musical refinement, and even more important, musical self-criticism." He showed his charges how to analyze the works of master composers and then asked them to do as well. To quote one lad:

> . . . it was always *our* fugues against what *Bach* had written. . . . With our Counterpoint exercises, he was never satisfied unless we came up with something as good as Palestrina, which was very difficult [and] at times very discouraging.

Nonetheless, after a few years of that sort of study, Robertson students got "a pretty good idea of what makes music tick, of what constituted great music and what was inferior."

Other collegians of this era remember Robertson as "a warm person who cared about students . . . one of the kindest, humblest men one ever would meet." Whereas many professors kept their office doors shut, Robertson's door always stood open, and if ever he saw a hesitant youngster standing outside his office, he would invite the youth in to chat. Rarely was he in his studio alone, but rather would sit at his desk orchestrating, carrying on conversations with half a dozen students at the same time, exchanging ideas, and expressing many of his personal feelings, his likes and dislikes, all of which were strong.

Regarding the development of the university's string program, Robertson had long realized that if he were to have competent string players, he would in large part have to teach them himself. Therefore, it was not long before he had amassed a large class of private pupils—both for violin and viola—whom he taught at odd hours on school days and all day Saturdays. He painstakingly planned individual programs of study for each one, more often than not composing and writing out by hand many of their exercises. These students came to him from throughout the state: from Cedar City on the far south; Logan and Tremonton on the far north; Price on the east; and Delta on the west. And eventually they were trooping in from the adjacent states as well: Idaho, Colorado, New Mexico, Arizona, Nevada, Wyoming.

His lesson fees were low, and in certain cases, according to one eyewitness, "so low you wouldn't believe the generosity." However, there were always a few students who really could not afford private instruction, and from them Robertson accepted payment in kind. It was not uncommon for him to receive a pound of home-churned butter, fresh fruit, and vegetables in return for lessons. The mother of one young girl regularly baked two loaves of whole wheat bread that she proudly delivered fresh and hot to the Robertson home every Thursday. Later, when Leroy and Naomi began to have a family, another lady asked to "baby-sit" their children, while yet another student paid for her lessons all through college by helping Naomi with the housework for a few hours on Saturday. In keeping with his thoroughgoing nature, Leroy kept meticulous accounts as to what was owed by whom: "_____ owes me 50¢"; "I owe _____ 50¢"; or simply, "_____, no charge." Indeed, many decades later, numerous students would tell Naomi that sympathetic Leroy had given them "countless lessons free."

A close bond developed between Leroy and these private students, and even after more than half a century, many would still remember how special their lessons were, how he always emphasized "the music," how he inspired them to do even better than what they thought was their best. Long after they had left BYU, they would write to this revered professor:

> . . . Right here I'd like to say that you have treated me grander and have done more for me than any other man except my father.

> You have done much for . . . music which no one knows anything about. . . . Your instructions will always be the peak of my training and I think the rest of your students feel the same way. You have given something that cannot be repaid in money.

The parents as well saw how Leroy was helping their children. Their letters to him disclose a deep and simple trust:

> I want to thank you for your help to _____. We all feel that she has accomplished a great deal. . . . I told her in my letter today that she must find more time to practice, even if it was necessary to drop some of her studies.

> . . . for your kindness to me I am going to reward you by placing in your care one of our sweet, talented, young ladies also [like you] possessed of a gentle even temperament, all of which is seldom found wrapped in the same parcel. . . . We are sacrificing her for a few months that she might return with even a finer touch and higher knowledge of that wonderful musical art you both possess. We are sure she will return to us as clean and pure as she leaves us.

Along with his private teaching, Robertson formed a number of chamber music ensembles as part of the string program, and he himself played in many of them. They performed at various school functions and even presented a few modest concerts. After hearing some of these fledgling organizations, President Harris insisted that they, i.e., Leroy, prepare "at least one string number" for the devotional assemblies regularly held each Tuesday for all BYU students. Although this required much extra planning for Leroy, it was time well spent. These instrumental numbers brought a beautiful variety to the devotionals, whose music heretofore had consisted mainly of light vocal pieces, with the more serious classical compositions generally being ignored. Robertson, who never "played down" to any audience, used these performances to introduce his listeners to the masterworks of Mozart, Schumann, Beethoven, Chopin, to name but a few. And in order that the students would more easily comprehend what they were about to hear, he would briefly explain each number beforehand. In no time, these presentations became an integral and much anticipated part of these assemblies.

One unusual performance for one of these string ensembles took place as a real pioneering effort. Young Earl J. Glade, who was just beginning to set up KSL Radio Station, asked Robertson to bring a string quartet to the station for one of its first broadcasts. The facilities can only be called primitive, for the broadcasting was done in a small shack situated on the roof of one of Salt Lake City's highest buildings, and to get onto the roof and into the shack, the players had to climb a ladder or two. For violin- and viola-toting instrumentalists this was not too easy; and for the 'cellist, it presented a real problem. However, with help, all four performers made it to the shack, and their concert went down in history as one of the first, perhaps even *the* first of "live-music" broadcasts in the Intermountain West. Thus began a tradition of collaboration between BYU musicians and KSL Radio that would continue for more than two decades.

However, above and beyond these notable contributions to the BYU Theory and String Instrumental programs, Leroy Robertson likely made his strongest impact on music—not only at BYU, but in the area at large—through his development of the Brigham Young University Symphony Orchestra. Once again remembering his own youthful hunger for symphonic music, and ever determined to create something better than what he had known as a lad, Robertson set out to build a respected organization that would some day be able to perform the best orchestral works of the greatest composers. It was to become a long, long labor.

Quite loosely organized before his arrival, the orchestra had been limited in its performances and repertoire by a lack of players. Robertson's first and most obvious task, therefore, was to find sufficient instrumentalists. These he sought anywhere and everywhere possible. He recruited players from the student body, the faculty, and even amongst the Provo townspeople, often paying some of the latter for their services from his own slim pocketbook. With the help of BYU bandmaster Professsor Robert Sauer—renowned composer of the popular song "Springtime in the Rockies"—he was able to enlist the best wind and brass players from the BYU band. As for the strings, by introducing certain of his own private violin students to the viola, he soon had developed a good corps upon which to build. Nor did Robertson's commitment stop with assembling the instrumentalists. When certain instruments—such as the piccolo and trombone—were lacking, he himself found and personally purchased them.

Orchestra rehearsals were held every afternoon from 5:00 till 6:00 P.M., the only hour that this whole motley crew could convene. Because he was working primarily with inexperienced youngsters, Robertson was first a teacher, then a conductor. In many cases he had to help them master their instruments, even the winds and brass. And as for repertoire, it was he who taught them their first symphonies, and overtures, he who gave them their "first real introduction to the higher realms of music." From the very beginning, they grappled with masterworks such as Beethoven's *Eroica Symphony*, of which their performance was likely a premiere for the region. This excerpt from a report about the BYU orchestra of 1925-1926 gives a firsthand account of their activities:

> Since the beginning of school the members of the organization under the able direction of Professor LeRoy J. Robertson have been working hard on a program that will speak well for the institution. The orchestra is unusually fine this year both in personnel and quality of work. . . . There is no doubt but what the attention of many students has been turned to College Hall during the time of rehearsal for Beethoven's *Third Symphony [Eroica]* with its fine, harmonious, and technical qualities.

From a purely technical standpoint, Robertson, with his remarkably keen ear, could unfailingly and quickly correct any wrong notes, be they flubbed, out of tune, or omitted. At one rehearsal, when a talented youngster newly "converted" from the trombone to the French horn, only pretended to play his part, Robertson simply put down his baton and stated, "The fourth horn is faking." On another occasion, when a young trombonist with a background in jazz "put a little vibrato in the slide," Robertson impatiently remarked, "Don't do that!" He endlessly drilled the string players till they could play together as one. "Violins, keep off that open D string," became his stock phrase.

However, although he corrected firmly and in an unforgettable way, he was never unkind, and would often lighten a tense moment by telling a joke or two. Once in a while, an unexpected "Damn" would explode from his lips, whereupon this staid professor merely explained to his startled charges that he allowed himself "one swearword per year if needed." In sum, the orchestra "rehearsed and rehearsed and rehearsed, worked and worked and worked."

But again as with his private students, Robertson was teaching these players much more than mere technique. Through his composer's understanding of the score, somehow he let the music unfold so that it was as if the composer himself—Bach, Mozart, Beethoven—were speaking. For the students this was a contact unknown before, and they came to perform "so far above their real ability to play that it was marvelous." Under Robertson, who was "a genius at holding people together," the orchestra developed a solid esprit de corps, a terrific morale. Long after leaving BYU, students would write nostalgically:

> I . . . long to be back at the good old Y and orchestra. . . . That orchestra will be the thing I'll miss the most. . . .

At first the orchestra was able to prepare and present but one concert per year, usually in the spring. These concerts—held in old College Hall—were triumphs and earned the group much support from all who heard them: the BYU administration, faculty, and students, as well as the people of Utah County.

Encouraged by this local reception, Leroy decided to take the orchestra on a few small tours, thereby making the BYU Symphony Orchestra the first organization to take symphonic music out to rural Utah and beyond. This was, in a sense, true pioneering, for no Utahn residing far beyond the Salt Lake City area had ever before had a chance to hear a symphony, there being as yet no radio broadcasts or orchestral recordings available. By introducing stockmen, farmers, and miners to classical music, Robertson was steadily building an ever-growing audience for such fare.

Fittingly, one of the orchestra's first excursions was to Fountain Green, Leroy's old home town. It was a grand occasion for everyone as his father, brothers, and three sisters invited the entire group to an outdoor party at the family homestead, treating them all to sandwiches and lemonade before the performance. All the citizens turned out for the concert, very proud that one of their sons could bring them this music. According to his brother, Doyle, however, "the best thing was how Leroy showed his respect for his family and the people of Fountain Green."

One unforgettable highlight for Robertson and the orchestra occurred when Dr. Carl Busch, renowned composer and conductor of the Kansas City Symphony, came to teach during the summer of 1927 as a visiting professor at BYU. To honor their noted guest, Robertson organized a "Grand Musical Concert" devoted solely to compositions by Dr. Busch, performed by various student and faculty groups from the Music Department. Dr. Busch graciously directed some of the numbers and also played first viola in a String Orchestra under Robertson's direction. This concert, described as "very much to the composer's liking," gave the region its first taste of contemporary American music.

Though Robertson was not able to study with Dr. Busch a great deal, he did show the eminent musician some of his scores, among which was his recently completed *Symphony No. 1*, or *Desert Symphony*. The Utahn's work must have impressed Dr. Busch, for he later would cite Robertson as "one of only three among all my students who I felt had a genuine talent and worked seriously" (the other two students being Robert Russell Bennett and William Dawson). Thus, just as he had with Chadwick in Boston, so did Leroy Robertson—once more isolated in the Rocky Mountains—make his mark on a renowned peer "from the outside." For Leroy, Dr. Busch would remain a constant inspiration throughout the years.

Meanwhile, on the home front, the summer of 1926 had brought a new challenge to Leroy and Naomi, for in August their first child was born, a little girl, whom they promptly named Alice Marian. Proud father Leroy loved to take this first-born with him wherever he could, and when at school, he often phoned home to inquire about his "little squawk-box."

Another significant family event occurred, when in 1927, the young couple bought their first home, a white stucco Spanish-style bungalow complete with red roof, located just a few short blocks from Leroy's Lower Campus studio. This little house, a pleasant, artistic, and beautiful place, soon became a real haven for many. With adequate space now available, the young couple immediately invested in a grand piano, using Naomi's upright as part payment. They also purchased a phonograph—the latest wind-up Victrola to be had—and gradually collected a few records: some "Pop" songs for Naomi and some "Classics" for Leroy. On the walls, along with Leroy's two beloved oil paintings, they also hung other original art works. Like their neighbors, Leroy and Naomi kept a vegetable garden, but unlike the others about, they landscaped the rest of their yard with many trees, shrubs, and rose gardens, thanks to the kind help of Naomi's older brother, Irvin T. Nelson.

From the beginning, the "Robertson White House" was often very crowded. There had long been a tradition in both Leroy's and Naomi's families to provide lodging for any relative wishing to attend school, and therefore, the Robertsons usually had a brother, sister, niece, nephew—or occasionally a needy student—living with them. A couple of daybeds and the living-room couch were constantly made up for someone or other.

Just one year after buying his home, Leroy made another very significant purchase. At last the violin came into his life that he had so long been seeking, an old Italian instrument that truly gave him the sounds he had heretofore been obliged to hear only in his imagination. Brought to Provo by Professor Sauer, this violin at once becharmed Leroy. He bought it outright and would never part with it for the rest of his life.

Then, just a few months later, there was yet another extremely important arrival in the Robertson household. In June 1929, a second child was born to Leroy and Naomi, another little girl, christened Renee. Leroy could not have been more thrilled.

Naomi relates that she never saw a father "more loving and tender" with his two small children, or more proud as they grew. Every evening he delighted in weaving separately for each one a fantastic bedtime tale of his own invention, much in the style of his Grandfather Robertson. In addition, he would sing, dance, make up tricks, and care for them in many, many ways. He did enjoy it, for he loved being with his children, and it truly gave him a much needed change of pace.

At Christmas time—just as he had done so many years before for his little brothers and sisters in Fountain Green—he now regularly made toys for his own little girls. One year he built a dollhouse, complete with furniture fashioned from wire clothes hangers for Marian; another year he made a little white doll's cradle for Renee.

There was but one persistent black cloud during these years. Leroy continued to suffer from the health problems that had plagued him during and immediately after his studies in Boston. He had much eye trouble, which innumerable sets of new eyeglasses never seemed to help, and terrible nervous headaches. He once wrote, "It just felt like I had a lump of lead in my stomach and an electric fan in my head." In an attempt to help put a few pounds on his thin, thin frame, Naomi would daily send a Thermos bottle filled half with milk and half with cream for him to drink between classes, but it proved to be a futile effort.

Nor did he ever relax his demanding schedule, not even in the summer, for these were the months when music teachers from throughout the Utah public school system came to study with him. Realizing that his own university work ultimately depended on the quality of students who advanced through the public schools, Robertson was very interested in helping these teachers. And they did become his grass-roots support in many ways.

However, no matter how busy he was, Leroy always found time and energy to compose. Much of it he did late at night after everyone had gone to bed and the house had become quiet, often staying up till well past 2:00 A.M. Sometimes of an evening he would go back to his studio on campus, where it was calm, uncluttered and comfortable, with warm radiator heat in winter and cool breezes in summer.

As a matter of fact, throughout his life he did all his composing so privately that the family was hardly ever aware of it. From time to time they might hear him playing certain passages over and over on the piano or violin, or they might see him intently writing at his desk in the living room, but they were certainly ignorant of the inner pressures and concentration involved. The interior drama that undoubtedly existed during this constant creation was rarely communicated to anyone else. Only in a few brief notes scattered here and there amongst his manuscripts did he hint at this unseen pain:

> Why does human being suffer
> line upon line
> precept for precept
> grace for grace

Nonetheless, it was always apparent when Leroy was working on a composition, for then he was wont to be preoccupied and distracted as he went about such mundane matters as driving the automobile or walking to school. With music continuously in some cranny of his mind, he would grab any piece of paper handy at the moment—an envelope, a scratch pad, or even empty staves on the page of some composition he was recopying—to jot down a melody as soon as it "hit" him.

These hastily notated sketches might sometimes be barely legible, but later, when he sat down to draft his pencil manuscript, "no composer ever made even an ink copy that looked quite so good," according to one colleague. Every measure, every beat was laid out across the page in perfect order. One of his copyists who would later make final ink manuscripts for him described his work as "meticulous."

Furthermore, Leroy Robertson was a practical composer in that he was always interested in the performer's point of view. He regularly sought the opinion of good instrumentalists when writing for an instrument that he did not himself play expertly, and would often ask them to try out various passages in many different versions so that he could hear the actual sound.

Compositions dating from these early years at BYU include many vocal numbers, some shorter orchestral works, and the afore-mentioned *Desert Symphony*. They bespeak his love of the land and the people about him.

As a composer, Leroy Robertson was considered by his associates to be a humble man, certainly not one to say, "I know it all," and they all saw in him "a man of deep spirit." Most certainly they had to agree that he was steadily and quickly making his mark as a foremost leader in the music world of Utah, not to mention the Intermountain West.

Chapter Eight

SAN FRANCISCO SOJOURN
AND TRAVELS TO OURAY

THE year 1930 proved to be very important in the life of Leroy
Robertson, for this is when he began his studies with the eminent
Swiss composer, Ernest Bloch, studies which, as Robertson later
observed, "marked a turning point in my career as a composer."

A longtime admirer of Ernest Bloch and his work, when Robertson first learned in 1925 that this great musician was coming west to
be director of the San Francisco Conservatory, he immediately set
out to find a way to study with him. The Utahn's persistent efforts
eventually paid off, and somehow he was able to obtain a leave of
absence from his teaching at BYU for March through August of 1930.
In typical Robertson fashion, many months before his scheduled
departure, he began contacting other important San Francisco musicians to ask about violin teachers and local symphony rehearsals. He
did want to make the most of this unique opportunity.

In the period just previous to his leave, Robertson was also
working on a score that he had been asked to write for a large pageant
then being planned by the LDS Church to commemorate the Centennial of its founding. To be presented in the great Salt Lake Tabernacle, and set to begin April 6, this pageant—entitled "The Message
of the Ages"—was to consist of tableaux depicting the history of the
Church's first hundred years, and Robertson's music was to accompany each scene. Scoring for full symphony orchestra, he composed
much original material, then also incorporated a few classical works
and certain Mormon hymns where appropriate.

However, although this would be Robertson's first symphonic
score to be performed in the Salt Lake Tabernacle, he was not present

for the event. In order to take full advantage of his anticipated six months with Mr. Bloch, he determined to leave as soon as Winter Quarter ended. Accordingly, in mid-March, he and Naomi loaded some household necessities and a few of Leroy's precious manuscripts into their newly acquired automobile, a Whippet—Leroy's pride and joy. Then bundling Marian and Renee into this "Green Wonder," they set off for California.

Because Donner Pass was still snowbound and impassable, the Robertsons were obliged to travel the longer route via southern Utah, across the Nevada and California deserts to Los Angeles, and then northward along the Pacific Coast towards the Bay Area. All in all, the trip lasted some ten days. At Oakland the little family had their first ferryboat ride across San Francisco Bay, a totally new adventure for them. In short order, they found a small apartment in Lomita Park, just south of San Francisco, and soon settled into a life quite different from what they had known in Utah.

Leroy immediately registered at the Conservatory and promptly began his studies with this great man whose teaching was to influence him for the rest of his life. Ernest Bloch's course, officially listed only as Harmony, consisted, among other things, of exhaustive analyses of J. S. Bach's *Chorales* and *Well Tempered Clavichord*, which showed the students how to critique and expand their own musical thinking. Leroy Robertson learned much more than mere compositional techniques, however, for Mr. Bloch was able to underscore in an illuminating way the deep spirituality that lay at the root of Bach's work. Thrilled as any explorer challenged by new worlds opening before him, the Utahn became both a devoted pupil of Bloch and an ardent disciple of Bach. Indeed, he would study and teach the works of the immortal Johann Sebastian till the end of his life, never ceasing to be amazed at what could be found therein.

It was at this time that Robertson started to compose his *Quintet in A minor for Piano and Strings*, a major opus which he would show to his teacher now and again. His notes concerning Mr. Bloch's comments about this work in its early stages are both cogent and useful for any writer:

Don't ever make a cadence because there is nothing else to do (because it is convenient). Let the idea have its full development.

In addition to studies at the Conservatory, Leroy attended rehearsals of the San Francisco Symphony whenever possible, a listening-learning experience held over from his Boston years. Through the symphony's conductor, Alfred Hertz, he even arranged to take some violin lessons with the concertmaster.

Simple family activities also occupied Leroy. He never tired of taking Naomi and their two children to the nearby San Francisco airport just then under construction. Here he would station the Whippet outside the high airport fence, and from this close vantage point, he and his family would watch in wonder and excitement as an occasional plane landed or departed the airfield. On one particular day, despite the damp gray fog rolling in and much to Naomi's dismay, he insisted on taking the family to the beach for a wiener roast with friends. It was a bit chilly by the ocean, but the food tasted good and the sound of the waves was tremendous. On yet another momentous day, he drove his family into San Francisco. After parking the Whippet on a very steep hill that descended straight into the bay below, he left his three charges for a few minutes while he ran a short errand. But upon his return, he could not find them. Although Naomi had spent her whole life in the high mountains of Utah, never had she seen anything so precarious as the hills of San Francisco, and fearing that the Whippet would surely topple into the yawning waters at their feet, she had made her little girls get out of the car and wait with her elsewhere. Another experience added a new dimension to Robertson family life when Leroy learned how to eat artichokes by watching someone enjoying this delicacy in a restaurant. That strange edible—prominently displayed in all the local grocery stores—had puzzled them since their arrival, for it was quite unlike anything they had ever seen before, and they really could not imagine what to do with it. But after Leroy demonstrated how to cook and eat this thorny thistle, the Robertsons henceforth made artichokes a favorite food at their table.

And so the weeks passed from March until early June. As planned, Leroy again registered at the Conservatory, this time for the summer session. But a scant two days later, he received a surprising letter from Mr. Bloch's wife, Margherite, stating that Mr. Bloch had suddenly decided to leave America and return to Europe, and that since he would be busy preparing for the trip and was also very, very tired, he could devote no more time to his students. Robertson was crestfallen. He had expected to remain with this master teacher at least another three months. Indeed, he felt that he was just getting a good start.

This terrible blow was perhaps softened only slightly by Mr. Bloch expressing his own deep appreciation for Robertson's "seriousness in work and fine musicianship and sympathy and understanding for his [Bloch's] aims and ideals." The composer from Utah might also have taken comfort in knowing that he had truly gained a special place in his teacher's heart, for just a few weeks earlier, Ernest Bloch had inscribed a photo of himself for this unusual student as follows:

> To Leroy Robertson
> One of the "very few"
> With great sympathy.

Greatly disappointed at having his studies cut short so abruptly, Leroy decided to return to Provo as soon as possible. However, for him these few months with Ernest Bloch had been the best days of his life, and he determined forthwith that somehow he would find a way to continue his work with this inspiring teacher-composer. Still restless and aching for more time to compose, he thought of applying for a Guggenheim award, but never really pursued the idea.

Once again at BYU, Robertson resumed his duties as a full-time professor, with about the same assignments as before. He now became, as one student later recalled, "the whole Theory Department." Inspired by his recent work with Ernest Bloch, he added a new aspect to his teaching by introducing detailed studies of Bach compositions. His students, literally steeped in this treasure-trove, saw how "Bach was possibly the only composer who made the notes go not where they wanted to go, but rather, where he, the composer, wanted them to go," and some realized, that they were glimpsing "the composer as creator, one who was at once both above and yet with nature."

As to his university orchestra, Robertson had now assembled a good-sized group of about sixty-five or seventy players. As usual, he programmed music of the highest quality, but which, at the same time, would appeal to those still unfamiliar with symphonic repertoire. His musicians could at last handle a concert that included a complete symphony, plus an overture or suite, and other shorter numbers. At times, he would feature one of his particularly fine violin students as soloist in a concerto, and on rare occasions he would present one of his own orchestral compositions. Their "big concert piece" of 1931 was Mozart's *Symphony No. 39 in E-flat Major*, while their 1932 pièce de résistance was Dvořák's *Symphony No. 5 (from the New World)*, both premieres for the region.

An especially memorable symphony concert occurred in early 1932 as part of a program that featured no less a Russian dignitary than the Countess Alexandra Tolstoy. One can easily imagine how thoroughly Robertson prepared his players in anticipation of their appearance before such an auspicious visitor. Among other numbers, they performed the entire *Nutcracker Suite*, which incidentally may well have marked yet another premiere for the people of Utah. Those remembering the occasion report that the Countess was "very thrilled with the orchestra's performance."

During these years the BYU Symphony Orchestra not only played more concerts locally, but also began to tour farther and more often. Although he occasionally had only a chamber orchestra ranging from twenty-five to thirty members, for the most part, Robertson took the full seventy-piece orchestra. Journeying north even into central Idaho and south to the borders of southern Utah, they covered what were unusually long distances in this era of narrow thoroughfares and slow-moving vehicles. In fact, as these intrepid musicians braved the still unpaved roads over Soldier's Summit to take their music to the people of Price in eastern Utah, they traveled in buses so decrepit that whenever they came to a dugway, all the orchestra members had to get out of the bus and push.

In these early and mid-1930s, yet another important facet of Leroy Robertson's influence on music gradually began to show itself throughout the West. He had now developed students who themselves were proficient enough to go into the various rural communities and teach just as he had done. At first a modest infusion, it constantly grew as his graduates—all carrying with them the high standards, ideals, and methods of their teacher—fanned out into Utah and the neighboring states. It is heart-warming to note that early on Leroy sent one of his best students to Fountain Green when his beloved home town needed a music teacher. And, thanks to Leroy's good auspices, this young man even lived at the home of Leroy's Uncle Jim.

However, although Leroy Robertson was now firmly established in his work at BYU and charting a clear course for himself in its Music Department, he nonetheless felt a deep need to earn the standard academic degrees to complement his diplomas from the New England Conservatory. He realized that attitudes were changing and that certification from a professional school would soon not be sufficient if one wished to be fully recognized by university academia. Therefore, already since the summer of 1926, he had consistently been enrolling in courses at BYU with the intention of eventually earning both his A.B. and M.A. degrees, and was now pursuing this goal more diligently than ever. The demanding class assignments required hours of daily study, which Leroy, however, very much enjoyed. According to Naomi, "If he was learning or creating something new, it was the greatest pleasure he could have."

One course he particularly liked was Psychology, where he directed his attentions to the "Psychology of Music." The following excerpts taken from the notebook he prepared on this subject reveal something of Robertson, the philosopher-educator:

> Intellect should not be confused with information. The one represents power and the other storage goods.
> Thinking is the elaboration of ideas in the mind to meet new situations and to seize new problems.
> A musician should have intellectual interests outside his art to acquire a sensible outlook and interpretation.
> The great musician is always a person of great intellect. . . . Although the form and content of the [musical] thought are different, it requires the same logical grasp as in mathematics or philosophy.
> The outer form of music is a symbol of the inner feelings,

ideals, or ideas of the composer, performer, and listener. It appeals especially to the imagination in that the symbols do not represent discrete ideas. Let it not be misunderstood, however, that music does not convey fine distinctions; "it is more definite than speech, and to want to explain it by means of words is to make the meaning obscure."

"The great artist has thought and lived great thoughts a long time before he breaks out into song."

During these early 1930s Robertson was also writing his master's thesis. Extracts from the "Introduction," with its pointed comments about music in relation to society, tell much about Leroy Robertson, the down-to-earth idealist:

> Music is the art of tone and rhythm. . . . But . . . the term itself is of no consequence . . . [Music] can be a medium of expression serving an outlet for the savage soul or it can warble the sick sentimentality of an up-to-date "crooner." It will respond to the fingers of an amateur pianist whose rich relatives make it a recital display of an expensive gown or it will drone out the longings of an unfortunate beggar at the corner. It will march with the High School Band or it will sing with the Symphony. It will ring in riches, fame and fat for the lucre-conformists of a commercial print shop or it will utter the cosmic message of a God-thrilled soul draining the body to death, the mind to insanity. It will tingle the sweet consonances of the maiden's prayer or it will prophesy in terrible dissonance the fate of a warped world.
>
> It is therefore of greatest importance to ascertain, if possible, the message of most value which this art has given and is giving, and to realize the best means of arriving at its interpretation. No true artist should be concerned about the external show of this message, neither should its material advantages, if there be any, impress him. He should only be deeply conscious of its fundamental correctness and the bit of cosmic reality which it dips from that deep flow of eternal truth.

In the conclusion of this thesis, Robertson casts a few well-aimed darts against the prevailing attitude towards music that ever seemed to surround him, and against which he so constantly and diligently fought:

> We are a race that indeed *races*. While nature fashions a mushroom, we erect skyscrapers. Impressive as they are, they have not as yet pierced the stars. . . .

It is paradoxical that we, a people who profess admiration for the truth, should have become misled in musical evaluation. We zealously preach purity of the physical but the cultural is taken without serious question.

* * * * *

In view of his academic load, it is amazing that Robertson found any energy for composing, yet he did. And at this time he began to draw on a new source of musical material that would enrich much of his work henceforth.

He had long been keenly interested in American Indian music, and when he met up with William F. Hanson, a fellow faculty member and well acquainted with the Ute Indian tribes at Ouray and White Rocks in eastern Utah, Robertson at last found someone who could take him into the society of this proud and exclusive people. With Bill Hanson as guide and interpreter, Leroy traveled for many years to these Ute reservations, where he was permitted to observe their ritual dances, hear and transcribe their chants. After each visit, Leroy returned home with pages and pages of melodies he had notated from the Sun and Bear Dances.

Through the years he would incorporate these haunting Ute chants into his compositions in an expressive and powerful way. However, rather than rendering an exact imitation of the Indians' manner of chanting, he chose to adapt their melodies to his own personal idiom, to place them, as he once said, "on the level of our Western art."[1] The first such work was an extended symphonic tone poem, *Timpanogos*, which contains not only Ute Indian songs, but also the beloved LDS hymn, "Come, Come, Ye Saints." Subsequent major works in which the composer would eloquently employ Indian themes are the *String Quartet in E minor* and the *Concerto for Violin and Orchestra*, among others.

---

[1] In making this remark, Robertson meant no disrespect, but was explaining how he coordinated these two disparate musical traditions. His original transcriptions would satisfy the demands of the most exacting ethno-musicologist as to accuracy.

Yet, despite this over-full life, Robertson was driven by discontent. He still longed for more study with Ernest Bloch, and at Christmas time, 1931—slightly more than a year after his sojourn in San Francisco—Robertson wrote to his esteemed mentor, still in Europe, to inquire about working with him once again. After what must have seemed a long five months, in early May 1932, a warm letter finally arrived from Mr. Bloch explaining his delay in answering and inviting Leroy to come to Europe at once. Mr. Bloch, who was now residing in a mountain retreat not far from Lake Lugano in the Italian section of Switzerland, enthusiastically described how Leroy could live in an excellent *pension* (boarding house) in the nearby village of Roveredo-Capriasca, and how he would likely be Bloch's only student for the entire summer. This was good news indeed.

When actually faced with the prospect of going to Europe, however, Leroy at first found the idea impossible. With the great depression of the 1930s in full swing, finances loomed as an insurmountable obstacle. If Leroy were to go on sabbatical leave, his already lean salary would be halved, and under those circumstances, how could any man possibly study in Europe and still provide for his wife and two children in Utah? An unexpected answer to their prayers appeared when Naomi was offered a full-time job as a sewing teacher at BYU. Even more good news arrived when they learned that Naomi's sister, Minnie Evalyn, could come to help run the household while Naomi was teaching all day at school. In addition, Leroy's brother, Joe, decided to come to study at BYU, and this meant that there would be a man around the house to do the heavy work of stoking the fires and shoveling the deep winter snows.

Leroy and Naomi discussed the problem from every angle. She felt that they could manage somehow, and they both realized that Leroy would never get another chance to study with Mr. Bloch, certainly not as his only private student. Furthermore, Leroy had now completed all requirements for his A.B. and M.A. degrees, and was scheduled to graduate in June, so this hurdle was out of the way. Finally, after much deliberation and planning, and after receiving much impassioned advice from others—both pro and con—Leroy decided to go.

Having once made up his mind, he was anxious to be on his way and was ready to leave as soon as Spring Quarter ended. On June 5, 1932, he played for the BYU Baccalaureate exercises one last violin solo, a composition of his own. At commencement, he received, with honors, his two hard-earned diplomas. Then, one week later, on a hot summer morning in mid-June, he departed for Europe and experiences that would leave their mark for life.

Chapter Nine

ALPINE MEADOWS AND STORM TROOPERS

LEROY departed Provo about noon. As Naomi and the two little girls accompanied him to the old interurban station to bid him good-by, there were tears in everyone's eyes. No one knew what the future would hold. They all took some comfort, however, in the fact that Leroy would not be journeying alone. Young J. J. Keeler—one of Robertson's theory and orchestra students—had decided to go to Germany to pursue organ studies, so teacher and pupil had arranged to travel together. At Salt Lake City, they boarded the east-bound train, stopped over for a few hours in Chicago, then went on to New York City, where they embarked on the steamship "Hamburg" for an uneventful crossing of the Atlantic. Leroy disembarked at Cherbourg while J. J. continued on to Germany.

At last in Europe, as he traveled overland to meet Ernest Bloch in Roveredo-Capriasca, Leroy was haunted by the fact that such composers as Mozart, Schubert, and Mendelssohn had each managed to write innumerable compositions of major proportions before dying in their early thirties, whereas he, Leroy Robertson, now already in his mid-thirties, had as yet produced but very few large-scale works: one symphony—still not finished to his liking; a *Quintet for Piano and Strings*, still being composed; and an overture, albeit a prizewinning one. To be sure, he could claim a large number of songs, anthems, hymns, violin solos, and suites, yet he could not help wondering, was he foolish to think that at his age he would indeed write something of significance? He could only answer, "I don't know why I am over here, but I will keep trying anyway."

Once in Roveredo-Capriasca, Leroy found the promised inexpensive lodging at the Pension Roveredo, a plain boardinghouse set into a steep cliffside that could be reached only by foot or bicycle. His room overlooked a canyon with trees, green alpine meadows descending to Lake Lugano a few miles distant, and the jagged Alps beyond. Roveredo-Capriasca itself, one of many small villages in the region, was located straight up the mountainside, not far from the Swiss-Italian border constantly patrolled by Italian soldiers ordered to shoot anyone who tried to cross.

Knowing that his studies with Ernest Bloch would stop at summer's end, Leroy wasted no time. The very day of his arrival he proceeded directly to Mr. Bloch's home, pencil and paper in hand, ready to resume his learning with this great composer-teacher. At this time, Mr. Bloch outlined a program of study and analysis that might well have overwhelmed a less ambitious, less well-prepared student.

All that wonderful summer, Leroy spent part of each day with Mr. Bloch and was treated like one of the family. Sometimes his lessons would last several hours, but other times, the two would just have a short session for their music, then go out wandering through the countryside to hunt mushrooms. It was during these hikes through the nearby meadows and ravines that the two composers discussed their beliefs and ideals not only about music, but about life in general. Bloch, well read in French literature and deeply philosophical, reinforced Robertson's own feelings concerning the need to hold to one's integrity and the danger of pursuing "'relations,' publicity, quick company, [and] the 'fads' of the moment, 'social success.'. . ." Indeed, Ernest Bloch forthrightly declared that "many sold their 'souls' in [so] doing, . . . and [thereby] lost the *only* treasure we possess: our own conscience and personality. . . . What can be the use of success, applause, approbation of others if deep inside one feels one has not been *true* to oneself?" Both men lamented, "Nowadays if one wants to be on the front page [i.e., get one's work performed], one must forever see people, pester conductors, and be a travelling salesman for one's own ware!" Both regretted the superficialities that seemed to be dominating music of the day. As Bloch would later write:

. . . I cannot act as *so many* so-called "modernists" do! . . . [with their] Charletanism, Emptiness, tricks already out of date, for the most. . . . People have nearly lost their heads! The old principles have been crumbling and they have nothing to replace them but fanatical theories in which I do not believe— . . . it requires great courage, perseverance, and faith to live in such an Epoch—and one must go on and do one's best, with no hope of reward or recognition.

Another quality that Robertson and Bloch held in common was a love of nature and a desire to live away from the world's great metropolitan centers. As Bloch explained:

. . . we [Mr. and Mrs. Bloch] decided to leave the cities . . . to find peace and . . . health in the mountains. . . . it is beautiful here, peaceful, quiet. . . . Then, I can work again, which is the most important thing for me. . . . In big cities there is too much *distraction*, the feeling of *intrigues*, of *lack of judgment*, *discrimination*, [and lack of] balance perturbs you too much.

During these precious months, Robertson of course directed his main efforts to composing, concentrating especially on the *Quintet for Piano and Strings*, begun so long ago in San Francisco. This routine of study and composing lasted until the end of September when Mr. Bloch left for Italy to prepare and conduct performances of his own compositions, and as planned, Leroy then also departed Roveredo and went on to Germany to continue his studies there.

Robertson had already arranged to study in Berlin with Dr. Hugo Leichtentritt, often called the "Father of Musicology." But, before committing himself to yet another period of intensive work, he decided to spend a couple of months in Pforzheim and Leipzig with some Utah friends. In Pforzheim he visited with John R. Halliday, a former student who was then serving a mission for the LDS Church. After about a month of rest and relaxation in this Baden city, Leroy then journeyed eastward to Leipzig to check on young J. J. Keeler, who was now enrolled as an organ student at that city's renowned conservatory.

Leroy remained in Leipzig for about six weeks. He and J. J. attended concerts of the Gewandhaus—one of Europe's leading orchestras then under the baton of Bruno Walter—and Leroy even managed to get a few violin lessons with that orchestra's concert-master, Edgar Wollgandt. He often visited Leipzig's grand cathedrals, his favorite being the *Thomaskirche* (St. Thomas Church), where Bach himself had once been *Kapellmeister* (music director). Here, he loved to listen to the organists, and was particularly enthralled when they played compositions of Bach, for then, the sounds echoed and re-echoed throughout the high vaulted ceilings, forming vibrant dissonances from which a beautiful consonance would emerge as the music came to rest. So impressed was Robertson by this phenomenon that he later sought to recreate this same effect in many of his own works.

As might be expected, the Utahn, constantly inspired by the great organ music surrounding him, became interested in composing for this instrument, and his principal organ pieces, including the *Fantasia for Organ* and the *Organ Sonata in B minor*, were at least germinated, if not finished, in Leipzig.

At last Leroy was immersed in a rich culture that from every side nourished his all-consuming need for music. Yet, he found it extremely hard to be separated and so far away from his family. Letters from home constantly kept him informed about life in Utah, but he longed to be there. Naomi was teaching every day, Marian enjoying first grade, and three-year-old Renee staying at home in the care of her beloved "Aunt Min." Leroy's brother, Joe, had indeed come to live with the family while attending BYU. In addition, another student took board and room with them, thus filling the modest Robertson bungalow to almost more than capacity. The Utah winter of 1932-1933 brought some of the earliest, deepest snows and coldest temperatures on record. Already in November, Leroy had received a plaintive letter from Marian, lamenting that Joe would not help her "make a snowmen" [*sic*], and that she wished her father were back home "to do it." Then, when Naomi's mother suddenly and quite unexpectedly died a few weeks later, leaving Naomi devastated, the Utahn wished more than ever that he were back in Utah to take care of his little family.

However, despite his loneliness and homesickness, he stayed in Germany, almost frantically taking in all the music the country could offer. In early December he left Leipzig for Berlin, and at once began his long awaited studies with Dr. Leichtentritt.

Profound, demanding scholar though he was, Hugo Leichtentritt has nonetheless been described by those who met him as "a very gentle soul," "most kind, cultured, and gracious." He resided with his mother in an unpretentious but well-appointed apartment, complete with balcony and a view to the street, of which both were very proud. Under Dr. Leichtentritt's direction, Leroy concentrated on the music of the Renaissance composers, copying by hand many of their works and thereby thoroughly learning the techniques of sixteenth-century counterpoint, new and necessary mind-expanding skills which he later would teach to his own students as they became ready.

While in Berlin, Leroy—ever in love with the violin and wishing to improve his playing—found, with the help of Dr. Leichtentritt, another great teacher, the renowned pedagogue and violin virtuoso, Carl Flesch. Though Leroy likely had but a few lessons with this acknowledged master of bowing technique, he was able to add many skills to his own playing which he would later pass on to future students. He also had the good fortune to pursue further violin study with Roman Totenberg, then recognized as one of Europe's most brilliant young concert artists. After a few months, however, Totenberg told the Utahn that he would be leaving Berlin for Paris, mainly to escape the increasing Nazi menace. As a special parting gift, Leroy presented his teacher with a newly completed work for violin and piano, "Lullaby from the Rockies," which he based on a Ute Indian melody. Totenberg graciously accepted the manuscript, and later included the "Lullaby" in his repertoire.

Not long after Leroy had begun his work in Berlin, J. J. Keeler came from Leipzig for a visit and decided to remain in the capital city to continue his organ studies there. The two friends shared living quarters, but since their particular interests differed, they were not together much of the time. Nonetheless, Leroy did feel responsible for young J. J. and watched over him like an older brother.

Eager to absorb as much music as possible, Leroy and J. J. attended concerts almost daily, often as the guests of Dr. Leichtentritt, who was also Berlin's foremost music critic. They frequently went to hear the Berlin Philharmonic, then under the direction of Wilhelm Furtwängler, and for the first time in their lives, saw many, many Wagner operas, for which Leroy seemed to have unbounded admiration. They also visited the great churches of Berlin, where they heard—also for the first time—Bach's *Passion according to Saint John* and *Passion according to Saint Matthew* as well as many cantatas. For Leroy, it was all "just like heaven." Furthermore, the two Utahns, almost inebriated by this rich culture, found it hard not to buy every music score and book to be had on all sides.

A quite different aspect of Leroy's musical activities in Berlin can be seen in his ongoing contributions to the music program of the LDS Church in that region. As he had done in Leipzig, so in Berlin, he arranged hymns and anthems for the congregations and choirs, and at Church functions, he often performed violin solos—many of his own composition.

However, despite all the wonders that Berlin offered, one very humble item of ever-increasing importance was missing in Leroy's life. Since leaving home, the Utahn had developed a nagging thirst for an ice-cream soda, a treat as yet unavailable in Germany, and he finally determined that this sad situation should be remedied. So, one day with a loyal friend in tow, he betook himself to an ice-cream parlor where he had become acquainted with the proprietor. After an impressive "hard sale," he was able to persuade the dubious man to make up this marvelous drink. Following Leroy's explicit instructions, the shopkeeper methodically proceeded to combine the necessary ingredients. Everything went well until, as his last and most crucial item, the newly recruited soda jerk added *das Spritzwasser* (club soda). Suddenly, the magnificent concoction began to fizz and sputter, then bubble wildly all over the counter and down onto the floor. Convinced that he had unwittingly created some terrible explosive primed to blow his shop to smithereens, the startled proprietor dashed panic-stricken into the street, shouting for the police. Needless to say, Leroy and his companion beat a hasty retreat and never again patronized that place.

The shopkeeper doubtless had good reason to be afraid, for in this winter of 1933, Berlin was becoming a dangerous place to live. Hitler and his Nazis, now established in the capital city, were fast consolidating their alarming power. By the end of January, Hitler had been named Chancellor of Germany, and a few weeks later, arsonists torched the *Reichstag* (House of Parliament). Dreaded Blackshirts, Hitler's elite Storm Troopers, filled the city. No one seemed to know what would happen next or how to prevent it.

Leroy and J. J., who resided in a Jewish neighborhood, witnessed firsthand the Nazis' ruthless destruction as Storm Troopers raged "all over the place, breaking into Jewish stores, caving in windows, dragging out shopkeepers, throwing goods out on the streets and looting." Even the two Utahns were accosted from time to time. For example, one day, after making some purchases in a Jewish shop, they found their path blocked by Nazi sympathizers —men and women—who, mistaking them for Jews, harassed them at the doorstep and kept them from leaving the building. Not one to be intimidated, Leroy stood his ground and cursed them roundly in very obscene English laced with swearwords so vile as to make one's hair stand on end. Rabble that they were, the crowd somehow understood. Backing away, the troublemakers apologized, saying that they were "not against the English." Leroy, still furious, quietly explained in his very good *Hochdeutsche* (Literary German) that he and J. J. were not even English, but Americans come to study in Germany.

On yet another occasion, as Leroy and J. J. sat one evening on the minuscule balcony of their apartment overlooking the street below, they suddenly heard shots ring out, saw a van drive up, and helplessly watched while Blackshirts roughly herded an entire family into the vehicle. No one ever heard anything from that family again. After this incident, J. J. chose to leave Germany and continue his organ studies in less dangerous London. But Leroy, determined to complete his year's sabbatical in Germany, opted to remain in Berlin.

As a matter of fact, Leroy's innate curiosity would not let him rest until he had seen Adolph Hitler close up and in person if possible, for he truly could not comprehend how this madman had been able to arouse the German people to such fury. Therefore, when it was announced that Hitler would be speaking one evening in Berlin's vast *Sportpalast* (Grand Sports Arena), Leroy devised a way to get past the redoubtable S.S. guards and into the building. He and a missionary friend made up some very fancy "press cards" which identified the two as "reporters" for the *Improvement Era* (an LDS publication). Once in the vicinity of the *Sportpalast*, they of course found every block cordoned off and all streets blocked by Hitler's Blackshirts. Hearts in their throats but undeterred, they bravely flipped out copies of the *Improvement Era* and flashed their "press cards" before the troopers at each blockade. So impressive were these credentials that they were somehow allowed to pass by. At the building's entrance, not only were they admitted, but promptly escorted to seats in the front row of the international press box situated directly above the speaker's platform. Hearing Hitler at such close range repelled Leroy and awakened in him a dreadful foreboding as to what lay ahead. This contempt and fear he continually expressed in several compositions dating from this time.

These months in Berlin proved in fact to be very productive for Robertson as a composer. He had always been able to write with great facility, but now, with few distractions, he was working with unbelievable fire and rapidity.

As usual, Leroy had melody after melody coursing through his head waiting to be developed into some opus or other. However, for many weeks, there had been one tune in particular—a driving and angry theme—that was really bothering him. Try as he might, he could not get it to evolve into any sort of full-fledged composition, and it just would not leave him in peace. Then, one day as he was casually walking down the street on his way to a lesson with Dr. Leichtentritt, another tune "hit" him. Realizing at once that he had found the companion (or foil) to his problem-melody, he stopped and whipped from his briefcase the ever-present manuscript paper; then, propping his foot on the ledge of a nearby shopwindow, with briefcase and paper balanced on his knee, he began to write as quickly as he could, oblivious to all else. The music came almost faster than he could notate it. When he breathlessly ceased writing a scant few minutes later, he had composed, nonstop, from beginning to end, the entire *Etude in G minor for Pianoforte*, a passionate and dramatic work in which he never changed a single note thereafter. Some twenty years later, citing Aristotle's definition of the "enthusiastic poet," Robertson would refer to this etude as having been composed by a person of "intense feeling who wrote in a transport of frenzy."

Other major works completed in Berlin are the *Quintet for Piano and Strings*, the aforementioned *Sonata* and *Fantasia* for organ, and two other *Concert Etudes for Pianoforte*.

After this winter of such intense activity, Leroy, however, was forced to slow his pace when in the spring he became very seriously ill. Truth to tell, in his effort to make every minute count during this year in Europe, Leroy had once again pushed himself much too hard. Already at the end of his studies with Ernest Bloch in Roveredo, he was suffering from general fatigue and nervous strain that constantly triggered a lot of upset in his system. And as he continued the same relentless schedule in Berlin, his health could only deteriorate. Finally he became so ill that in desperation he urgently sent for Naomi.

As soon as she received his call for help, Naomi immediately arranged to stop her BYU teaching several weeks in advance, got permission to give her exams early, left the children and household completely in care of Minnie Evalyn, and departed for Europe the first week of May. Because she had to cross the United States by bus, and the Atlantic and North Sea by steamship, it took about two weeks for her to reach Berlin.

Meanwhile, Leroy's condition had steadily worsened, and ultimately he was in such pain that he was rushed by ambulance to the hospital. Diagnosed with acute appendicitis, he was operated on at once, but then lay for days critically ill, fighting with all his might for his life while he awaited his beloved wife.

Knowing that he would not be able to move from his bed for some time, he asked John R. Halliday—his missionary friend now transferred from Pforzheim to Berlin—to go meet Naomi at the ship, which was to dock at Hamburg. Upon finding her, John explained to the bewildered woman what had happened and took her directly to Berlin and the hospital. With his "Bonnie" at last nearby, Leroy began to regain his strength, and was soon well enough to leave the hospital, though still too weak to be up and about very much.

At this critical point in Leroy's convalescence, the young couple was kindly invited to use an extra room in the LDS German Mission Home by Mission President Dr. O. H. Budge and his wife Margaret, who had both become well acquainted with Leroy through his Church-related music work. The Mission Home was located near the *Tiergarten*, Berlin's beautiful and famed zoological gardens, and every day, Naomi and Leroy strolled through the tranquil park, each time going a little farther than the day before as Leroy slowly grew stronger. From their room, evening after evening, they could hear the nightingales sing, music they never forgot.

At the earliest possible moment, Leroy took Naomi to a performance of a Wagner opera, *Die Meistersinger*. After the overture, her reaction to this new experience was somewhat neutral, but Leroy, completely entranced, could not help murmuring, "That was worth the whole trip."

Also, as soon as he was able, Leroy took Naomi to meet Dr. Leichtentritt, who invited the young couple for lunch and a boat ride on one of the many lakes around Berlin. At this time, Dr. Leichtentritt also wrote a "Letter of Recommendation for Leroy Robertson," in which he detailed Leroy's studies in Europe and praised him as:

> not only a talented musician, well informed in his art, intelligent, eager to increase his stock of knowledge, but also an artist in the proper sense of the term. He possesses the rare gift of finding satisfaction in working as an artist for art's sake mainly.

When Leroy had sufficiently recovered, he and Naomi embarked on a bit of European travelling, a delayed honeymoon, as it were. First, they went to Denmark, where, in the land of her forebears, Naomi readily spoke the Danish learned from her father, but not used since childhood. Leroy then took Naomi to meet Ernest Bloch, who was once again living near Lake Lugano. After a warm reunion with this dear mentor and his family—one mixed with many heartfelt goodbyes—the "honeymooners" journeyed on to Salzburg and Vienna, where Naomi discovered to her dismay that the Danube was not really "blue."

Next came Paris, with stopovers en route at Milan, Prague, Dresden, Leipzig, and Frankfurt-am-Main (in honor of Goethe).

Once in Paris, with tickets obtained through the help of another Mormon missionary friend, they spent an evening at the Opéra, which likely impressed Leroy much more than did the Eiffel Tower. Then after a brief visit in London with J. J. Keeler, in early July they boarded a steamship at Southampton, homeward-bound at last. Stopping but briefly in New York and Chicago where they splurged to visit the 1933 World's Fair, they excitedly caught a coach-car bound for Utah, penniless but happy.

Because Minnie Evalyn had closed their Provo residence for the summer and had taken the two little Robertson girls to the old Nelson home in Milton, Leroy and Naomi detrained at Morgan, the nearest station. Reunion with family and friends was a thrilling event for everyone. Even neighbors in Milton danced up and down the street at the news of their arrival. Renee, not recognizing this father who had been absent for so long, ducked her little blond head and refused to leave the protecting arms of her "Aunt Min." But Marian ran joyfully to him, hardly daring to believe that he had truly come home at last.

It was near summer's end when the Robertsons—Leroy, Naomi, and their two children—returned to Provo. Once again in the "White House on Third North," they all awaited the beginning of another school year.

Chapter Ten

PRIZEWINNING AND PIONEERING

AFTER his year in Europe, Leroy seemed to enjoy his work better and generally be more satisfied than before. Every Saturday he relaxed a bit by playing a vigorous game of volleyball with other faculty friends, and because he soon established himself as one of the keenest and most aggressive participants, everyone wanted to play on "his" team. At home, he began to teach music to his two little girls, calmly showing Renee how to draw a tone from the violin, finding suitable piano pieces for Marian to learn, and even composing simple songs for them both to sing. Sunday evenings he lit a fire in the living-room fireplace and gathered his family around for sandwiches and hot chocolate while they listened to the weekly Detroit Symphony broadcast of the ABC Ford Sunday Evening Hour. As he later wrote:

> Although the times were uncertain with wars, government scandals, and a serious depression, we lived fairly content in an atmosphere of friendliness, frugal security, and common sense. People were free to express themselves and much was said but not all of it was listened to.

As before, he taught, performed, and composed, never allowing himself an idle moment. Coming home from school every day with his arms full of papers, he would immediately sit down to write.

He was now putting into final form the works he had written while in Europe, namely, the *Quintet*, the *Fantasia* and *Sonata for Organ*, and the *Concert Etudes for Pianoforte*, all of which may be described as major compositions. For the most part, the only thing he had yet to do was to make clear, definitive copies. But this, in reality, was an unusually big project, for, with no automatic copying processes such as xeroxing and computers then available, every single copy had to be written separately, entirely by hand, note after note, page upon page. He often labored at his desk far into the night patiently drafting his flawless pen and ink manuscripts.

However, during the latter part of 1934, Leroy Robertson suddenly faced far more pressing problems than either his teaching, performing, or composing. Naomi had developed a severe ear infection that finally required drastic surgery, and for several months thereafter, she lay near death. Scarcely able to lift her head, if ever she did chance to open her weary eyes, she would see Leroy kneeling at her bedside, humbly and quietly praying. With the help of Mrs. Josie, a warm-hearted Hungarian lady and the mother of one of his students, he cared for his wife and children as best he could. Only in the late evening hours, after the whole household had settled down, did he turn to copying his music.

Nonetheless, by early spring, when Naomi at last began to recover, Leroy had readied many final copies of his "European" compositions, and now and then sent them to a few musicians who he thought might possibly be interested in them.

Of these works, the organ compositions were the first to be performed, with J. J. Keeler premiering both the *Sonata* and *Fantasia* during two different 1934 concerts. Then, in the spring of 1935, Alexander Schreiner featured the *Sonata* on one of his regular noon organ recitals at UCLA. While the composer described this work as singing of "the hope and vitality of the new West," Mr. Schreiner, in comparing it favorably to the music of Ravel and Stravinsky, termed it "modern music of a rather radical order."

The *Sonata for Organ* went on to win for its composer the grand prize of $50.00—no small amount in those depression years—in a statewide contest for the best composition by a Utah composer. This contest, named for Helen Sheets, was supervised by Tracy Y. Cannon, director of the McCune School of Music, who wrote to Robertson that the judge found his work "far superior to any other entered . . . and that Mr. Robertson is a serious, splendid musician . . . who by all means should have the prize." While Leroy Robertson had long been recognized in Utah as a fine violinist, teacher, and director of the BYU Symphony Orchestra, winning this award greatly enhanced his reputation as a composer throughout the region. He happily accepted the prize and used this financial windfall to buy a matching hat and coat for each of his little girls and dinner for the family in a Salt Lake City restaurant.

However, a few months later, it was another of these "European" works, the *Quintet for Piano and Strings*, that brought Leroy Robertson his first truly wide acclaim. In early May of 1936 he received word that it had won first place in a nationwide contest conducted by the Society for the Publication of American Music. Selected from more than two hundred manuscripts submitted by composers from throughout America, it had received the publication award, which meant that the *Quintet* would now be published for both national and international distribution. Robertson shared this award with Easterner Quincy Porter. Only one other person with ties to Utah, Arthur Shepherd, had ever been so honored.

The news of Robertson's winning stunned the music world, for whereas Quincy Porter was already a composer of established reputation whose works had been performed and recorded in the East, Leroy Robertson was virtually unknown beyond the Rocky Mountains.

It is true that just months before, he had been elected to membership in the prestigious Society of Arts and Sciences headquartered in New York City, in recognition of his "contribution to the arts as an exceptionally fine musician, composer and director." But, in all honesty, his work had as yet had little impact east of the Mississippi. The *Quintet*, bursting upon the scene unannounced, almost as if from nowhere, had made its way to the top solely on its own merits. Characterized by the judges as "vigorous in expression . . . [and] an original contribution in music," it received five of six votes in the preliminary judging and a unanimous decision in the final auditions. All of the Society's officers expressed to Robertson their admiration for his work and their joy in discovering it.

Robertson immediately wrote his good friend and former mentor, Ernest Bloch, telling him the good news and asking permission to dedicate the *Quintet* to him. Bloch responded at once with a warm letter of congratulations and thanks:

Your letter made us very happy ... and I hope this will be an encouragement to you and an incitement to go on further, as you did, *with no haste and no concessions to the "taste of the day."* ... you were so kind and faithful to dedicate [your *Quintet*] to me—I assure you that I am extremely *moved*—You know me enough to understand that I appreciate only "true values" in this poor, tormented, blind world ... and I am always touched when those who have been *near* me do not forget.

A few months later the *Quintet* was published and immediately scheduled for its premiere the following spring at the 1937 Biennial Convention of the National Federation of Music Clubs to be held in Indianapolis.

Leroy arranged his work at BYU so as to attend this concert as well as a few rehearsals. He was, in fact, extremely anxious about the whole affair. He felt very responsible for his "brainchild" and wondered how this work from an unsung Westerner would be received. Would it "say anything"? Would the performers like it? Would all those notes he had put on paper actually sound like the music he had heard in his head?

He need not have worried. The *Quintet* was given an inspired reading by pianist Rudolph Reuter and the Chicago String Quartet, much to the joy of all concerned: performers, composer, critics, and audience. There was general agreement that here was a significant work deserving of many performances, a needed and welcome addition to the repertoire. Sensing that "the music had sprung from strong inner convictions," the critics praised Leroy Robertson as "a composer who has much to say, and who knows how to say it; ... [who] has a decided melodic gift and a feeling for dramatic emphasis ... a composer who will be heard of in the future."

Immediately after its Indianapolis premiere, the same musicians again performed the *Quintet* in Chicago. Robertson could not remain in the East to hear this concert because he had to return to his work and family in Utah. However, a former BYU student then in Chicago reported to him that the critics found the *Quintet* to be "one of the most arresting things to come out of America."

During the year that had elapsed between the announcement of the *Quintet*'s award in May of 1936 and its performance the following

April, many other significant events occurred in the life of Leroy Robertson.

First of all, just a few weeks after the *Quintet* prize was reported, Robertson went to California to study with Arnold Schoenberg, that giant among twentieth-century composers best known as the creator of the twelve-tone system. Despite his musical successes, Robertson had long felt relentless academic pressures to get his doctorate, and when he discovered that Schoenberg was going to be teaching at USC, he made arrangements to study during the first Summer Session of 1936 with this eminent Austrian, feeling that here was a man from whom he could learn much.

The Utahn avidly attended every class, and later recounted many vivid anecdotes about the famous composer-professor. For example, on the first day, when a South American student gushed, "Oh, Mr. Schoenberg, I must tell you that every composer in South America is using nothing but your twelve-tone system," Schoenberg drily replied, "Is that so? And what are they *saying* with it?"

During class, when lecturing to his students, Schoenberg would incessantly pace back and forth, head bent while he spoke. At each side of the classroom he kept a strategically placed ash tray holding a burning cigarette, and as he reached the cigarette at either side, he would stop talking just long enough to take a puff. Somehow he timed everything so that both cigarettes stayed lit, a fact that always amused the Utahn. When not lecturing, Schoenberg would sit at the piano to play and examine the students' projects. His comments about their work could be extremely pointed, yet illuminating. One day, while looking over an assignment submitted by one student, he suddenly stopped and asked, "What have you done here?" "I've inverted the theme, Mr. Schoenberg," came the student's timid reply, whereupon Schoenberg tartly queried, "Have you ever tried to carry a glass of water upside down?"

Robertson fared very well with this somewhat imposing professor, and the relationship between the two soon became one of mutual respect and friendship between composers. Since Schoenberg did at first ask all of his students to compose something according to the twelve-tone system, Robertson obligingly wrote a few pieces in that idiom and easily satisfied Schoenberg that he had mastered the technique. Thereafter, however, Robertson continued to compose —with Schoenberg's approval—in his own already well-developed style.

One day Robertson showed Schoenberg some graphs he had made of two Beethoven symphonies, which were similar to certain thesis projects he had been devising through the years for his own graduate students. Schoenberg, himself a great admirer and student of Beethoven's works, immediately grasped the significance of these charts and invited Robertson to his home, where they discussed and studied these graphic analyses at greater length. The friendship grew, and although Robertson had to return to Utah at the end of the summer, their joint research was to continue for many years. They even intended to collaborate in writing a book based on their findings.

After such an association, Robertson was likely puzzled to discover that Schoenberg had given him a grade of "C" for his summer's classwork. However, some ten years later, much to Robertson's surprise and gratification, Schoenberg sent him a copy of the following letter, written to the USC registrar:

> In regard to the grades of Mr. Leroy J. Robertson in courses 108a SS 1936 and 208a SS 1936 I would like to make the following explanation:
> Since this was my first class in America, and since it was the first time that I had had to grade students, I was not accustomed to do it and was embarrassed by this requirement. Therefore I asked a friend what I should do. He recommended that I give everybody "C," for he said that this is a passing grade. Thus the grade of "C" is not a personal evaluation of Mr. Robertson, whom I know as an excellent musician. I recommend that you give him an "A" in both of these subjects, because I know he is [a] serious composer.
> Signed. . . .

Another important event during this year of excitement occurred a few months after Leroy's return to Utah from California, when he learned that Roman Totenberg would be performing his "Lullaby from the Rockies" on a League of Composers Concert to be aired

over the NBC Network from New York City.[1] Since this marked
the first nationwide broadcast of any Robertson work, it marked a
milestone for this composer from the Rocky Mountains. Unfortunately, no Utah station carried the broadcast. But even though Leroy
was disappointed at not being able to hear the performance, he was
glad to renew his contact with Totenberg after so many years.

Then, during this frigid midwinter of 1937—just a few days after
the Totenberg broadcast and just a few weeks before the *Quintet*'s
premiere—yet another thrilling event occurred in the Robertson
household, one that in many ways eclipsed all the others. A third
daughter was born to Leroy and Naomi. No father could have been
more pleased or proud. Indeed, on Valentine's Day—just three weeks
after her birth—Leroy carefully cut out a little paper heart, lovingly
inscribed it "To Suki from Daddy," and placed it by the pillow of his
as yet unnamed baby daughter. He did not want his smallest child to
be without a valentine when her older sisters were receiving so many.
Soon thereafter, he lovingly christened her "Karen Naomi."

* * * * *

Although elated by his successes with the *Organ Sonata* and
Quintet awards and the Totenberg performance, Leroy Robertson
had come to know that a large part of his life would always have to
be committed to his students and the building of music in the West.
In this regard, he likely drew encouragement when he read these
words from Ernest Bloch:

> It is fine . . . that you can devote your life, as you do, educating
> and stimulating, even with modest means, those who surround
> you—Such activities, as yours, are more useful and more
> necessary, and by far more *enduring* than those of the "virtuosi"
> of all kind, who with their great talent and brilliancy often rather
> *obliterate* the Love for Art and Beauty—for their *own* personal
> success—I have always been sure that it is the work you . . . and
> a few others scattered through America do, in all abnegation and

---

[1]The reader will remember Totenberg as the brilliant young violinist
with whom Leroy had studied while in Berlin, and to whom he had given
a manuscript copy of this violin work.

sincerity, which *will*, in due time, really *build up* America—It is
not always *grateful*, I know, and many of my "disciples" have not
the courage nor the *honesty* to stick to it.

As Leroy Robertson thus continued to build the Music Department at BYU, he added many classes based on material he had studied
in Europe to the established curriculum, and soon he had organized
a course of study leading to a master's degree in Music Theory, the
only such degree to be granted by any institution in the Intermountain West at that time. The Theory program steadily grew, so
that in a very few years there were more students in graduate classes
alone than had previously been enrolled in all of the elementary
classes combined. Of course Robertson realized that very few of
these students would be composers. But he felt nonetheless that such
theory training was vital to all musicians, "especially . . . our teachers
who become musical leaders in the various communities . . . first,
because it is necessary that they properly evaluate the music they
choose to teach, and second, that they teach it effectively."

Robertson was expanding the Chamber Music program as well.
He had now developed enough skilled players to form many different
string quartets, trios, duos, etc. Their College Hall recitals came to
be an almost weekly event, especially in the spring, and the chamber
works of Handel, Haydn, Mozart, Beethoven, and Brahms, among
others, were fast becoming standard fare for Provo audiences.

One Chamber Music program of unusual interest took place
when the BYU Faculty String Quartet appeared on KDYL Radio for
one of Utah's first closed-circuit experiments in what Robertson
termed "some strange new invention called 'Television.'" During the
telecast, studio lights glared so brightly that he had to wear dark
glasses in order to see the music, and even then he was nearly blinded.
With performers obliged to work under such conditions of extraordinary light and intense heat—which could harm both eyes and
musical instruments—Robertson afterwards wondered how anything
practical or useful could ever come of this strange idea.

In addition to his regular university work at this time, Robertson now took on yet another task. Since he could always offer very
precise and helpful instructions, music teachers throughout the area

—of whom many had once been his students—invited him to come and judge the diverse music contests then being organized in the schools. One of these competitions was held each spring in Grand Junction, Colorado, for the high schools of the Western Slope, i.e., that part of Colorado west of the Continental Divide; and for many years Robertson went by train to that city to adjudicate the various activities of the contest. One assignment he particularly enjoyed was the sight-reading event "because," as he observed, "the way the kids read was so much more interesting than what was on the printed page." One year when the band from Steamboat Springs—then but an obscure town high in the snowbound Colorado Rockies—played while marching on skis, it provided a show that took everyone by surprise, a sight that Robertson would describe with a chuckle for many years thereafter.

However, as a teacher, Leroy Robertson probably continued to make his most visible contribution with his ongoing development of the BYU Symphony Orchestra. In these mid- and late 1930s, the group averaged eighty-two members and boasted a full complement of instruments, including even a harp. This was indeed very different from the days "before Robertson" when, as one colleague later reminisced, "I was the only 'cello playing the part on my baritone [horn]." Students were coming not only from communities scattered throughout Utah and the nearby states, but from the West Coast and Canada as well.

Because Robertson fervently wanted everyone in the area to become acquainted with symphonic music, he systematically began to expand the orchestra's activities in: programming; frequency of concerts; and building wider audiences.

As to the programming, he added a new dimension by inviting world-renowned concert artists to appear with the orchestra. It truly required a lot of courage to ask virtuosi of international stature to perform with his amateur musicians, and they all—Robertson included—"sweat blood" as they rehearsed and readied these concerts. But it was worth the effort, for players and audiences alike thrilled at each performance.

The first of many artists to play with the orchestra was Australian-born composer-pianist, Percy Grainger, who, in 1938, appeared in a concert that was successful in every way. Indeed, Mr. Grainger averred that he had never expected to find such good musicians in the Utah hinterlands. Thereafter, at least one or two great virtuosi appeared annually with the BYU Symphony Orchestra. These concerts attracted audiences from throughout northern Utah, many of whom wrote to express their pleasure:

> . . . I expected an enjoyable entertainment, but I did not antici-
> pate being so thrilled. You surely train your people to surpass
> amateurs. . . . I have never heard a violin section with a lovelier
> tone.

> I think you have a most remarkable organization. . . . I couldn't help
> but feel the work that you are doing . . . has a far-reaching effect in the
> cultural development of this whole section.

By now, Robertson had also increased the orchestra's schedule far beyond the single annual concert of years past. They not only performed for their loyal Provo audiences, but made musical forays into the nearby public schools, into Salt Lake City's Temple Square, and toured as well throughout the entire region.

Robertson's special concerts for the area's school children were true pioneering ventures. Never before in the Intermountain West had there been any such youth concerts. Often playing to as many as 400 young listeners, the orchestra brought them a new and unexpectedly happy experience. As one school official commented:

> Until your two concerts for the Provo City Schools, I little real-
> ized the real beauty in the music of your Symphony Orchestra.
> It was an inspiration.

For their Temple Square appearances, the BYU Symphony Orchestra played both in the great Tabernacle and the Assembly Hall, often in special programs that also involved statewide organizations. For example, at various times they combined forces for concerts with all-state high school choruses; and they also participated in an ambitious Lincoln Memorial Program with such success that the fledgling Utah State Institute of Fine Arts, which sponsored the affair, began to dream of even greater activities for the Fine Arts in Utah on a scale never before envisioned:

> By such contributions of time, energy and talent as you
> [Robertson] made, we hope that the Institute will be able to build
> a powerful movement for the advancement of culture and the
> development of Utah's artistic resources. . . . Here's to the day
> that the State will have a gallery of masterpieces, a permanent
> orchestra and opera house. With a little luck and some work,
> and such examples as you so freely gave, that day is not far off.

On more than one occasion, the BYU Symphony Orchestra
performed with the Salt Lake Tabernacle Choir, earning praise from
the choir's exacting director, J. Spencer Cornwall, both for their
thorough preparation and their "special pride in working out this
assignment as perfectly as possible."

One program, performed both in Provo and Salt Lake City
during Eastertide, 1936, deserves special mention because of its
memorable musical and spiritual impact.

Robertson—no doubt remembering his studies with Ernest
Bloch and his days in Leipzig and Berlin—had long wished to present
Bach's *Passion according to Saint John*, a work never before heard in
the area either in its entirety or with orchestra. But, strange to tell,
when he proposed this somewhat daring idea to his BYU colleagues,
he immediately met with strong opposition from some vocal teachers
who felt that the singing of such a demanding composition might
harm their students' voices—not to mention the fact that they saw
Robertson as intruding into their domain. Very soon the whole
Music Department was divided into "pro-" and "anti-Bach" forces. A
BYU Bach Club, composed mainly of Robertson's students and a
few visionary faculty friends, spontaneously formed. With their dedicated help, Robertson assembled the needed soloists and chorus—of
course he already had the orchestra—and patiently taught them the
intricate score. As one devoted "pro-Bach" member stated, "We all
got together [and] rehearsed till we were 'blue in the face.'"

When concert time arrived, they were able to give, according to
one critic, "exceedingly fine performances [that had] a sense of
perfection." The event was a triumph for all concerned, and letters
of congratulation poured in—many from non-musicians—terming it

"the finest program that has ever come to Provo," and "one of the most distinguished musical performances ever given in these parts." One of those many non-musicians penned:

> . . . I was thrilled from the time the first strain of music was produced until it was all over. I feel sure that your contribution . . . by way of gradually building up an appreciation for very fine music is sure to eventually bring good results.

Leroy Robertson, with his uncompromising standards and determination, was setting a new tone for all the people.

In addition to their school concerts and Salt Lake City appearances, the orchestra was now touring on an even more ambitious scale than ever before, travelling oftener and farther to communities as distant as Rexburg, Idaho, on the north and Cedar City, Utah, on the south. When these junkets lasted overnight—as they often did— the townspeople of the communities en route would provide meals and lodging in their homes for the "visiting artists." Sometimes the local sponsors would sell tickets to the orchestra concerts and then use the proceeds to help music organizations in their own area, usually the high school band. On occasion, the proceeds might also go to other community services such as child welfare.

Transporting some eighty-plus energetic young musicians and their instruments in the three university buses then available required organization, patience, and humor. And Robertson always stood close-by to supervise the entire loading procedure and make sure that all the players and instruments were present, accounted for, and ready to go. The smaller instruments went inside the buses to be held on their owners' laps. But the larger instruments, such as the tympani and double basses, had to be carried on top, and loading them was a tense operation. One person—usually the driver—would climb a ladder attached to the back of the bus, and once topside, he would carefully take each instrument as it was gingerly handed to him by its anxious caretaker and then place it in a special rack. After securing his ungainly cargo, the driver would next cover everything with a worn tarpaulin as protection against the elements. The loaded bus, with students waving from the windows and instruments bouncing on top, did make quite a sight as it went bumping along the roads, tarpaulin flapping in the breeze.

Occasionally during a long trip, orchestra members received a special treat, such as one day in early spring when, before an evening concert in southern Utah's Panguitch, Robertson granted permission to a number of students who had never seen Bryce Canyon to visit this great natural wonder of peaks and crevasses. As the buses approached the canyon, snow covered everything except the road, while at the canyon rim, deep late-afternoon shadows were creeping over the glistening white-capped red pinnacles, making "one of the most beautiful sights ever to be seen," the bus driver would later recall.

It was during these late 1930s that the BYU Symphony Orchestra further extended its concert horizons, going far beyond the Intermountain Region by means of a number of radio broadcasts. They performed in a series of Sunday evening programs that aired over KSL Radio, and then "went network" with two Easter morning programs carried nationwide over the Mutual Broadcasting System in 1939 and 1940. These network broadcasts mark the BYU Symphony Orchestra as the first symphonic organization from the entire Intermountain West ever to be heard all across America. Numerous letters of praise poured in from regions far distant: Alberta and Ontario, Canada; Montana, Minnesota, Wisconsin, Illinois, Ohio, and Kentucky, to name but a few. The comments, of which the following are typical, must have pleased Robertson greatly:

> I have heard many orchestras including college orchestras in the east. I have never heard a college orchestra play with such harmony, feeling, and technique.

> The *Lohengrin* (finish) was as delicately done as if by professional symphony players. We . . . marveled at the results you are able to get out of your students.

> Your part in the broadcasts was a great inspiration for all of us who believe in the artistic and spiritual strength and vision of the American people, and not in the least of those who live in the open country.

The BYU Symphony Orchestra under Robertson's direction now equaled any similar organization in the area, and was actually considered by many to be the first. More importantly, by means of the orchestra, Robertson was communicating to the listeners his own deep commitment and fervor for music. As one colleague wrote:

> It seems last night that I enjoyed the orchestra more than I have ever done. But of course, it seems that way almost every year. [Then, quoting Lawrence Gilman]: ". . . the supreme interpreter *is not commanding music*: instead *the music is commanding him*—filling him with a divine humility, a divine ecstasy of revelation, a divine excess of love."
> I am sure you imparted some such feeling to your audience last night.

However, despite these successes, for Leroy Robertson, directing this orchestra meant not only painstaking, but also painful work. As soon as he had developed a student into an almost professional musician, that student would either graduate, leave school to get married, or go on a mission for the LDS Church. The annual losses in personnel were tremendous, and with student enrollment changing even from quarter to quarter, the orchestra was often more than three-fourths new. Robertson was, in a sense, always starting over.

Another very discouraging aspect for both Robertson and his students was the fact that after their studies at BYU, these players had virtually no way to earn a living in Utah as performers. Many of his most skilled students simply left the region to join, or as Robertson put it, "feed" the great symphonies of metropolitan centers throughout the country. Some, on the other hand, chose to make their living in other professions. He used to say, rather wistfully, that he seemed to "have had a great deal to do with making physicians."

Realizing that building a truly great symphony orchestra depended on maintaining a large corps of excellent players that would essentially remain the same over an extended period of time; and realizing that to do so would require that such players have some financial recompense, already as early as 1935, Robertson forthrightly proposed the establishment of a professional orchestra in Utah, "not only to keep Utah musical talent at home, but to fill the need of a state impoverished in fine orchestra music." He envisioned that such an orchestra could be made up mainly of Utah musicians and centered in Salt Lake City, which he felt was the only community large enough to support it. Meantime, while pioneering the idea that musicians should be paid for their work—a tenet very much against the prevailing Utah ideology—he tried to find teaching positions for those young musicians he had trained who wished to remain in the profession and were trying to find a niche for themselves. In his own humble circumstances, he could not offer a great deal, but he consistently tried.

* * * * *

During these late 1930s, Leroy, as always, was driven to compose. He was now working primarily on his *Symphony No. 2*, subtitled *Trilogy*, a work that was taking on epic proportions. Having long since resigned himself to the fact that he would never hear it in his lifetime since he would never have access to an orchestra capable of performing it, he decided to follow his inspiration and not be bound by the conventional restrictions of instrumentation and orchestra personnel. Guided by his incomparable composer's craftsmanship, he wrote strictly as the music itself demanded.

This second symphony constantly possessed him—even every day when he came home for lunch. During this hour, he would eagerly bundle baby Karen into her warm blue velveteen coat and bonnet, and then no matter what the weather, would take her for a "walk around the block." All the neighbors watching him as he slowly went by gently cuddling the little child in his protective arms, beheld this as the act of a loving and devoted father—which indeed it was. Little did they realize that as this man plodded along the sidewalk day after day with his little girl, he was actually working out in his mind different passages of the *Trilogy*, his attention far removed from the world about him.

At the university as well, his students would find him composing this symphony during any free time available. Often he would invite them into his studio to show them what he was doing, and as he explained the music, he would sit at the piano simultaneously conducting, playing, singing, and whistling, though those who heard him said "it was not really whistling." He repeated phrases over and over, listening as if to test the sounds and solidify them in his mind. For the students observing him, the most impressive aspect, however, was not Robertson's playing, singing, and "whistling," but rather, the faraway look that came into his eyes, described by one as "a look into the cosmos." Those around him could not help but sense that this composer had a great line of communication to something far beyond the usual workaday human experience.

Sadly, it was at this time that Leroy's father, Jasper, died after several long months of suffering. The noble father—who, so long ago with his bare hands had built the family home in Fountain Green; who by his example had taught his children integrity, courage, and steadfastness; who through his widower's despair had held the family together for so many years—that dear father was now gone.

Along with his younger brothers and sisters, this oldest son grieved and grieved, but without great visible drama, just quiet acceptance of the inescapable. Once again, Leroy somehow channeled his feelings into his work.

By early fall, 1939, he had completed the *Trilogy*, was preparing for another year of teaching, and had even planned a short vacation with his family to Yellowstone Park (which would become about the only vacation he ever took). But, just as he, Naomi, and the three children reached Idaho Falls on the first leg of their trip, newsboys were jostling each other on every street corner, shouting, "Extra! Extra! Extra! Hitler invades Poland." World War II—foreseen and dreaded by Robertson so many years before in Berlin—had begun. Too upset to prolong the trip, he took his family home at once.

For the Robertsons, Christmas 1939 was simple and somewhat solemn. Ah yes, Santa did bring presents. There was still a fire burning in the fireplace, good food on the table, and peace over America. But, as the decade ended, Leroy Robertson feared what inevitably lay ahead.

Chapter Eleven

CREATING A MECCA FOR MUSIC

WITH the world he had known suddenly tearing itself apart by war, Leroy Robertson felt a more urgent need than ever to preserve and create music. He at last began consistent work on the oratorio based on the Book of Mormon that had been brewing in the back of his mind since his teens.

The first hurdle in the vast project was to decide which sections to take from this complicated scripture in order to construct a meaningful libretto. For months on end, immediately after supper, he would get out his worn copy of the Book of Mormon, and then, settling into his comfortable living-room rocker in the very midst of all the family hubbub, he would study for the rest of the evening, marking appropriate passages and words in the text. The constant comings and goings of his wife and children did not bother him in the least, and the family became accustomed to walking around him as he worked on what he lovingly called the "Good old 'And it came to pass.'"[1]

Once he had the text in order, the music came almost unbidden. As he would later observe, "As soon as I could get a libretto which would work, the music was there. I didn't have to worry about the music at all."

His students as well as his family saw the *Oratorio from the Book of Mormon* germinate and grow. Indeed, he composed one of its most inspired numbers while teaching a class of Advanced Theory. For a

---

[1]Many passages throughout the Book of Mormon begin with the phrase, "And it came to pass. . . ."

final exam, he had given the students one of his own chorale melodies to harmonize, and after they had submitted their work, he, as usual, went to the chalkboard to show them a few of the possibilities for solving the problems involved. Just as he picked up the chalk, the words of the Lord's Prayer came to his mind along with the chorale melody. At once he began to write, but so fast did the music come that he could scarcely keep pace. While the students watched in amazement, this teacher, caught up by inspiration, notated nonstop a complete choral setting for this prayer, straight through from the beginning "Our Father" to the final "Amen." He was just transcribing the last notes when the bell rang to signal the end of class. And while the students left the room in wonderment, practical Leroy grabbed a bit of manuscript paper and rapidly copied the music from the board before the janitors could come in and erase it. At home later that evening, he quietly commented with a faraway look in his eyes, "I think something great happened today."

This simple statement proved to be a modest assessment of the work, for it soon became one of Robertson's most beloved and widely performed compositions. After its premiere in 1940 during the second nationwide Easter Sunrise broadcast, requests for the music came in from across the country. Encouraged by this reception, Robertson sent the score to his friend, A. Walter Kramer, of Galaxy Music Corporation, who immediately responded.

Galaxy had long since decided not to publish any settings of this text because, as Kramer wrote:

> Most people who have set it have set it as though they did not know what the prayer meant. But we found yours so excellent, so devotional, so finely executed and so genuine an expression of these great words that the Committee [on Publication] threw its rule away and made the kind of exception that every committee should make when it meets the real thing, rule or no rule. . . . We are delighted to publish your setting and will send you a royalty contract in the near future.

After publication, the work gained such acclaim that it went into its second printing within less than a year, and has maintained its popularity ever since.

In other efforts to preserve great music in Utah throughout these wartime years, Robertson—with the help of a few loyal colleagues—instituted one special and very different project that would soon make Provo and BYU a mecca for music unique in the Intermountain West.

This was the annual BYU Summer Chamber Music Festival, which for many years would center around the renowned Roth String Quartet. The Roths had first performed at BYU in 1937, and soon thereafter Robertson—who always regarded the string quartet as the purest and highest form of musical expression— was able to convince his colleagues of the need and value of such a festival. In this endeavor he worked particularly close with Herald R. Clark, dean of the BYU College of Commerce, and chairman of Provo's very successful and long-standing lyceum series.

From a modest and tentative beginning in 1939 consisting of only three quartet concerts, the festival schedule increased within five years to more than sixteen concerts, with other artists subsequently augmenting the quartet offerings.

Quartet leader Feri Roth later recalled their 1939 meeting with Robertson as follows:

> Scorching heat met us when our train arrived in Salt Lake City. . . . An awkward-looking, tall, bent, soft-spoken man met us at the station to drive us to Provo. He carried our bags to his car. He really worked hard with those many heavy suitcases in that murderous heat. He wore a hat [when outdoors, Robertson, like his father, always wore a hat] and sweated enormously, but without a murmur he did his chores. During the ride I learned that he was . . . [a leading professor in] the Music Department of the Brigham Young University. "This is something," I thought, "for a modest provincial teacher."

Some of the festival highlights occurred in 1945 and 1946 when, for the first time in the region, the Roths featured the complete cycle of Beethoven String Quartets and the six Mozart Quartets dedicated to Haydn. To complement these concerts, Robertson taught extra daily classes wherein he analyzed in great detail each quartet, illustrating his lectures at the piano, with recordings, and unique anecdotes. The fortunate students attending these classes were thus able to hear each quartet at least three times in one week, an experience never to be forgotten. For several years, KSL Radio also broadcast the programs to a wide listening audience. Never before had the people of the area heard such a rich concentration of chamber music. Though the audiences varied in size, and certainly did not always fill the hall, there was soon a hard-core group of aficionados from the entire region who would never miss a concert.

What attracted such musicians to BYU year after year? It definitely was not the money, for the budget was very low and uncertain. Indeed, Robertson and Clark had to scrap bitterly each year for every penny allotted to the Festival. But, these artists, like Robertson and his colleagues, were idealists, who, from the very onset, believed in the project. Feri Roth, ever the optimist, wrote to Robertson immediately after the first festival:

> I am sure that everything will be all right for next summer. . . .
> We are doing also everything to make Provo a great place for Chamber Music.

Moreover, Provo was indeed a beautiful place for the musicians to spend a few weeks in midsummer, and the townspeople treated their visitors royally. In addition to several parties after each concert (the quartet members preferred to separate immediately after such intense labor), various Provoites hosted picnics in the nearby canyons and boat excursions on Utah Lake, all replete with fresh home-cooked food provided by Naomi and other Provo culinarians.

At this time, due to the war and the construction of Geneva Steel, lodging simply was not to be found anywhere in the region. As a result, various citizens took the visiting musicians as guests into their homes. Summer after summer Leroy and Naomi made room for quartet violist, Julius Shaier, while Feri Roth—himself accustomed to the most elegant of international luxury hotels—genially resided at the home of local physician, Dr. and Mrs. Lloyd L. Cullimore. As ties grew closer each year, these artists seemed more like family than mere fair-weather acquaintances.

One summer, quartet 'cellist Oliver Edel brought his bride to Provo for their honeymoon, much to everyone's delight. Another year, the wife of second violinist, Jeno Antal—herself an excellent artist—painted a portrait of Naomi, all of which helped Mrs. Antal pass the time while her husband was at the daily quartet rehearsals and gave Naomi many interesting hours of visiting. Leroy would prize this beautiful portrait of Naomi for the rest of his life, both for its subject matter and the friendship it represented.

Now, to put it mildly, the life of any serious musician can be nerve-racking. And playing at least three concerts per week in the four to six weeks given over to these Summer Festivals placed immense strain on Feri Roth. During one particularly intensive season, he consulted with Dr. Cullimore, asking how to achieve a bit of relief from this constant nervous pressure. The good doctor advised Roth to get some regular physical exercise, whereupon Leroy, learning of Feri's predicament, promptly proposed that this magnificent quartet leader come every day and mow the Robertson lawn. Roth did indeed accept the offer, and as his graceful, white, musician's hands pushed the old Robertson lawnmower back and forth, cutting wide, crooked swaths in every direction, this ultra-elegant artist would grin and say, "I'm moaning the lawn." No one can honestly claim that Mr. Roth enjoyed such exercise, but it did seem to release a certain amount of tension for him, and the Robertson lawn never underwent so much unusual "moaning" either before or afterwards.

If these musicians liked Leroy Robertson as a friend, they also admired him as a composer. Already during the Second Summer Festival, the Roths and pianist E. Robert Schmitz gave the Utah premiere of Robertson's prizewinning *Quintet for Piano and Strings.* Hoping to prepare local audiences for this performance, Utah newspapers quoted from comments previously published at its Indianapolis premiere:

> The work is so different some of you will not like it; it is beyond anything we have heard. But if this young man could devote himself entirely to composing . . . he might well become as great a composer as Beethoven.

As might be expected, local reactions to the *Quintet* were mixed, with some hailing it as "the experience of a lifetime," and others complaining at its "ultramodern" dissonances.

Meantime, with Feri Roth's encouragement, Robertson had already begun to compose a *String Quartet*, his first effort in this exacting medium. For material he turned to the eloquent Ute Indian chants and haunting ballads of his pioneer grandmother, Melissa, all melodies from his early life, and truly of the Mountain West.

Much of the *Quartet* was written at Aspen Grove, high on the eastern slopes of Mount Timpanogos, where BYU regularly held its second session of Summer School. While his children enjoyed a wonderful vacation climbing the steep mountain trails or romping with friends through the alpine meadows, Robertson, when not teaching, sat writing at an oilcloth-covered table in the very plain two-room cabin similar to all others used by the faculty. Occasionally, he would set up a table outdoors under the shady trees.

By early summer of 1940 he had the *Quartet* nearly finished and ready to show the Roths. Feri Roth, proud to be on hand as this work neared completion, immediately claimed it as his own. In early fall, after transcribing the final copy of this long and brilliant score, Robertson modestly wrote to Roth, then in New York City:

> A few days ago I sent you the new *Quartet*. . . . Now, my dear Feri, I have done the best I know how with this *Quartet* hoping it will be worthy of you and the fine boys in your ensemble. Please, won't you all write and tell me what you think of it.

After a few months, when the Roths had had a chance to study it, he received this reply:

> You can be very happy . . . about your *String Quartet*. It is a fine work. . . . The themes are thoroughly American. I can see the Great Salt Lake Valley and the surrounding country, and the music gives one the feeling of vastness. . . . I hope that you will have great success with it.

The Roths themselves premiered this new *Quartet* the following summer and kept it in their regular repertoire henceforth.

When they performed it in 1944 as part of New York City's formal concert season, it was cited as "one of the best chamber works heard in New York this season," and was immediately nominated for the prestigious New York Critics Circle Award, along with works by Randall Thompson, Aaron Copland, and Andrew Imbrie, then a sergeant in the U.S. Army. For any composer such a nomination was as important as the award. Thus, although the award finally went to Sergeant Imbrie after tight balloting, Leroy Robertson knew he was once more making his mark in the East. The NBC Quartet—which had been chosen to play the Robertson work at the special concert wherein the nominated compositions were repeated for Circle members only—termed the *Quartet* "a superb opus . . . [which they] studied with all the devotion and care possible," and with which they were "overjoyed."

When the Roths had first premiered the Robertson *String Quartet* at the 1941 BYU Summer Festival, they also featured a premiere of a new *Quintet for Piano and Strings* by Arthur Shepherd, with the composer himself at the piano. At this time, Shepherd brought his wife and son, Grazella and Peter, and they all visited with the Robertson family in Provo. What had heretofore been merely a more or less professional relationship grew into a close personal friendship.

Robertson had long admired Shepherd, whom he first knew only by reputation. To the younger Westerner, born and reared in isolated Sanpete, Arthur Shepherd had the air of a sophisticated English patrician who—though not unapproachable—stood on a very high pedestal. They later became better acquainted only when Shepherd journeyed west from his adopted home in Cleveland, Ohio, to visit Utah relatives.

It has been recounted that during one of Shepherd's Utah visits, Robertson arranged to show him the recently completed *Trilogy*, whose complicated score Shepherd read and flawlessly played at sight, much to everyone's astonishment and admiration. Only now and again would he pause to ask Robertson, "Why these notes?" and then nod in agreement as Robertson explained his reasoning.

After the 1941 Summer Festival featuring both the Shepherd and Robertson works, the elder composer, upon returning to the East, warmly wrote to the younger:

> . . . I am so delighted, at "long last" to discover Provo or that part of it which bears *your* particular imprint, and which you have put on the map.
>   I tell you in all sincerity that it is an immense gratification to me to know that there is a man and artist of your calibre to point

the way and keep a guiding hand on the musical culture of our people.

Then, without making any specific allusions, Shepherd expressed his understanding of the unique problems one confronts as a serious musician in the Mountain West:

> I think I realize in a measure the difficulties and handicaps that beset your efforts. That you are achieving such fine things as composer and instructor, in spite of these conditions, is very impressive evidence of your worth and integrity.

Thereafter, Shepherd unstintingly promoted Robertson works among musicians in the Great Lakes Area, and at one time, even invited Robertson not only to send a composition for performance in the Fine Arts Series of Western Reserve University, but also to participate in person, writing:

> ... We both [Mrs. Shepherd and I] think of you and your charming family and beautiful mountain backdrop with a lifting of hearts. You gave us a happy experience. We would like to return the compliment.

For his part, Robertson encouraged performances of Shepherd compositions in the West, and also recommended that Shepherd be given the Utah Academy Award in Arts, describing him as "an extraordinary pianist, conductor, composer and scholar. . . . He is the most outstanding musician Utah has produced."

Though usually separated by many miles, these two composers would henceforth maintain a warm friendship.

*   *   *   *   *

During these years, a big change had taken place in the Robertson household. The family moved from their beloved "White House on Third North" to a larger two-story home of purple brick surrounded by a deep yard complete with flower gardens, vegetable garden, and a chicken coop that might hold a few chickens on occasion.

The reason for this move to a larger home readily became apparent. In midwinter 1941, the Robertson's last child was born, a son, whom they christened James Leroy. Once again, no father could have been more thrilled. On the momentous day of his only son's birth, instead of teaching, Leroy proudly led all of his classes, one after the other, to the nearby ice-cream parlor, and treated everybody to cones, milk shakes, and malts. As a BYU professor, he did not care to pass out the proverbial cigars, but he surely did buy ice cream.

Just as he had with his other children, so with his infant son, Leroy often walked the floor to comfort and quiet him. And to this lively boy in his arms, he always sang over and over a special little tune to the nonsense syllables: "Hi Doo, Deedle Doo, Hi Doo, Deedle Deedle Doo. . . ." One day, a friend overhearing Leroy thus singing as he cradled Jim, remarked, "Robertson will compose an entire symphony on that melody someday." In a sense he did, for the haunting air was later to figure prominently in the *Concerto for Violin and Orchestra*, and again in his last major work, the uncompleted folk opera, *Pegeen*.

The year 1941 rolled on, and Leroy Robertson was pursuing his usual schedule of teaching, performing, and composing. Then, suddenly on December 7, the Japanese bombed Pearl Harbor. The United States entered World War II.

Forty-five years old and father of four, Robertson was not called to serve in the armed forces, but many of his students—boys over whom he had watched like a father or older brother—were now volunteering or being drafted. They wrote him poignant letters from all corners of the world: Alaska, Hawaii, India, Central America, France (described by one as a "very beautiful farm country"), and Egypt (where "the wind continues to blow 24 hours a day").

Each letter evidenced in some way these boys' persistent dedication to their professor and his ideals. Some loyally apologized for not giving him more notice of their departure and ruefully wished that they would not be gone too long:

> . . . I hope it isn't so late that it has caused you trouble. I imagine you were planning on having me back to play in the Orchestra. I hope the war will not take all of your students away. It seems as though the war will destroy all the good things that we once had.

> Your Tympani player is now in the Navy. . . . I hope and pray I can come back to be under your baton again . . . and to think I would have been a Senior this year.

One boy, who loved his violin so much that he took it with him into the Army, soon discovered that he had little chance to touch it:

> There just seems to be no time for such things. Especially now since I am in an armored division and a member of a tank crew.

Another lad chose to donate his violin to the BYU Symphony until his return, saying, "It isn't worth much but you can let some student use it who hasn't a fiddle of his own. . . ." Some, when applying for a specialized branch of the service, asked their professor to write them a recommendation.

To a man, they missed "the wholesome enjoyment of being part of the Symphony," and lamented that the pop tunes currently pounding their ears would "drive one to a 'Section Eight,'" or "a sane person crazy." However, they doggedly did their best to seek out something better. One boy told of his joy in finding a fellow violinist from Brooklyn with whom he was planning a recital, "practice time permitting." Another lad, on a short leave to Cairo from his desert post, "had the privilege of hearing the Cairo Symphony"—quite unusual R and R for a young serviceman on his own in a big world capital. Though not a student of Robertson, one Utah youth wrote from the Yukon requesting scores to a few Robertson compositions, explaining that he needed something to study that would relieve his mind. One inductee eloquently summarized for all these boys the importance of music:

> Music, a creative life, seems irreplaceable once one has come to know it. The compensation it offers in human experiences and emotions and mental fullness seems far to outweigh any material privation. All this is of course probably old stuff to you. At this moment it is again vitally new to myself.

The sentiments expressed in these letters sharply contrasted with the general attitude of the military towards music and musicians, and while Robertson usually sent the servicemen newsy reports about the BYU Symphony Orchestra and their other friends, on one occasion, he could not contain his discouragement and disgust:

> I see they [musicians] . . . are considered quite non-essential. . . . It seems a pity that the Fine Arts have come to be so degraded in

America. I don't know what the country is fighting for if the bureaucrats kill our culture. Surely no one objects to fighting and working any place to help prosecute the war—but these damned inferences make it seem that the country is still as inconsiderate as ever of everything artistic. I suppose Kate Smith is ample representation for us.[2]

When news arrived of one of his "boys" being killed, he grieved as if he had lost one of his own family:

Something is wrong when a fresh innocent child like that has to be sacrificed on the altar of stupidity and crime. . . .

School went on of course, but not as usual. The BYU Symphony Orchestra was, as Robertson wrote, "quite crippled because of the war." With all college-age men now in the military, there were not nearly so many players as before, and the orchestra became nearly "all-girl." To get the minimum personnel necessary for even a small group, Robertson literally had to scour the countryside. Just like his first years at BYU, he once again was enlisting players from the faculty, the public schools, and other interested Provo citizens. Despite severe gas-rationing, Robertson even drove his own car cross-town every afternoon to fetch needed high school students to round out the orchestra for rehearsals. With such a diverse collection of players, scheduling conflicts were inevitable so that rarely was there complete attendance at any one rehearsal.

Nonetheless, thanks to Robertson's stubborn dedication, the BYU Symphony Orchestra kept an ambitious concert schedule. Preparing a different program about every six weeks, they continued to present premieres of many standard classics heretofore not heard "live" in the region. With touring virtually halted because of gas-rationing, they had to limit most of their concertizing to Provo. Here, however, they always played to large audiences. The people seemed to need this music.

Two of their most unforgettable concerts were a memorial service

---

[2]Kate Smith, a corpulent soprano, was the very popular radio and television star who introduced Irving Berlin's anthem, "God Bless America."

for Provo men killed in the war, and another program played just after VE Day when Robertson and his "troops" performed Tchaikowsky's *Pathétique Symphony* in a rendition so compelling that the listeners did not applaud at the end.

Then suddenly came Hiroshima and Nagasaki, and World War II was over. Even before his "boys" mustered out, Robertson had found modest employment for some.

* * * * *

During these wartime years, despite his being confined almost exclusively to Provo, Leroy Robertson's reputation as a musician had continued to grow on state, national, and even international scenes. He was elected to the Utah Academy of Science, Arts, and Letters; to the National Association for American Composers and Conductors; and selected to serve as one of three committee members to choose all the string quartet music for the National High School Competition Festivals Manual.

But, more important to him, no doubt, was the fact that his compositions were being performed with increasing frequency not only in Utah, but also throughout the American continent and Europe.

Throughout the 1940s and 1950s the *String Quartet* continued to receive many performances everywhere, not only by the Roths but other notable string quartet organizations as well. In fact, just seven days after Pearl Harbor, it had received its nationwide premiere in an NBC broadcast by the Walden Quartet.

Along with the *String Quartet*, the prizewinning *Quintet* and the *Two Concert Etudes for Pianoforte*—all written so many years before in Europe—were also now being heard worldwide. The *Etudes* especially found a champion in young Hungarian pianist Andor Foldes, who not only gave them their East Coast premieres, but also performed them on virtually every continent except Antarctica. Other fine pianists became interested and played them as well. Yet, despite their popularity, Robertson was unable to get them published because, as he wrote, "I am in a bad location [Utah] with little or no time to promote them." Also, needless to say, supplying all the requested copies at his own expense was at that time very costly.

During these years yet another work from Robertson's European days took on a new appearance when he orchestrated the *Sonata for Organ*, likely made in response to an inquiry from Arthur Shepherd as to whether Robertson might have any symphonic work that could be suitable for high school groups, "practical, not too taxing and not of maximum symphonic calibre." Under the title, *Prelude, Scherzo, and Ricercare on Two Themes* (actually named after the *Sonata*'s three movements), it was first performed at the Convention of the Music Teachers National Association held in 1941 at Minneapolis.

Other Robertson works introduced to audiences outside Utah at this time were his *Three Songs from the Shadow*, composed soon after his return from Europe, and first shown by the composer to world-renowned tenor Jussi Björling, who lauded them as being "well written for the voice and possessed of high artistic value." Nonetheless, there is no record that Björling ever sang them. Moreover, it must have been very disappointing when, a few years later, after receiving an urgent request from Helen Traubel's accompanist and vocal coach, Harry H. Voge, to send these songs posthaste to the great soprano, Robertson could not get the necessary copies made and shipped in time. Miss Traubel wanted them for her upcoming European tour, and although the composer rushed the printing and sent everything via air mail, Miss Traubel had already left the country before the music arrived in New York. Afterwards, she was no longer interested. However, the last song of the three—"Joy, Shipmate, Joy!"—eventually became very popular, with many performances in New York and elsewhere.

During these wartime years, the earlier Robertson compositions had not been the only works to attract attention. As always, he had many new works whirling around in his mind, and almost simultaneously several large works were developing: the *Concerto for Violin and Orchestra*, the *Rhapsody for Piano and Orchestra*, the *Overture to Punch and Judy*, not to mention the *Oratorio from the Book of Mormon*, which continued to occupy him greatly.

Of these works, the *Rhapsody* was likely the first to be put into final form. Written for and dedicated to Andor Foldes, who had long ago asked Robertson for a major work, the *Rhapsody* was premiered in the fall of 1944 before an enthusiastic Salt Lake City audience by the Utah State Symphony (the immediate precursor to the Utah Symphony) with Foldes playing the brilliant piano part. Robertson himself had been invited to conduct the performance, and his work—both as composer and conductor—elicited favorable responses from the orchestra personnel and management, who termed it "a great boost to the music lovers and musicians alike." The following spring, the *Rhapsody* earned for its composer the coveted Utah State Institute of Fine Arts Award.

After the Utah premiere, Foldes—who always claimed the work as "his"—untiringly promoted the *Rhapsody* everywhere, especially with the publishers and broadcasters in New York, where he was influential in getting Carl Fischer Inc. to place it in their rental library. A few years later, Foldes and the CBS Symphony, Leon Barzin conducting, broadcast the *Rhapsody* nationwide on the CBS Invitation to Music Series. This performance brought many letters of praise to Robertson from across the entire country, even from the "Top Brass" of CBS. But a letter from colleague and longtime friend, Alexander Schreiner, was likely valued as highly as any:

> The *Rhapsody* was perfectly thrilling. . . . You packed the piece with gorgeous emotional drive and brilliant life . . . , a real match for Foldes' performing powers.

A few months later, the tireless Foldes announced yet more wonderful news:

> After long deliberation, Karl Krueger selected our *Rhapsody* for my appearance with the Detroit Symphony.

Other pianists did express interest in the *Rhapsody*, and young Reid Nibley later performed it much to Robertson's liking. However, after a few years, this much acclaimed work would seem to fade into oblivion as other projects caught the composer's attention.

One major composition to follow closely upon the *Rhapsody* was another work for string quartet, the *American Serenade*. Robertson, himself, wrote of it:

The *American Serenade* is a sort of "Western" divertimento. . . . It is light and tuneful and is sometimes programmed as a contrast to the more serious works predominant in the string quartet repertoire.

In my home town, the sheepherders, most of whom were "unemployed" during the winter months, spent several nights of each week at parties, dancing to the music of the fiddle and banjo; sometimes the dances became quite exciting and boisterous, and this is reflected in the "Finale" of the *Serenade*.

Composed in 1944, it was premiered by the Roths during the 1945 Summer Festival, and then immediately programmed by the same players for the National Composers Congress sponsored by Roy Harris in Colorado Springs. Leroy and Naomi drove from Provo with friends to attend the Colorado concert, which occurred —as Leroy always noted with pride—on VJ Day.

A popular work, the *Serenade* was subsequently performed to much critical acclaim not only by the Roths but many other string quartets throughout North and South America and Europe. After a Los Angeles performance, it was reported to Robertson that famed violinist Toscha Seidel asked, "Where is that man Robertson? He is a genius!" Such adulation no doubt pleased the composer, but he likely took it with a grain of salt.

*　*　*　*　*

Despite this consistent and ever increasing success of his compositions, in the eyes of his family Leroy Robertson remained their dependable, steadfast father who just happened to be preoccupied with music. He still danced around for his children, and sketches of new melodies can be found along with grocery lists on the same shred of paper. It is typical that the following notes appear at the bottom of a pencil manuscript page of the *Overture to Punch and Judy*:

Phone Roth; Train leaves at 4:00; Order a load of coal.

His BYU colleagues likewise still regarded him as a quiet, yet demanding university professor, devoted above all to his students and his teaching. The theory classes now had record enrollments on all levels, and his significant graduate program was increasingly attracting students nationwide. His private students continued to appear on regularly scheduled concerts, usually held Sunday afternoons, while the chamber music groups—still supervised by Robertson, but now under the immediate direction of Robertson graduate student, Louis W. Booth—were attaining prominence due to their touring and bi-weekly broadcasts over KSL Radio.

But once again, it was Robertson's work with the BYU Symphony Orchestra that still seemed to attract the most attention. The postwar orchestra had rapidly regained its former size as returning servicemen and other fine players joined its ranks, and concertizing increased as the group, in addition to many local performances, toured extensively throughout the Western states.

During one of these tours, which featured pianist Andor Foldes playing the aforementioned *Rhapsody*, they presented eleven concerts in eight days, travelling from Logan on the north to Mount Pleasant on the south, a most ambitious undertaking for full-time students.

During this tour something very unusual occurred. After the fourth concert, Robertson—having assured himself that everyone was properly housed for the night—abruptly departed to make a hasty flight to San Francisco, where his prizewinning *Quintet* was to have its West Coast premiere at the hands of pianist Lev Shorr and the San Francisco Quartet. Robertson had truly been concerned about leaving the orchestra in mid-tour, even for a few days, but encouraged by his colleagues, he could not resist going. After all, it was in the City by the Bay that he had first conceived the *Quintet* while studying with Ernest Bloch so long ago, and this particular concert thus held a double meaning for him. Once again the work was hailed by the critics.

During Robertson's brief absence from the orchestra, former student Lawrence Sardoni, now a part-time faculty member, took over the baton. The tour continued as planned, and Robertson was soon back on the podium conducting as usual.

Subsequent orchestra concerts that season featured the Brahms *Symphony No. 2*, another "live" premiere for Utah. Referring to Robertson's interpretation of this work, Lowell Durham—just returned from his own doctoral studies—reported:

No man had such understanding of the music, and there was no symphony orchestra in this state except the BYU Symphony . . . no doubt about it.

Musicians from throughout the country—even from the Philadelphia Orchestra—continued to label the group "one of the finest college orchestras," and asked Robertson to send them a few of his programs for their perusal.

After decades of unremitting labor, Leroy Robertson had indeed built an orchestra of the highest calibre, one of which the whole region, or anyone else for that matter, could be proud. With this group, he had literally paved the way for what was to become the Utah Symphony.

Yet, at the BYU Commencement Exercises, 1946, Robertson again did something quite unforeseen by anyone. After conducting the orchestra for the "Processional" March and a special number —which had become the tradition since Robertson first came on the scene—he stepped off the podium and temporarily entrusted the baton to an aggressive and talented orchestra flutist, explaining that the administration was requiring him to be up front and exit with the other faculty members during the playing of the "Recessional." Leroy Robertson then quietly walked away from his players and never again conducted them in public. There was no fanfare, no announcement, no official farewell. He did not even say "Good-bye." After more than twenty years, he simply left.

Many would ask, "Why, after such success, and with such a good orchestra, after so many good years, and after bringing us so much good music, why, why leave now?"

Perhaps Robertson was tired. He certainly had been pushing himself to extraordinary limits. And truth to tell, he had never really enjoyed conducting. The nervous strain made him literally ill before every performance, and he found little relief afterwards. His eyes, which had caused problems since his Boston days, continued to trouble him greatly; his composing schedule had become increasingly heavy; and, at last, in Lawrence Sardoni, he had found an excellent musician and conductor who would be able to maintain the orchestra's high standards and enthusiasm. Furthermore, it was actually a very natural time for Robertson to step away, for, after fourteen years, he had finally been granted another leave of absence, and he ardently wished to resume his Ph.D. studies at USC.

Because his four children, in the midst of their own schooling, could not easily be transferred, and largely because it was financially impossible to take the whole family, Leroy and Naomi decided that he should go alone to California. To help out the budget—now pinched by Leroy's reduced salary plus his own extra expenses of tuition and living in Los Angeles—Naomi provided board and room to a BYU student, much as she had done years before when Leroy went to Europe. Leroy, having found a small room near the USC campus, officially resumed his California studies in September 1946.

Arnold Schoenberg, now in his seventies, was no longer at USC, so Robertson—who really had to get all of his work "on the books," i.e., get official credit for all his studies—registered for classes with another great Austrian composer then teaching at USC, Ernst Toch. As before with others, Robertson easily impressed this eminent composer-teacher with his own abilities, and during the classes, which actually became private lessons, both Robertson and Toch developed a great admiration for each other. Robertson appreciated Toch as a master-teacher of Mozart, whereas Toch described Robertson as "a full-fledged composer, and a very good one at that . . . who excels both in creative gift and craftsmanship."

Having chosen English as his secondary subject, Robertson also took courses in Literary Criticism, and here he became enthralled with the great thinkers of antiquity, notably the Greeks. His class notes, with their added personal comments, witness how he identified with them, and these few statements, cited at random, show what caught Robertson's attention:

> Man's highest goal is happiness . . . man's highest good is "reasonable activity"; i.e., actively demonstrating (conducting orchestra). You cannot be happy by withdrawing from life.
> What a high-minded man despises is of much input in human life.
> Poets (writers): must stop where nature stops.
> Stick to the subject:
> "If one begins to draw a cypress tree,
> It should not turn out to be a storm at sea."

Remembering his own humble beginnings, Robertson noted:

> Stefan Zweig—best to have rough and tumble combat. If one knows only the rarified world, when [that is] gone—nothing left.

At USC Robertson not only took classes, but also taught one or two courses of Music Theory. This letter from a USC student shows how effective he was:

> I want you to know that I enjoyed your classes immensely. . . . I feel I am a much sounder musician from the few short weeks I spent in your classroom. It was truly a privilege to be one of your pupils.
>
> Perhaps I can carry on with the work next term. If so, you can look for me in one of your classes, you may be sure.

At Christmas time Leroy left his studies to come home for a short holiday, and then returned to California in early January to complete the first semester, which had been for him a great success. However, he did not remain at USC to pursue his Ph.D. as originally planned, for a pressing composing commitment was calling him back to Utah.

Just one year previous, in February 1946, Robertson had been told by the LDS Church First Presidency to finish his *Oratorio from the Book of Mormon* and ready it for the Church's upcoming 1947 Centennial Celebration of the Mormon Pioneers' arrival in Utah.[3] This assignment had come at a very special and private dinner given for him and Naomi by these august authorities, during which, at their request, Leroy sat at the piano, sang, played, and explained parts of this composition. Before the evening ended, the First Presidency informed him that they wanted the *Oratorio* to be the central showpiece of the summer-long festivities then being planned.

For Leroy to have the Church sponsor a performance of his *Oratorio* was a dream come true in many ways, for it showed official recognition of such serious music and of him as a composer. Above all, it meant that this epic work would be heard.

---

[3]At this time the First Presidency consisted of President George Albert Smith, and Counselors J. Reuben Clark, Jr., and David O. McKay.

Since that memorable evening, Leroy had spent every available hour working on it, but by this midwinter of 1947, he realized that if he was to meet the deadlines, not only of composing but also of getting scores and parts copied in time for rehearsals and performance, he would need to devote all his efforts to the *Oratorio* only. So important was the project to him that he left USC and returned to Utah to concentrate solely on completing this work.

Once again in Provo when Leroy inquired about using his old studio at BYU, he was informed that it was now occupied by someone else, and that there was, in effect, no room for him on campus. Undeterred, he set up a card table at home in an upstairs bedroom and proceeded to write nonstop, hour after hour, day after day, almost round the clock. Evenings, when this bedroom was occupied by a sleeping child, he sat in the living room midst the ongoing family turmoil finalizing the last big numbers, oblivious to all else.

The work progressed rapidly. By early spring he had it nearly all composed with only a very few pages yet left to score. Then, one day, as he casually picked up the newspaper, he read an announcement that left him dumbfounded. The featured work for the forthcoming Centennial was to be a musical, *Promised Valley*, with music composed by Crawford Gates, one of Robertson's most gifted students. The *Oratorio from the Book of Mormon* had been replaced, and no one had bothered to inform Leroy Robertson.

He never said a word about his feelings to anyone, not even to Naomi. "I have often wondered how Leroy felt . . . ," she would later write. He was happy for Crawford, who had always been like part of the Robertson family, and was happy that one of his students had been given this task.

But Robertson's own disappointment could only have been most keen, his heart broken. He simply put aside the nearly completed score—now apparently forgotten by the Church authorities—and left it lying as he went on to other projects.

Once again he turned to the *Violin Concerto*. And after all, another year of teaching at BYU would soon begin.

Chapter Twelve

TRILOGY, O *TRILOGY*, THOU "WAYWARD CHILD"

THE school year of 1947-1948 started off as usual for Leroy Robertson, but soon seemingly unrelated events began to coalesce that would change the entire picture and make this a pivotal year for him.

First, there was his meeting with Maurice Abravanel, newly appointed conductor and musical director of the recently formed Utah Symphony in Salt Lake City. The two musicians had actually become acquainted a few months earlier, when Abravanel, en route from New York to San Francisco, had stopped over in mid-June to meet with the symphony board before finalizing his contract. At that time, he had asked among other things, "Is there any composer in Utah?" When told of Leroy Robertson in Provo, he asked to meet the Utahn, and an appointment was set up.

Because of an earlier scheduled meeting with Dean Herald R. Clark, Abravanel arrived at Robertson's office only in the late afternoon, a time when the room—with its high ceiling and very tall, narrow windows shaded by trees—was very dark. So dark was it, in fact, that Abravanel would later recount that at this first meeting he could not distinguish Robertson's face. But after the customary introductions, Abravanel immediately asked Robertson if he had any orchestral scores that might be considered for performance.

Taking a deep breath, but without saying a word, Robertson went to a cupboard and brought out the *Trilogy*, his massive *Second Symphony* which Abravanel later described as "an enormous thing that was bigger than the table." Quite taken aback by its size, Abravanel next inquired if Robertson might have something for an orchestra not quite so large. Once more without saying a word,

Robertson then showed him a more recent score, the *Overture to Punch and Judy*, whose charm Abravanel saw at once:

> Ah, I liked it right away. I took a quick look while he was waiting, a very quick look, but I liked the texture and construction. It was full of music, very good music.

After studying the score further upon his return to New York, the new Utah Symphony maestro informed Robertson that he would indeed like to program *Punch and Judy* at one of his first concerts of the 1947-1948 season. This news, of course, pleased Robertson, but remembering the general disappointment with the preceding year's conductor, Robertson did observe, "Let's wait and see what Abravanel can really do." A few months later, after hearing Abravanel's first concert with the Utah Symphony, Robertson would happily remark, "He is one of the greats."

Leroy Robertson had many reasons to be interested in the Utah Symphony and Abravanel. A large number of his students, past and present, were now members of the group, and he truly hoped that at last his longtime dream of a professional orchestra in the state might be realized, not so much for his own private gain as for the musicians and audiences of the region.

However, Robertson's attentions were centered on his teaching at BYU and his ongoing composing of the *Violin Concerto*. And, at the same time, neither could he dismiss the *Trilogy* from his mind. After Abravanel's sharp reaction to its large dimensions, he wondered more than ever what would become of this work. Would it continue to lie on the cupboard shelf, forever unheard?

He was particularly concerned because about two and a half years earlier—in the spring of 1945— he had entered this symphony in a great international competition, the Symphony of the Americas Contest sponsored by Henry H. Reichhold in Detroit, and had as yet heard nothing of the outcome.

The very circumstances of his entering this competition had created some drama for him and Naomi at the time. It was Conrad B. Harrison, then music critic of the *Deseret News*, who informed Leroy about the contest. Open to all composers of the Western

Hemisphere, it offered sizable cash awards to the three top winners —$25,000 for the first prize—and performances by the Detroit Symphony. All entries were to be submitted under a pseudonym so that each work would be judged only on its merit, not the composer's name.

Robertson, however, was reluctant to enter. As usual, he felt extremely pressed with his composing and teaching commitments; furthermore, the two final pages of the *Trilogy* yet needed a bit of revision; and most important, the contest committee required two copies of the score, and there was no way he could get such copies printed in Utah. Even by pushing himself to the very limit, how could he ever meet the fast approaching deadline which was scarcely one month away? Undeterred by Robertson's objections, Harrison insisted and persisted until finally the reticent composer agreed to give it a try. Somehow he found time to adjust those last two pages. Then, sending his only score under the pseudonym "Nostrebor" to good friend A. Walter Kramer in New York, Robertson asked him to get the necessary copies photostated and put into the mail as soon as possible. It was nip and tuck all the way, but Kramer did succeed in getting the two copies made, bound, and posted just barely before the midnight deadline. Robertson's *Trilogy* thereby became an official entry.

Now, in 1947, two years had gone by, and still there was no word from anyone concerning this contest or his scores. Quite sure that the competition had long since been decided in someone else's favor, in mid-September Robertson wrote to the contest committee requesting them please to return his two copies of the *Trilogy* score. After all, those photostats had cost him a great deal of money, he loved this symphony, and he wished to have it back home. By return mail came a reply. The contest had elicited many more scores than had been anticipated, and therefore the judging had taken much longer than planned. Final results would be announced November 2, on the ABC Ford Sunday Evening Hour broadcast, and would he kindly allow the committee to keep his score till then? Upon reading the letter, Robertson shrugged slightly, then pursued his daily tasks of teaching, composing, and more teaching.

Then, Friday, October 31—just two days before the scheduled announcement of the winners—as Robertson was in the midst of giving a late-afternoon violin lesson, his studio phone rang. Somewhat annoyed at the interruption, he answered, only to hear a very matter-of-fact voice on the line asking: "Are you Leroy Robertson? Are you a citizen of the United States? Are you a Professor of Music at Brigham Young University? Do you reside at 55 South Fourth East, Provo, Utah?" After Robertson affirmatively replied, the mysterious voice simply said, "Thank you," and thus ended the conversation. Perplexed, Leroy finished his day's teaching, went home, and told Naomi about the strange phone call, whereupon she reported that this same person had also phoned her at the house with similar questions. They both wondered what it might mean.

The following day passed very slowly. Leroy gave his Saturday lessons as usual, but could not completely dismiss the phone call from his mind. Did it possibly have anything to do with the Reichhold contest? Might the *Trilogy* perhaps have earned an honorable mention?

Sunday—the day of that long-awaited announcement—was chilly and gray. Clouds moved in, and the first winter snows were threatening. About noon the phone again rang, and this time it was pianist Andor Foldes calling from New York, himself so thrilled he could hardly speak. All New York was abuzz with the news: Leroy Robertson had won the Symphony of the Americas award! Robertson, listening in disbelief, could only reply that he had as yet heard nothing official. But, he wondered, could Andor be right?

The Robertson family, not knowing what to expect and trying to pretend that nothing extraordinary was about to happen, went about their customary Sunday activities. Naomi had to attend the regular afternoon Church meeting because, as an officer in the LDS Relief Society, she was scheduled to address the congregation that day. Leroy, however, decided to remain at home. If indeed he was among the winners, he would be notified sometime before the Ford Sunday Evening Hour, which aired locally at 6:00 P.M. To make the time pass, he copied manuscripts and paced the floor. A light snow had begun to fall, increasing the tension at 55 South Fourth East.

Then, suddenly, at exactly 4:00 P.M., the big front doorknocker banged loudly. Leroy, breathing hard, his lips tightly pursed, steadily walked to the door and opened it to see a shivering Western Union boy standing with a telegram. Himself shaking with emotion, Leroy took the telegram, tore open the envelope, and read:

> Please accept my personal and heartfelt congratulations on the occasion of your selection as the first prize winner in the competition for the Reichhold Symphonic Award for the Western Hemisphere. . . .
> Best personal regards.
> Henry H. Reichhold.

This tall Utah composer, usually so calm and deliberate, could not contain his joy. Literally jumping three feet from the ground —higher and faster than anyone had ever seen him move—he shouted, "I won. I won first prize. I won. I won!"

Determining forthwith that Naomi should be with him for the nationwide announcement, he rapidly bundled six-year-old Jim in an overcoat, took him by the hand, and tramped with his son through the snow to fetch Naomi. As the little boy trotted along beside his fast-striding father, he asked:

"Dad, did that telegram say you won $25,000?"

"Yes, son," answered Leroy.

"Well," Jim continued, "If you get it in nickels, can I have one?"

A few hours later, this Provo family eagerly grouped around the radio and heard Leroy Robertson named as the grand prizewinner in the Reichhold Symphony of the Americas Contest, with second and third prizes going respectively to Camargo Guarnieri of São Paulo, Brazil, and Albert Sendrey of Los Angeles.

Immediately the Robertson phone began to ring. Friends, colleagues, relatives—it seemed that everyone was calling from everywhere across the land. Telegrams were arriving almost nonstop, and the big front doorknocker just kept on banging as nearby friends came to offer congratulations, good wishes, small gifts, and lots of ice cream and cookies. The celebration lasted until twelve or one o'clock in the morning. That evening many neighbors said they now knew why the lights in the Robertson home were always burning till well past midnight.

And in that early Monday morning, after the partying ended and things grew quiet, the lights of the Robertson home once again stayed lit. Leroy had to sit up yet a few more hours to finish copying orchestra parts for his *Overture to Punch and Judy*. As promised, Abravanel had programmed it on one of his first Utah Symphony subscription concerts, and its first rehearsal was scheduled for 9:00 A.M. that very day.

Yes, in late November 1947—right in the midst of the ongoing *Trilogy* excitement—*Punch and Judy*, as it came to be called, was premiered in the Salt Lake Tabernacle by the Utah Symphony and Abravanel, and thus became the first of many Robertson compositions to be played under the baton of this conductor.

Among Robertson's most popular compositions, *Punch and Judy* was later described by one New York critic as a "composition for children with plenty of standing room for grownups." Robertson himself—who had deliberately portrayed the two famous puppet characters in a gentler than usual fashion—characterized the work as "an attempt to bring back the simple world of childhood to an adult age that is involving itself more deeply each day in the modern complexities of life." Indeed, whenever he spoke of this overture, as he often did, he was always proud to point out that the striking little Carousel melody—so poignantly given to the oboe near the end—had been sung to him, complete with words, many years before by his second daughter, Renee, when she was but a small child three or four years old.

However, during those November and December days of 1947, it was indeed the *Trilogy* that kept commanding the greatest attention. The unprecedented award captured the imagination of everyone. Even Robertson was amazed when he learned of the competition's vast scope. More than 400 musicians from seventeen countries had submitted scores, including every major composer in North and South America. In addition to the three top prizewinners, eight composers—from Canada on the north to Chile on the south— received honorable mention. The judges for the various national juries and the final international jury had consisted of some of the hemisphere's most eminent musicians.[1]

Many colleagues and friends affirmed that they were not at all surprised about Robertson capturing the award. Among the countless letters he received at this time, one of the most valued likely came from his old Pleasant Grove High School music teacher, who simply stated:

> It would be useless for me to try to find words to tell you how I feel about your success, all I can say is congratulations. . . .

Another that must have bolstered the composer's courage came from Dr. Karl Krueger, conductor of the Detroit Symphony soon to give the *Trilogy* its premiere:

> I was sincerely happy that your score won the decision of the judges. You may not know it, but I had requested, at the time the contest was announced, that I have no vote except in case of a tie. I did, however, read through all of the scores for my own interest and yours was my first choice from the start. I can honestly tell you that one of your background and qualities is worthy of receiving this distinction.

With the Reichhold award, Leroy Robertson suddenly skyrocketed to international fame and became a sort of folk hero. The media, fascinated by his early years as a sheepherder, labeled him, albeit somewhat inaccurately, a "Utah Cowhand." Pictures and articles about him appeared in publications large and small throughout the country. The size of the award itself—the largest ever given till then for a piece of classical music—made headlines everywhere.

In New York, wherever musicians congregated, they were talking about Leroy Robertson. He was immediately invited to participate in a discussion and hear performances of some of his other works for

---

[1]Members of the United States national jury were: Eugene Goosens, former music director of the Cincinnati Symphony Orchestra; Valter Poole, assistant music director of the Detroit Symphony Orchestra; Fritz Busch, music director and conductor of the Metropolitan Opera Association; and Rudolph Reti, pianist and composer. The international jury consisted of: Dr. Karl Krueger, chairman; Roy Harris, Dr. Eric Delamarter, Herbert Elwell, Dr. Howard Hanson, and Donald M. Swarthout.

a session of the Composer's Forum, sponsored by the New York Public Library. Reluctantly he had to decline because of his ongoing work pressures and what was then the formidably long distance from Utah to New York. Publishers and performers heretofore uninterested in Leroy Robertson and his compositions now sought him out either to inquire about other completed works or to offer him commissions for new ones.

BYU was also quick to honor its famous professor. In late November, just before he was to leave for the Detroit *Trilogy* premiere, the administration held a public "Program of Tribute" for him. Though a winter storm was raging throughout the entire state that would have kept most people home, the large Joseph Smith Auditorium filled with family members, close friends, high public dignitaries, and, as President Harris stated, "others who have just come night after night and day after day when good things have been presented for the hearing."[2] The very ecumenical program featured musical numbers and speeches by some of the most prominent citizens of the state, of whom many had known Robertson for years.

Near the end, Robertson himself slowly rose to address the audience. So excited and moved was he by their genuine friendship that an almost boyish enthusiasm propelled his words, which, curiously enough, took on his boyhood Sanpete accent. After personally recognizing many who had come, he suddenly confessed, "In these last twenty years I have been practicing 'polygamy,' [and] Mrs. Robertson has known all about it." When the laughter died down, he went on to explain how he really had two families: Naomi and their four children, and another "family" that consisted of his compositions, his "brainchildren." He then named and characterized each of his major works, just like any proud father telling about his offspring. Finally he spoke of the *Trilogy*:

> Of course [it] was lying around all the time [and] wouldn't do anything. I couldn't get anyone to take an interest in that "child." . . . It seemed to be rather "wayward" . . . and I think when you

---

[2]This particular Joseph Smith Building has now been demolished.

hear it, you will find it really isn't as "polite" as you might expect
. . . it really isn't a very polite work.

Elsewhere he had termed this symphony, conceived at the outbreak
of World War II and certainly the largest and most comprehensive of
his works to date, "almost prophetic in its message."

Robertson then told of his early struggles, his disappointment at
having to refuse the Rome Prize and of never being in a position to
apply for a Guggenheim fellowship; of his difficulties in finally
getting to Europe on his own; and of his constantly asking himself,
"Why, why was he driven to compose?" But now, at last, *Trilogy* and
its triumph were answering these questions, vindicating all his
stubborn efforts, and confirming for him that there "was some force
working back of the whole thing." He concluded:

> And I want to say I am very, very thankful it has all worked out
> this way, because somehow perhaps this environment and this
> choice of things have helped to put into the *Trilogy* the thing that
> I sincerely hope will justify this award. That is the main thing.

For this humble Utah composer, who had "long despaired of ever
hearing his *Trilogy*," joy was mixed with awe. All in all, he "couldn't
quite realize it, but [felt] quite happy about it," he mused a few days
later.

His thoughts, however, were not focused on the substantial prize
money, nor on the widespread recognition that had at long last come
his way. Rather, he was concerned with the immensity of launching
such a major composition, and could not help but wonder if his symphony would indeed measure up to everyone's high expectations.

Already the very day after being named grand prizewinner, Leroy
had begun to prepare for the *Trilogy* concerts in Detroit which were
scheduled for mid-December. The ABC network, the magazine
Musical Digest, and the Detroit Symphony office asked him to write
a life sketch and program notes about the *Trilogy*. In addition
—surprise of surprises—the program directors requested that he say
a few words during the nationwide broadcast about his prizewinning
symphony and its composition. Friends observed that he seemed
more worried about this speech than the *Trilogy* performance itself.

Leroy and Naomi left for Detroit in early December, about one week before the scheduled concerts, and as they travelled by train across the snow-covered lands, they eagerly but anxiously contemplated the week ahead, a time they would never forget. Once in Detroit, their days were filled. Leroy had meetings with Dr. Krueger, Mr. Reichhold and various symphony officials; and there were many festivities for him and Naomi. Soon after their arrival, Leroy learned, much to his relief, that the big score had arrived in good time, that all parts had been copied, and that the great orchestra was well prepared. And most important, the players liked his work.

Upon hearing it at rehearsal—for the first time ever—and then at another rehearsal just before its first public performance, Robertson opined that his ten-year-old symphony might be "a bit unbridled . . . untamed," but added, "I am rather certain if I had written it now in the smoother style I have seemed to find in maturity, it wouldn't have won the prize."

The *Trilogy* had three public performances at the hand of Dr. Karl Krueger and the Detroit Symphony. The first two, which were part of the regular subscription series, were well received, with the audiences at both concerts shouting for the composer. However, it was the Sunday radio premiere that everyone across the country was eagerly awaiting.

The broadcast proceeded as outlined with introductory announcements, followed by a few remarks about the contest from Dr. Krueger. Then, as he had been asked, Leroy Robertson stepped to the microphone:

> A composer should not be taken too seriously when he speaks in some other medium than that of music. In attempting to say anything concerning my *Trilogy*, I can only give you its background.
>
> It was composed in Utah about ten years ago.
>
> Each of my grandparents came from a different part of the world: one from Sweden, one from England, one from Illinois, and one from Utah. I have studied music and composition in Utah, California, Boston, and Europe.
>
> Utah's early population was made up of Indians, missionaries, trappers and explorers. These were a rough-and-ready people, but they developed an honest code of the range which is still followed.

The spirituality of Mormonism was later superimposed upon this vigorous life of the West.

Nature indulges in various moods in the valleys and peaks of the Wasatch. Just now Mount Timpanogos is a great white monument rising more than 12,000 feet. . . . In a few months this mountain will be bursting with springs of freshly melted snow coming through banks of moss and flowers. Above the aspens, the pines point to formidable ledges of rock, the backbone of the Wasatch Range.

At the foot of Timpanogos is a calm freshwater lake leading to the soft western hills and on to the quiet expanse of our American Desert.

Perhaps some of this has become a part of the *Trilogy*.

I wrote it according to the laws of absolute music. But above this, there must be a greater law which all art strives to express.

There was a long silence. Dr. Krueger then mounted the podium and the solemn opening phrases of *Trilogy* sounded forth. As the last chords brought *Trilogy* to a close of this moving interpretation, the audience broke out in loud and sustained applause. Dr. Krueger went offstage to bring back the prizewinning composer, and then, with the audience stilled, the announcer, on behalf of Mr. Reichhold, presented the unprecedented and much publicized first prize to Leroy Robertson. With great emotion and dignity this quiet Utahn thanked the performers and Mr. Reichhold, simply stating, "Words fail me." He then concluded:

I only wish it [the award] had fallen into the hands of Mozart or Schubert. Since it comes to me, I shall consider it a sacred trust and sincerely hope that the *Trilogy* and other works will measure up to the glorious challenge and responsibility.

The excited audience again broke forth in vigorous applause lasting some five minutes or more, and recalled the composer at least three times.

Next day, the Detroit music critics, without exception, echoed the audience's enthusiasm, writing:

Trilogy is a pure adventure in the realms of tone . . . a constant blooming, forever bursting with surprise . . . fresh and free and altogether American.

. . . the heart and soul of the composition is . . . all-Robertson, and therefore all-American. There are climaxes . . . as moving as the snowy peaks of the West that gave it birth, . . . a gusty sort of humor that springs only from American soil, . . . also a dignity that is incomparable.

Immediately following the Detroit performances, and for months thereafter, letters and telegrams of congratulations poured in. They came from friends and strangers deriving from all walks of life and from every part of the land. Professional musicians—composers and performers alike—praised the *Trilogy* and asked Robertson how they might obtain some of his other compositions. But Robertson likely took his greatest delight from the straightforward and vivid comments he received from non-musicians, ordinary folk who wrote:

> None of us [are] experts, but people who enjoy music like yours.

> . . . we could hardly wait for your number. It was grand . . . electrifying. . . . Like the heavens all aglow and then suddenly thousands of bright stars darting and falling, here, there and everywhere.

> By Gosh! that is great, just as good as any symphony or orchestra number I have ever heard.

Alfred Human, editor of *Musical Digest* and closely connected to Mr. Reichhold, summed up the opinions of those who had been in charge of the contest:

> . . . we all feel that in Leroy Robertson we have truly discovered a treasure. . . . The scoffers who had been inclined to rebuff any kind of work which would carry off the award seem to have been silenced by the sheer worth of the score. Frankly we were puzzled before the broadcast and immediately following as to what the general reaction would be. . . . We find that invariably the layman responded instantly, . . . that your music reaches the ear of the average music lover as well as the musician. For all this we rejoice.

Leroy's feelings at this time must have been overwhelming. To have even heard his *Trilogy* was a dream come true. Then, to have it given such understanding and beautiful performances by Dr. Krueger and his highly skilled players was an added joy. Finally, to have this "wayward child" receive such universal acceptance surely gave him much needed satisfaction and reassurance. He had reached the apex of his musical career thus far.

A day or so after the Detroit concerts, Leroy put Naomi on the train heading west towards Utah while he journeyed eastward for a whirlwind trip to Boston and New York. In Boston, his old alma mater, the New England Conservatory, had declared in his honor a "Leroy Robertson Day," and here, at the school he had not seen since his graduation in 1923, he had a happy reunion with old friends and former teachers. He also had a heartwarming and impressive visit with Dr. Hugo Leichtentritt, who had long since emigrated from his beloved Berlin to America and was now living in extremely modest circumstances after retiring from Harvard. In New York, Leroy had to confer about certain recording and publishing contracts, and he also met informally with some of the "cream of New York's music life." A fierce winter storm, however, suddenly brought everything to a standstill in the area, and this prevented him visiting with many friends and acquaintances.

Leroy arrived home just in time for Christmas, and a joyous Christmas it was. For the first time in his life, Leroy felt wealthy enough to be a bit extravagant, and he sent a dozen red roses to Naomi and to each of his daughters and sisters, not to mention both the mother and wife of Dr. Karl Krueger as well as Mr. and Mrs. Reichhold.

Then, in early January, less than a month after the Detroit performances, Maurice Abravanel and the Utah Symphony gave the *Trilogy* its Utah premiere. Although the Maestro had blanched at the size of the score just six months earlier, he now felt that the *Trilogy* would be attractive to Utah audiences. Moreover, he had always seen the work as "full of music, full of music, from beginning to end, . . . sincere, honest, expressive music, . . . [the score] of a totally committed, totally honest man, . . . a real composer."

Composer and conductor worked closely together for this performance. Robertson was able to secure permission for the Symphony to rehearse daily in the Tabernacle, something heretofore unallowed. For his part, Abravanel studied the score with great devotion, and though himself delayed in New York by a terrible blizzard and forced to return to Salt Lake by train, he did get back to Utah in time for all rehearsals amidst a flurry of mostly local media coverage. The Utah Symphony gave it a dramatic reading to a sold-out house. Robertson, who had so long dreamed of having a professional symphony in Utah capable of performing such compositions, wrote:

> I am sure that you feel my pride in having an orchestra of our own able to give such a work as the *Trilogy*. Only those who know the demands of such a work can fully realize how far we have arrived in Symphonic music this year.

Sadly, however, despite its initial triumphs, the *Trilogy* did not go on to take its place in any standard orchestral repertoire. The jury had infuriated the musical establishment of the East by choosing this symphony from the West, and they certainly were not interested in promoting something from "an outsider." And living in the West, as he chose to do, Robertson was not really in a position to promote it himself. Furthermore, the *Trilogy*'s very size and scope daunted most conductors. For example, at one time, it was scheduled for performances in Brazil, but these never took place because sufficient players to handle the work could not be amassed. And most important is the fact that Robertson—like his mentor, Ernest Bloch—deplored hawking his works. He much preferred to spend his time and energy creating rather than selling.

Trilogy, like his other compositions, would stand on its own merits and be judged, for better or worse, through time.

Chapter Thirteen

THE DIFFICULT DECISION

THE early months of 1948 continued to bring one exciting event after another into the life of Leroy Robertson. Close upon the heels of the *Trilogy*'s Utah premiere came the performance of another Robertson work in Detroit when the Detroit Symphony Orchestra, Dr. Karl Krueger conducting, and pianist Andor Foldes played the *Rhapsody for Piano and Orchestra*. Everyone involved, including Leroy, regretted that he could not leave his work at BYU to come and hear it, for this composer, so shortly before unknown to the people of Detroit, had now become almost one of their own. The work, new to Detroit, was well received by musicians, critics, and audiences alike. Foldes summed up the general reaction when he wrote:

> The performance was a great success and the audiences really went wild.

Other honors, both local and national, kept coming nonstop: receptions, concerts featuring his early works, and honorary life membership in the National Federation of Music Clubs.

Now much sought after, Robertson suddenly found himself at a crossroads. Everywhere people were asking, "What will Robertson do now? Will he remain at BYU or will he leave for 'greener pastures'?" It had been no secret that for many years he had been offered positions to teach elsewhere, both in and out of the state as well as in Canada, positions he had thus far refused, sometimes to Naomi's bitter disappointment. But now, "numerous lucrative and enticing offers" were constantly arriving from universities, conservatories, and music schools throughout the country. Robertson was continually facing the problem of whether to stay or go.

Actually, the very idea of leaving BYU distressed him greatly. This was a man of great conscience, and he spent many, many sleepless nights agonizing over the consequences of any action either way. At times he would discuss at length the pros and cons with a few of his closest confidants, and even consulted with some of the General Authorities of the LDS Church.

Robertson had many reasons to continue at BYU. After nearly a quarter century, he had developed a university music program which was ranked among the foremost throughout America. Furthermore, at BYU he felt he was in a strong position to contribute to the music program of the LDS Church, one of his lifelong concerns.

Nor was the BYU Board of Trustees unaware of his value to the institution. In an effort to ensure that he would not leave, the trustees authorized newly appointed President Howard S. McDonald to match any salary offer, no matter how large. Also his teaching load would be greatly reduced, or, if he wished, he could simply devote full time to writing and be designated "Composer in Residence." As a final incentive, they promised to give his name to the new Fine Arts Center proposed for construction in the not-too-distant future as part of a projected campus expansion.[1]

In addition, prominent community officials—who naturally wanted to keep Utah Valley the cultural oasis that Robertson had helped create—were interested in having "their dear Professor" remain at BYU. Last but not least, Robertson and his family had established deep and long-lasting friendships among the people of Provo, which would make any departure very difficult.

On the other hand, however, Robertson felt that although his years at BYU had been good, he had "come to a dead end." Contrary to popular opinion he was not and never had been "Head of the Music Department," so his authority to act and make plans never matched his vision. More important, in those days preceding jet travel and satellite communication, Leroy Robertson, the composer,

---

[1]The Fine Arts Building that might have borne Robertson's name is the present-day Harris Fine Arts Center.

felt isolated from the musical mainstream. There were very few musicians in Utah who could understand or play the music he had written and yet intended to write. And he longed to be near a truly professional symphony orchestra. In his eyes, such a group would always be basic to the music program of any community, for it provides the skilled players necessary not only for symphonic literature, but also for chamber music, opera, ballet, etc.—each a medium important to any serious composer enamored of the larger classical forms as was he.

However, while Robertson was attracted by many of the offers coming his way, there was but one that caught his attention for very long, and this was the position as head of the Music Department at the University of Utah in Salt Lake City. He determined that, after all, he really did not wish to take his family and leave Utah, their home and the place where he had literally given his life to bring good music to the people he loved.

And although he would, in a sense, have to begin all over to build the University of Utah Music Department, he found one unique advantage. The Utah Symphony, under the direction of Maurice Abravanel, was making fast strides towards becoming the professional orchestra that he had so much wished to see in Utah. And as head of the Music Department at the university in Salt Lake City, he would be in a firm position to help this fledgling organization, which everyone knew would need strong backing if it were to survive the next crucial years. Indeed, as part of his plan, Robertson envisioned that the Symphony could "have a home on campus." Here, they would be guaranteed rehearsal space, which they did not have at the moment, and the Symphony's principal players could become adjunct faculty members, and thereby increase their teaching potential by giving private lessons to University students.

But, even as he considered these possibilities, Robertson was still undecided about whether or not to accept the post in Salt Lake City. Foreseeing good and bad results either way, he kept asking himself, "In the long run, what will it mean to BYU, and, on the other hand, what will it mean to Utah and the Utah Symphony if I come to Salt Lake City?"

Of course, there was one key person to consult before making any final decision, and this was Utah Symphony Maestro, Maurice Abravanel. He would certainly be playing an important role in any such projected plans.

Accordingly, one late January afternoon following a Symphony rehearsal in the Tabernacle, the two men conferred together in a long and frank chat. As they sat side by side on one of the benches just in front of the great organ, with pale winter sun filtering through the high windows, Robertson spoke first:

> I have been invited to come to the University of Utah. But leaving BYU is a very serious move which would mean exchanging something good for something much less good, a lot of hard feelings, and who knows what else. But, if you, Maurice—despite the enticing offers you have had from Houston and other places—if you will stay, then I will take this position where I can truly be able to help this struggling Symphony.

Abravanel quickly replied that although the Symphony was on shaky ground financially, he had refused Houston and had promised to remain for at least a few more years. With this reassurance, Robertson immediately responded, "In that case, if you will stay, I will come. I will make the move."

Thus began what was to become a long and productive relationship for Leroy Robertson, Maurice Abravanel, the University of Utah, and the Utah Symphony, a relationship that would soon prove to be of great benefit for music throughout the Intermountain West.

Though still in no "official" position to do so, Robertson then formally proposed to University of Utah President A. Ray Olpin that "an effort be made to identify the Utah Symphony and its gifted conductor, Maurice Abravanel, with the University of Utah." Underscoring Utah's need for such a symphony and the advantages to be gained from such a connection, he proposed that the University's role would primarily be one of assistance in promoting the welfare of the orchestra (not fund-raising). For its part, a professional orchestra on campus would complement the threefold development envisaged by him for the Music Department.

President Olpin, a man of great vision, agreed. A rudimentary plan was then quietly set in motion by these three principal proponents. President Olpin and Maestro Abravanel dealt with the public out front while Robertson unobtrusively acted in the wings as catalyst. At the final Utah Symphony concert of the 1947-1948 season, President Olpin publicly invited the Utah Symphony to come "make its home on the campus of the University of Utah."

Shortly thereafter, in mid-March, local and national publications headlined the news: "Leroy Robertson Named Head of the U. of U. Music Department."

Reaction was loud and immediate. BYU as a whole felt betrayed, could not understand why, if he chose to leave, he would go to this rival university in nearby Salt Lake City. After all, how could this move enhance his connections to the big musical centers of the East and West Coasts? Nonetheless, a very few Utahns did realize that Robertson was making the transfer "in the unselfish interest of bettering music standards in this entire Intermountain West." Across the nation, musicians were delighted, seeing it as "a prime opportunity to develop a central music force and activity for the whole . . . region." One colleague from the East wrote, "I dare say you will go to town."

In the midst of all this furor, Leroy Robertson merely wished to complete his tenure at BYU quietly teaching and composing as he had always done. However, he could not avoid some notoriety. The Paganini Quartet announced plans to perform the *American Serenade* during the forthcoming BYU Summer Music Festival. And at its final concert of the year, his beloved BYU Symphony Orchestra —now under the direction of Lawrence Sardoni—concluded the evening with a performance of Robertson's *Overture in E minor (Endicott)* as a sort of farewell salute.

A few days later Robertson received a courteous letter from Thomas Giles, retiring head of the University of Utah Music Department, in which Professor Giles predicted "a series of ever-increasing glorious triumphs for you and your staff."

Then, the last day of June 1948, Leroy Robertson calmly completed his twenty-three year stint at BYU not only as a constant and consistent leader in the Music Department, but also as one of that university's most popular and prominent faculty members. The following day, July 1, he officially assumed his new duties at the University of Utah in Salt Lake City. Little could anyone guess what triumphs and troubles lay ahead.

1 Leroy Robertson's Birthplace: Home of Jasper and Alice Robertson, Fountain Green, Utah, 1897. Foreground, left to right: Hanna and Edwin Robertson; Jasper and Alice, holding infant Leroy; Will and Melissa Adams with their two youngest children. Note in the background, a relative holding Jasper's prize team of horses, the barn, and the knoll.

2 Leroy Robertson with his younger brother and sisters during Jasper's mission, Fountain Green, ca. 1912. Left to right: Joe, Leroy, Macel, Ora, and Wanda.

3 Robertson, near the time of his High School graduation, ca. 1916.

4   Naomi Nelson, ca. 1923.

5   Robertson, ca. 1923.

6   Ernest Bloch, ca. 1930.

7   Robertson in Berlin, 1933.
Left to right: an unidentified friend,
Robertson, and J. J. Keeler.

8   Utah premiere of Bach's *Passion according to Saint John*, Provo Tabernacle,
1936.   Standing in foreground, left to right: Richard P. Condie, Margaret
Summerhays, and Robertson (next to organ).   Seated at the organ is J. J. Keeler.

9   Robertson working on a score, Aspen Grove, ca. 1939.

10   Robertson with pianist, E. Robert Schmitz and members of the Roth Quartet
at the Utah premiere of Robertson's *Quintet for Piano and Strings*,
Provo Tabernacle, 1940. Clockwise: Schmitz at the piano, Rachmael Weinstock,
Feri Roth, Robertson, Julius Shaier, and Oliver Edel.

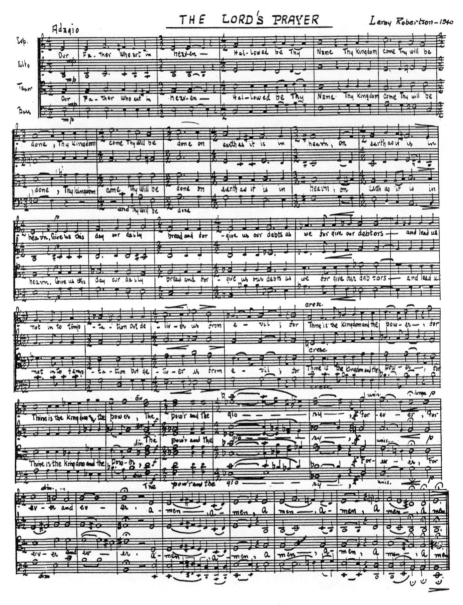

11   Robertson's original manuscript of the "Lord's Prayer."
© Copyright 1941 by Galaxy Music Corporation.
Used by permission of ECS Publishing, Boston

12 Brigham Young University Symphony Orchestra, Joseph Smith Building, Provo, Utah, 1945. Robertson is standing center front.
Note that due to World War II, the group is nearly "all-girl."

13 *Left:* Robertson at home,
holding his prizewinning
Trilogy score,
Provo, 1947.

14 *Below:* The Robertson Family
at home, Provo, 1947.
Left to right: Karen, Naomi, Leroy,
Jim, Renee, and Marian.
Note Robertson's well-worn copy
of the Book of Mormon on the
table in the foreground.

PART III

IN THE VALLEY OF THE GREAT SALT LAKE

Chapter Fourteen

NEW PROFESSOR ON CAMPUS ONCE AGAIN

ALTHOUGH the Valley of the Great Salt Lake was not far from Provo, Leroy Robertson's move to the University of Utah meant a big change for his family. They would be leaving behind everything they had known—friends, schools, neighbors.

One of Leroy's first priorities was to find a suitable home for Naomi and their four children. This proved to be no easy task, for three years after World War II, housing in the Salt Lake Valley was still at a premium. And more than once, by the time Leroy could fetch Naomi from Provo to look over a home he had located, the property would have been sold. Finally, in desperation, Leroy just used his own judgment, chose and bought a house right on the spot without consulting his wife or anyone else. It was a rash act, but turned out to be a wise decision. The home in which he would live the rest of his life, and which would henceforth become the center of activities for the Robertson family, was another "White House," this time a large brick English-style cottage not too far from the University. The Robertsons made their big move to Salt Lake in midsummer, and immediately began settling into a life both different from, and yet similar to what they had experienced in their beloved Provo.

Leroy would henceforth be highly occupied with his professional duties, and would inevitably spend much energy composing. Yet, he somehow would also have time for his family. In the early evenings, as they all sat together around the dinner table, he would alternately recount and listen to the different stories of the day. Then after dinner, he would go to "his chair"—always placed in the dining room right in the midst of the family traffic—and remain buried in his ongoing studies and writing. But as the children and Naomi skirted past him, he always seemed to know what was going on. And how he did love his children and their mother.

For example, one afternoon as he was sitting in his chair composing, the sound of a basketball being dribbled just outside the nearby window bothered him intensely. This incessant, nonstop noise finally became so distracting that he could no longer concentrate. So he went out to ask the offending dribbler, "Please, go play somewhere else." But when the annoyed composer saw that the determined basketball player was none other than his own son, Jim, all irritation vanished. With a grin on his face, he returned to the house, remarking, "That Jim really knows how to handle a basketball." Settled back into his chair, he comfortably resumed his composing, no longer upset by that ever bounce-bounce-bouncing ball.

On another afternoon when he came home from work, Karen was practicing her piano lesson. Quietly passing by his little daughter, and careful not to interrupt her, he commented to Naomi, with a soft smile, "What a beautiful tone that child has."

As for the University, the news of Robertson's coming had generated tremendous excitement, with townspeople, colleagues, and students alike eagerly awaiting this much publicized musician. Sensing that music at the University of Utah was about to take a different direction, many flocked to enroll, and weeks in advance, music classes had filled with earnest scholars, performers, and would-be composers, most of whom, for the first time, seriously began to consider music as a profession.

Robertson, in turn, came to his new job full of enthusiasm, committed to the great task ahead of upgrading the Music Department and arranging a home on campus for the Utah Symphony. According to Maurice Abravanel, Robertson did indeed change the whole atmosphere regarding music, and this was felt not only in the University, but throughout the entire community and surrounding area.

At one of his first meetings with President Olpin, Robertson learned that, among his many duties, one of immediate priority would be to organize a show-piece marching band, one that could rival that of Ohio State University, which at the time had one of the most spectacular marching bands to be found anywhere. President Olpin even demonstrated with great enthusiasm how that famous band would end its show by spelling out, in script letters, "Ohio," with the grand climax being one tuba player running across the field to dot the "i." Robertson, rising to the challenge, quickly replied, "President, we promise you that if we go into this band business, we'll have a band that will script-write 'Utah,' and *four* tuba players will run out to cross the 't.'"

In organizing such a band, Robertson certainly had no time to waste, for President Olpin wanted it ready to perform in early September when the University of Utah football team would be playing the mighty Trojans of USC in the Los Angeles Colosseum. A phone call from Olpin to a former colleague at Ohio State resulted in Robertson's recruiting the best man Ohio State could recommend, Ronald D. Gregory.

When he arrived in August, "Greg" had barely five weeks to get a band together and ready to perform. But this young bandmaster proved to be a genius at rallying students, and in no time had amassed a group that quickly grew from sixty to 120 members, something heretofore unheard of. They loyally and spiritedly rehearsed every night, working to master not only the music, but also the renowned "Gregory March," which consisted of bringing the knees up "just high enough to hold a plate so one could eat from it, and prancing precisely eight steps to every five yards," as one band member explained.

While Greg was busy teaching the band to perform, Robertson discovered that he had yet one other important hurdle to surmount. There simply was not enough money in the budget to purchase the special band uniforms so dearly needed to show off these energetic musical high-steppers at their best. Lack of funds, however, did not stop Robertson, who—as he had so often done in the past and would continue to do in the future—merely substituted imagination for money. Search of an old and almost forgotten storage space uncovered a cache of somewhat bedraggled crimson jackets which Robertson immediately sent off to the dry cleaners, and which came back looking bright as new. Each band member then furnished his own pair of white duck pants, and Greg, ever the showman, added red spats as a finishing touch. There was never a sharper-looking band.

Robertson used to peer in at rehearsals to see how things were progressing, and when the time finally came for the band to make its foray into Trojan territory, Robertson, feeling a bit of fatherly responsibility towards his young musicians, decided to travel to California and witness the performance.

The game was set for a Friday night, and the band would present two shows, one before the game, and another at half time. At the pregame appearance, as the band exited the ramp and came onto the field at about 144 steps per minute, the crowd went wild. No one in the West had ever before seen anything quite like that. Then at the half, as the University of Utah ensemble concluded its show by scriptwriting "Utah" with the four tuba players crossing the "t," exactly as Robertson had promised, the Utes had clearly won the "Battle of the Bands" (though their team did lose the game). The former USC band director even wrote to Robertson:

> . . . your Utah Band was fine. One can certainly tell that the band members have had good training. My loyalty had to be divided because I had to be in favor of S.C., . . . but I wanted to tell [your bandmaster] that the band looked beautiful on the field.

After this auspicious launching, the band program continued with good success. Its influence spread throughout the region, and soon university and high school bands alike were following the lead of the University of Utah marching band. In keeping with Robertson's philosophy of reaching out to and involving the public, the University began inviting school bands from throughout the state to participate in an annual Band Day on campus, where they could all learn to march and play together. One year, much to everyone's delight and surprise, the band kids spelled out—in block letters that filled the field at Rice Stadium—LEROY ROBERTSON.

Of course, the band was but one of many programs demanding Robertson's attention. His main concern was to adapt the curriculum of study so as to meet national standards, and to do this, he started from the ground up. Proceeding from the basic premise that the students needed to know more music than had hitherto been offered or required, he sought to give more advanced work in those courses already on the books as well as add new classes to round out the studies. To this end, Robertson tirelessly worked with the administration persuading them to offer music students not only the usual academic degrees in Arts and Sciences, but truly professional degrees as well, such as a bachelor's or master's in Music. In short order, he succeeded in getting these plus even more specialized degrees established, and within a few years after his arrival, the University of Utah became the first school in the Intermountain West to award the Ph.D. in Music—a truly remarkable milestone.

For such a full-scale expansion, Robertson obviously needed to augment his faculty. Several fine musicians of national and international repute were inquiring about teaching in the department, but Robertson, rightly or wrongly, opted to work with the musicians at hand. To add to the staff already on campus he recruited—by dint of much patience, persuasion, and persistence—a few excellent teachers who had recently returned to Salt Lake City after spending several years elsewhere; and eventually he was also able to develop qualified instructors from among his best graduate students.[1]

To assist with the ongoing administrative details and inevitable office red tape, he personally chose young Lowell M. Durham to be his executive secretary, a move that freed Robertson for what he termed the "artistic supervision" of the department.

According to those who worked with him, Robertson was a somewhat unorthodox administrator with a very personal, almost inborn style. He held few faculty meetings, formed few committees, and tended to assign projects to certain carefully chosen faculty mem-

---

[1]Among the excellent local teachers whom Robertson recruited, one may mention Dr. Helen Folland; violinist Albert Shepherd; pianists Reid Nibley, and then Gladys Gladstone. For names of full-time music faculty during Robertson's tenure as department head, the reader may consult University of Utah catalogues of 1948-1949 through 1961-1962.

bers, while he himself remained in the background. As he once explained, "I never appoint anyone to do a job until I am absolutely sure he is fully prepared to do it well. Then I let him alone."

Some programs that Robertson enlarged or inaugurated with his faculty are: private lessons, which, thanks to the Utah Symphony's arrival on campus, soon became available for all instrumentalists; Chamber Music, with its highlight being the annual midwinter Chamber Music Festival featuring visiting artists, faculty members, and students in performance together; the University Symphony Orchestra, which, in a few years, grew from a group of sixty players to ninety, presenting regular concerts both locally and throughout the state; the Opera Workshop, designed to give vocalists experience in performing opera; and the presentation of great choral-orchestral works with the combined University Choruses and Utah Symphony. Some special programs were held only during Summer Quarter and designed to impact immediately the whole community. Among these were the annual Choral Workshops set up for high school chorus teachers and their students, and directed by some of the nation's outstanding choral conductors including Peter Wilhousky and Roger Wagner. As Robertson hoped, such programs would soon have wide ramifications. Indeed, after a few years, the local high school choral directors developed a special High School Honor Chorus, consisting of the best high school students throughout the state. This highly select choral ensemble would present a public concert at the University and join with the University Chorale for several performances throughout the year. In 1958, the Music Department would expand this Choral Workshop into a statewide Summer Music Camp for high school students and offer not only choral, but band, orchestra, piano and chamber music instruction as well.

Another summer event was the appearance of the Paganini Quartet in Kingsbury Hall. These quartet visits made exciting moments for the Robertson family not only because they programmed Robertson compositions, but also because Henri Temianka, leader of the group, always spent hours practicing his violin in the cool basement of the Robertson home, which, he claimed, "had the best acoustics anywhere to be found."

Guest choral director Peter J. Wilhousky succinctly expressed the goal of all these projects when he wrote to Robertson:

> I hope that our joint efforts . . . will result in an awakened appreciation of better music.

As one might expect, Robertson put a great deal of emphasis on the study of Music Theory for all music students regardless of their special interest. And, according to Maestro Abravanel, under Robertson's direction these classes changed from "something that was a nuisance . . . to something of great importance."

As to the graduate program, it became Robertson's bailiwick. Heretofore nonexistent, it had to start from scratch, and at the beginning of his tenure, Robertson himself taught all of the courses. In fact, he bore this "giant-sized teaching and tutoring load . . . almost single-handedly for more than a decade," Lowell Durham would later aver.

Leroy Robertson, now in his early fifties, had been teaching music in one way or another most of his life, and had been in a formal academic setting for at least a quarter of a century. One may well ask whether, after so many, many years, he could still bring freshness and enthusiasm to this task. With not only regular students but faculty members attending his classes, could he yet find something new and worthwhile to impart to those coming to learn?

One faculty member who regularly visited Robertson's classes answered quite simply, "I think he was a great teacher." No matter what the specific subject, Robertson's own excitement about making music pervaded everything. Students would later opine:

> With Robertson at the "U," we were discovering music for the first time.

> He was the first person to give us an insight into what music can really do *to* and *for* a human being.

Many recounted, "He started with Bach, stayed with Bach . . . , and branched out to other composers only when he felt we were ready." But whether this composer was examining the works of Bach, Mozart, or Schoenberg, he was forever delving into something different.

Can anyone present forget how satisfied he was when he figured out the thinking of Stockhausen and his *Elektronische Musik* (Electronic Music), which during the fifties represented the very latest in musical experimentation? Or can anyone who chatted with Robertson ever forget the boyish excitement and thrill he evinced even during his very last year of formal teaching as he analyzed with his students Bach's *Musical Offering*?

From time to time, Robertson would pull out and explain one of his own scores, usually a work in progress. This made exciting moments for his students, for, as one remarked, "We felt we were being initiated into the secrets, the inner workings . . . [of] what went on in the brain of a real composer."

As he taught, Robertson—ever strict and unyielding in his demands—endeavored to show how and why "every note had to be written for a purpose, in the right place, for the right reason." In so doing, he was attempting as always to develop in his students a basis for a scrupulous self-criticism, which for him was essential to any artist. He truly started his charges at ground level so that, as one remarked, "When you were finally 'up there,' you knew what was happening"; or, as another stated, "He just wanted to make certain that we were very, very, very well prepared to function as professionals, be it in teaching, performing, or composing."

Interestingly enough, this master composer persistently refused to schedule any class called "Composition," for he felt composers were born, not made. As he once wrote, "The poet [composer] must have 'celestial instruction.'" But he then added elsewhere, "This 'gift of heaven' does not come without learning." Therefore, along with meticulous criticism, he offered his students broad precepts to ponder, precepts he had gleaned from his own studies:

> There is no good or bad art. There is only clear or unclear thinking.
> Extravagances in art persuade few.
> In all speech, words and sense are as the body and the soul . . . [and] without [sense] all words are dead. Sense is wrought out of experience, a knowledge of human life and actions, and also, of the liberal arts.
> Our composition must be more accurate in the beginning and

end than in the midst, and in the end more than the beginning,
for thru the midst the stream bears us.
The artist: a true aristocrat, must never pervert his art; has
tremendous responsibility.

Through the years, Robertson changed his teaching ways very
little. At the University of Utah, his classes were small, rarely num-
bering more than ten, which enabled him to critique regularly the
work of each individual student. A man of few words, he avoided
flowery explanations, but rather would make his point with some
striking analogy, often seasoned with the dry Sanpete wit that somehow never left him. For example, one day, as a student came out of
Robertson's class laughing and laughing, a curious colleague asked,
"Now, what did he say?" "Well," chuckled the student, "he looked
over a class member's assignment, and then sort of told this story":

> You know, the other day I was going to my safety deposit
> box, and that's a lot of trouble. . . . You have to go downtown,
> get to the bank, sign in, get the attendant to open the safe and
> bring the bank key. Well, when I got through all those prelimi-
> naries, I realized I'd forgotten my own key. All my efforts came
> to naught for want of that crucial, final key. . . . Your
> composition is a lot like that.

Usually his comments were less involved, as for example, when a
bewildered student gravely asked, "How do you analyze and figure
out all these musical structures and forms?" Robertson simply replied
with a bemused smile, "You listen, just listen." On another occasion,
when an orchestration student submitted a needlessly elaborate and
impractical arrangement that produced little sound, he laconically
observed, "This work resembles a mountain in labor giving birth to
a mouse." And again, while checking over a submitted work, he
placed a sharp (#) before one of the notes, thinking that the student
had merely overlooked it. But when the student objected and
pointed out that "changing this note destroys the strict mathematical
imitation," Robertson gravely answered, "The music comes first, not
the imitation." Indeed, his highest praise was to comment, "That is
very musical."

His students agree that in his teaching Robertson was careful not
to impose his own unique style of composing, but rather, encouraged

each one "to go ahead and do his own thing." As he once wrote:

> Custom is the most certain mistress of language [music]. Yet we must adventure.

From the beginning of his tenure at the University of Utah, Robertson, in order to complement his own teaching, would invite other renowned composers and scholars to lecture at the school, sometimes only for a few classes, sometimes for an entire quarter. Not only did these men offer differing viewpoints and approaches to music, but even more important to Robertson was the department's direct contact with these great musical personalities. This, he felt, was "vital for the development of our students and faculty."

Even before the Music Department had adequate facilities on campus, Robertson encouraged his dear friend and former mentor, Ernest Bloch, to come lecture in Salt Lake at the beautiful McCune School of Music. The two composers had not seen each other for nearly sixteen years, but when they met, they picked up right where they had left off, discussing their ideals, philosophy, and music's place in the life of humankind. Music teachers and students filled the hall to hear Mr. Bloch, who—white hair shining above his brow—sat at the piano playing, humming, and explaining certain "Preludes" and "Fugues" from Bach's *Well Tempered Clavichord*. As he played, this master teacher-composer might occasionally miss a note, but never did he cease communicating what lay behind those notes.

In April 1951, Robertson also signed up another of his former teachers, Arnold Schoenberg, to come spend a few weeks at the University. Not only would Schoenberg be lecturing, but he and Robertson would also be working on the book of analysis they had projected so many years before. Tragically, Schoenberg died in mid-July, just a few weeks before he was scheduled to arrive in Utah. This certainly must have been a terrible loss to Robertson, for he had long looked forward to this collaboration. However, as was his wont, he hid his disappointment and went on to other work.

As another means of giving his students wider exposure and more experience with the outside world, Robertson arranged for the

University of Utah to participate in annual composition symposiums which brought together student composers and performers from the large West Coast universities: USC, UCLA, Stanford, and UC at Berkeley, among others. During these get-togethers, the participants would hear and discuss each others' compositions, and with so many diverse backgrounds and teaching methods represented, the critiques could be very spirited.

In general, although the Utah students were very experimental in their thinking, they tended to base their composing upon time-honored techniques of harmony and counterpoint, whereas the Californians, on the other hand, were working almost exclusively according to Schoenberg's twelve-tone system—then the rage among "modernists." On one occasion, a heated argument arose as to which style was more pertinent for music coming from this mid-twentieth century. After listening to the dispute for a while, Robertson himself settled the matter with one succinct sentence:

> It is a sign of maturity when we're not afraid of either the old or the new.

And in concluding a symposium held at the University of Utah—wherein some performers and composers ran around the piano, striking the instrument's back and top and crawling underneath to hit its underside, all while leaning over to pluck the strings—Robertson again dryly remarked, "I wonder if we have not changed the patron saint of music from Saint Cecilia to Saint Vitus." All in all, the Utahns were able to hold their own with the California students, as was noted in this letter from well-known composer John Vincent:

> Your Utah compositions showed to great advantage at the recent symposium. Your group represents some of the more sane and substantial influence both musically and in leadership.

As for the violin, of the countless students Robertson taught during his University of Utah years, there was but one whom he took as a private violin student (in contrast to his BYU years). This was a young lad who, like Robertson, had grown up on a farm doing heavy labor, all the while loving music and playing the violin. The busy department head, remembering his own boyhood, seemed to feel a deep personal kinship with the youth, opened doors for him to pursue his music studies, and indeed changed his life. During the lessons that followed, the older man often told the gifted youngster of his own early life in Fountain Green, of his struggles and successes. After only one year, Robertson—really too busy for this extra task—sent the boy on to study with Harold Wolf, the current concertmaster of the Utah Symphony, and never again did he teach violin.

It may be of interest to note that although Robertson scrupulously avoided imposing upon students his own unique composition style, he apparently felt that there was but one way to play the violin. One pupil has related that many years after his violin studies with Robertson, when he once performed the "Meditation" from *Thaïs* (a Robertson favorite), a lady in the audience came to him and said, "I know you studied that piece with Dr. Robertson because that is exactly the way he taught it to me."

As has been mentioned, Robertson always had taken a personal interest in his students, and now at the University of Utah, he became almost like a second father to many of them. He constantly inquired about their welfare, their families, their plans. The Robertsons well remember how one evening he came home terribly worried about one young student who, for a whole week, had been coming to class wearing a jacket with leather patches on the elbows. He feared that the boy's parents had, for some reason, withdrawn their financial support. The concerned professor was reassured only when his own children—much more aware of changing fashions than was he—explained that patches on sleeves were "the latest," and that to have such a jacket was a mark of wealth, not poverty. Nonetheless, Robertson remained very skeptical about it all, and watched over the boy with extra care for quite some time.

Practical man that he was, he not only offered his students counsel, encouragement, and abundant time, but also would somehow find them financial aid so they could remain in school through many critical periods in their lives.

This interest in his students continued long after they had left the University, and in looking at the records, one might say that he sort of spotted where each one should go. He just seemed to sense where they would best fit in order to contribute as musicians, whether as teachers or performers, and they all seemed happy in their work. As one student would later write, "I've never been sorry to have left the business world"; or, perhaps even more important, as another penned:

> You have pointed the direction . . . by which I can now proceed to find my real self and to express it with my own individuality. You have given me some concrete keys of criticism which I can apply to the free outpourings of my still youthful and romantic spirit.

On the other side of the coin, let it be said that Leroy Robertson's uncompromising standards were not understood by every student who came his way. There were a few who refused to accept what he offered, and every now and again, some even complained to the dean that Robertson was not teaching what was needed. Nonetheless, this singular professor held to his priorities and did what he had come to know was best.

*   *   *   *   *

Along with setting up and developing the Music Department's many new programs of study, Robertson also faced two other problems caused by this rapid expansion. The department desperately needed more adequate quarters and a library suitable for serious research.

Upon his arrival on campus, the Music Department occupied a very small building that had originally served as the University's heating plant. Located at the extreme northwest corner of the lower campus, it contained but two classrooms, one of which led to a dark little office in the rear. Such facilities obviously could not meet the needs of the growing department. Within six months, therefore, Robertson had arranged to have his department move across campus into six wooden barracks that had once been part of Fort Douglas. Spread over half a mile, these buildings, very spartan in their construction, were large, drafty, badly lit, and had poor acoustics for music. Installing fluorescent lights and hanging huge panels of coarse brown fish-netting improved the lighting and acoustics somewhat, but, at the most, these accommodations can only be described as primitive.

Nonetheless, precisely because there was nothing else to do, the musicians willingly bit the bullet and concentrated on making good music. Indeed, in retrospect, many of them would come to regard this time in the barracks as the golden years. After all, they had clean air to breathe, unhampered views of the valley in all directions, and a lot of space so that they were able to keep out of each other's way.

In any event, however, such quarters could never be considered permanent, and when Robertson learned that the old Student Union Building was to be vacated upon completion of the new Olpin Student Union, he set out to get the older edifice for the Music Department. He could envision this elegant, majestic building—in combination with nearby Kingsbury Hall—as the hub of a beautiful music complex. Of course, many other department heads were likewise eyeing these facilities, and the competition did become fierce. But the Music Department perhaps had an edge over the others because, for several years, all department concerts had been presented in the old Student Union ballroom, a tradition which Robertson wisely continued. To further his cause, he also enlisted the help of the prominent musicians who had been coming to teach in the department's summer programs, and they began writing to President Olpin about "the desirability of converting the Union Building into a Music Center."

After numerous heated meetings of the University administration and Board of Regents, the Music Department eventually won the coveted building, and during the summer of 1957—nearly ten years after Robertson's arrival on campus—the happy musicians moved into their new home, now renamed Music Hall.[2] Robertson selected

---

[2]This building, still occupied by the Music Department, has since been renamed Gardner Hall, after University President David P. Gardner, in keeping with a subsequent University tradition to name each building around the quad (now known as President's Circle) after a University president.

as his studio-office-classroom a large wood-paneled room with views to the south and west. This was the first bit of luxury he had known during his long teaching career. And he purposely placed his desk so that whenever he sat writing—be it correcting papers, drafting department projects, or composing—he could look westward, out over the city to the distant Great Salt Lake. Oh, how he loved that room!

Robertson's further plans for the building did not develop quite as he had hoped, however. Almost before everyone got settled in, President Olpin approached Robertson with the following problem and plan: If the University could immediately match a grant available from the federal government, it could have the first public television station in Utah. Olpin did not have the funds, but he could instead offer space, and so he asked, "Would Robertson give up part of the basement in the Music Building for this project?" The decision was doubly hard, for this also meant that money already appropriated for much needed and carefully planned remodelling would go rather to fix up the television facilities. Robertson realized that, in the short run, the Music Department would certainly lose quite a bit. But he also knew that if the University did not grab this chance, the TV station would go elsewhere, and that, in the long run, everyone —musicians included—would lose much more. Therefore, he swallowed hard and relinquished the space and funding. According to Lowell Durham, who was party to all the details, the resultant KUED owes its existence to Robertson and his foresight.[3]

Another example of Robertson's ability to put things in perspective and work things out for everyone's ultimate benefit occurred a few years later when he gave much needed room on the main floor to the new Ballet Department just being established under the direction of Willam Christensen. Robertson maneuvered so that his musicians could manage for a while, knowing the community's gain would be greater than the Music Department's temporary loss. And temporary it was, for when the Ballet School moved to other

---

[3]If Durham's opinion be exaggerated, one can say that, at the least, KUED's beginnings would have been postponed many years.

quarters, the Music Department regained this space.

* * * * *

As has been mentioned, along with organizing the department's many programs and finding suitable facilities for them, Robertson was also concerned with a third great need, that of building up a music library adequate for serious research. He set about solving this problem in an unusual and very personal way.

Ever since his studies in Berlin with Dr. Hugo Leichtentritt, Robertson had been impressed with the extraordinary library of this eminent mentor, who through the years had acquired innumerable precious texts, scores and manuscripts. After his 1947 visit with this great scholar, then living in very modest retirement at Cambridge, Robertson conceived the idea of helping Dr. Leichtentritt by having someone purchase his extensive collection. Realizing, however, how much this dedicated scholar would still need his valuable editions, Robertson suggested that Dr. Leichtentritt consider sending only a token shipment of books each year in return for a fixed stipend, with the entire collection becoming available only upon his demise.

Dr. Leichtentritt was at first reluctant to part with his cherished books, but he did find the idea alluring, and as evidence of what he could offer, he outlined a brief sample of his catalogue, a sample that was mind-boggling to any musician residing in the music-book-deprived desert of the Wasatch Front.

Sometime in early 1948 Robertson approached Leonard Kirkpatrick, head of the University of Utah Libraries, with his revolutionary plan. By summer's end the deal was struck, and in late 1948, the first of many shipments arrived from Dr. Leichtentritt. The volumes henceforth continued to come regularly. In fact, just before his death in 1951, Dr. Leichtentritt "was just packing another case to be sent . . . when total weakness overcame him," as his sister, Regina Buchwald, wrote to Robertson. After his death, Mrs. Buchwald continued sending Robertson valuable materials, all of which he turned over to the library. By 1958 the Leichtentritt Collection—to be kept intact as one unit in memory of this eminent scholar—filled an entire wall on one floor of the old George Thomas Library.[4]

This marked only the beginning of Robertson's efforts to expand the music library. Budget permitting, he went on procuring more and more standard works, as well as the most recent scholarly publications in music. Within a few years he was able to describe the University of Utah music collection as "one of the most selective libraries in America."

And that, in a nutshell, is how Leroy Robertson set about building a Music Department at the University of Utah that would soon earn both national and international respect—high respect to be maintained for years to come.

---

[4]Sadly, and much to Robertson's dismay, when the library was later moved to the larger Marriott Library, the Leichtentritt Collection was dispersed throughout the stacks, and many "old books" were cast aside in favor of "newer editions." Numerous invaluable first editions and manuscripts, not to mention Leichtentritt's invaluable notes scattered throughout, were thereby lost. Recently, however, efforts have been made to find what remains of the Leichtentritt Collection and again place the volumes together as one unit.

Chapter Fifteen

A REMARKABLE ALLIANCE

ONE of Leroy Robertson's most vital concerns at the University of Utah involved the presence of the Utah Symphony on campus. Making this "Home for the Symphony" had been his prime precondition for accepting the position in Salt Lake City, and once having decided to come, he fully committed himself to the success of this Utah Symphony-University of Utah affiliation. According to Abravanel, although President Olpin had been enthusiastic about such a venture from the beginning, had he been left on his own, he might have cooled off without Robertson in the picture. As the Maestro would later emphasize, it was Robertson who proceeded to work things out "in his own, quiet, stubborn, sheepherder's way."

Solving the problems of this unusual collaboration ultimately fell on the shoulders of both Robertson and Abravanel. And, in noting the vast differences in their backgrounds and personalities, one may well wonder how such divergent persons could ever team up on anything. Maurice Abravanel—born, reared and educated in cosmopolitan Europe, and already a well-known conductor in the international music world—was a gregarious, outspoken individual who liked to be in the spotlight. Robertson, on the other hand—born and reared in Utah's mountains, well-educated but largely self-taught—was a reflective man, one who generally preferred to be composing, teaching, envisioning and initiating projects in the background; one not prone to speak very much. However, these apparent contrasts were of style only, which paled before the common ideals and goals that bound them together.

To his joy, Robertson discovered that, like himself, Abravanel had settled in Utah to build a great music center, while the Maestro found in Robertson "not specifically this or that," but a man with whom he could talk; one who, like himself, was opposed to "the incredible amateurishness" that had seemed to prevail for so many years. For Abravanel, this association with Robertson became a very stimulating experience because of the Utahn's "untampered individuality," whereas in Robertson's mind—as has been mentioned—Abravanel on the scene was "one of the 'greats.'" Constant allies, they strengthened each other, and as Abravanel would later aver, this mutual support "went back and forth, it went back and forth."

Both men envisioned a whole musical culture, that included not only frequent symphony concerts, but also regular performances of opera, ballet, and the smaller chamber organizations. And in this total picture, both viewed the Utah Symphony as the crucial ingredient and catalyst, for they knew that only such a group of highly trained, professional musicians would be able to produce the quality of music they were hoping to create.

Therefore, both men were determined to secure the Symphony's position not only in Utah but throughout the Intermountain Region, with Abravanel being directly concerned with his players, while Robertson would be working out the myriad details at the University. Each man, in his own way, worked with community leaders on all levels, which was indeed necessary, for it must be admitted that during these years the Symphony was in a bad financial state.

In this alliance, Robertson's immediate responsibility was to find adequate rehearsal space on campus for the new arrivals. At first, the Symphony used one of the old Fort Douglas barracks. Then, when the Music Department took up residence in their newly acquired Music Building, the Symphony was given the big ballroom, now converted into a rehearsal and concert hall. Robertson made these facilities available to the Symphony whenever needed. Be it morning, afternoon, or evening, first priority always went to Abravanel. Moreover, Robertson gave the Maestro use of his own office in the Music Hall, there being no other space available for Abravanel.

Robertson made a second unprecedented move when he put the Symphony's principal players on the Music Department faculty, and also involved them in various concerts sponsored by the Music

Department.

Together, Robertson and Abravanel developed many brilliant projects with the University and Utah Symphony. There were annual choral-orchestral performances of many masterworks never before heard in the area; chamber music concerts in Kingsbury Hall that soon evolved into the larger "Contemporary Concerts"; seasons of summer shows in Rice Stadium featuring both a Broadway musical and an opera; very modest spring or winter seasons of opera in Kingsbury Hall; commercial recordings; and eventually ballet, thanks to the arrival of Willam Christensen.

The collaboration of the University Choruses and Utah Symphony—one of Abravanel's and Robertson's dearest projects—had actually been initiated by Abravanel the year preceding with a striking performance of Beethoven's *Ninth Symphony*. But the preparation had been a lonely, arduous battle for Abravanel, who had to take the full responsibility of teaching the students their parts; and these youngsters, undisciplined in every way, "really had no idea of the music." Yet, this concert, which marked the finale of the 1947-1948 Symphony season, was a great success. And Robertson absolutely insisted on making such concerts a tradition.

However, one sudden and unexpected hitch in these plans arose when the LDS Church announced that no choruses other than the Tabernacle Choir would be permitted to sing in the Tabernacle, which by now had become the established site for the Symphony's regular subscription concerts.[1] Abravanel's first response was, "Okay, let's call these Choral-Symphony concerts quits." Robertson, however, adamantly refused, arguing:

> It's an incredible educational opportunity for the students to work with Abravanel and the Symphony, and the people have never before had a chance to hear these works performed with a real symphony. We'll continue in Kingsbury Hall.

Because he was as committed as Robertson, Abravanel agreed.

---

[1] One exception to this policy was the annual performance of the *Messiah* by the Oratorio Society Chorus and Orchestra.

To launch this new collaboration of the University of Utah Choruses and Utah Symphony, Abravanel selected Beethoven's *Missa Solemnis*, which immediately provoked a rebellion among the University choral teachers. As vocalists, they unanimously protested to Robertson, complaining:

> The students will never accept this work. No one understands the Latin text; the vocal lines are impossible to sing and will ruin the students' young voices; it is simply too complicated to comprehend and put together.

Even the students—following the lead of their professors—likewise joined in the protest. But, once having made up his mind, Robertson resolutely supported this undertaking, simply turned a deaf ear to any and all grievances, and did not give in. "Not one split second did he give in," reminisced Abravanel.

In fact, Robertson himself took over the joint choral rehearsals, and in short order he amassed about 500 singers who presently were singing their hearts out. Two weeks before the performance, Abravanel came in to take over the final rehearsals. And as the Maestro directed the choruses, the ever present Robertson unobtrusively took his violin, went among the students, and played their parts with them to help them out while they sang. Robertson playing his violin among the students in this way struck Abravanel as "very old-fashioned, but touching, so touching that it was marvelous, it was marvelous."

No doubt, the preparation of this composition created much work for everyone, and did cause a lot of hardship, but in the end, it proved worth the effort. After the concert—which marked a premiere of the *Missa Solemnis* in the entire region—all the students came backstage thrilled. Standing on the stairs, they kept saying, "This cannot be the end. We must do it again." And due to popular demand, a second performance was given the following Sunday afternoon.

Subsequent collaborations between the Utah Symphony and University of Utah Choruses followed similar lines. But old traditions do die hard, and Robertson had a long uphill battle in these ventures. Year after year, he and Abravanel were obliged to take over the choral rehearsals in order to ensure that the singers were adequately prepared. Abravanel speaks:

> It took a long time and a lot of hard work, but always Robertson was there very strong helping out, always, always he was there. . . . Without him, it could not have been done.

These two friends knew that once the students learned their parts and heard the orchestra—which would arrive only for the final two or three rehearsals—they would invariably become the most enthusiastic of all the participants, and rightly so, for at last they were singing real music. For the first time in their lives, they were performing Verdi's *Requiem*, Bach's *Passion according to Saint Matthew*, Honneger's *Joan of Arc at the Stake*, to name but a few works, most of which had never before been heard in the West.

At about this time, Abravanel arranged with Westminster Recording Company to make a commercial recording of *Judas Maccabaeus*, the first Handel oratorio other than the *Messiah* ever to be recorded, and as he again states:

> Without Robertson around, I would have been given twenty-five reasons why it could not be done: "The teachers don't have time to teach the music; we can't use volunteer singers because they are too busy with other choruses; we have no facilities suitable for recording, etc., etc., etc."

But once again Robertson worked things out—"he always made it possible." A good-sized chorus, selected from University of Utah students and other citizens, and a small chamber orchestra, drawn from the Utah Symphony, recorded the *Judas Maccabaeus* in the Assembly Hall, and thus was launched the first of many Utah Symphony recordings made with the help of the University of Utah.

Eventually, it became evident that performing such works in Kingsbury Hall was a big problem. Limited space crowded the singers and orchestra mercilessly; acoustics were less than ideal; and in order to get the full Symphony audience seated, two performances had to be given. The obvious solution was to do these works in the Tabernacle, which at the moment seemed impossible. Abravanel grew discouraged, but, as he says, Robertson persisted, "Oh no, we won't give up."

Convinced that these concerts were too important to be lost to the community, Robertson and President Olpin went to newly installed LDS Church President, David O. McKay, to explain their situation and personally request that choruses other than the Tabernacle Choir be allowed to sing in the Tabernacle from time to time. Interestingly enough, President McKay was surprised to learn of this restriction, and at once gave permission for the University of Utah Choruses to perform in the Tabernacle with the Utah Symphony. Henceforth, these chorus-orchestra performances took place in the Tabernacle.

During Robertson's first year on campus he inaugurated another venture: the University's sponsoring of two special Utah Symphony concerts in Kingsbury Hall. These performances initially involved only Chamber Orchestra, and featured works by baroque composers, but one highly successful variation to this programming came in 1956 with the Mozart Cycle, given in commemoration of the 200th Anniversary of Mozart's birth. Unbelievable as it may seem, Abravanel and Robertson, with the added help of President Olpin, had to push this through in face of great opposition from others in the University.

One season, Abravanel decided to devote one of these Kingsbury Hall concerts to modern works only, and to everyone's surprise, statistics showed that more people came to hear Stravinsky and Milhaud than Bach. Robertson then proposed that only "Moderns" be featured on both programs, to which Abravanel agreed, and thus the landmark "Contemporary Concerts" were born, all funded by the Music Department. On occasion, the Symphony performed works by local composers, many of whom were Robertson's graduate students.

Of all the Utah Symphony-University of Utah collaborations, however, it was the Summer Festivals held annually in Rice Stadium that likely reached the largest numbers of people. An outgrowth of the successful 1947 centennial production, *Promised Valley*, they featured both a Broadway musical and an opera.

The idea of presenting an opera initially horrified many members of the Festival Committee, who felt that such highbrow stuff would be disastrous from a box office point of view. But Abravanel and Robertson insisted and persisted. These productions, with the professional orchestra, topflight soloists, and good staging—albeit out-doors—would be the first time for the people to experience really superlative operatic performances in Utah.

By placing opera alongside a popular Broadway show, Robert-son and Abravanel saw this as a chance to get the general public interested in such classical fare. And indeed, these two allies were proved right, for the Summer Festival operas were done so well that they soon attracted as big an audience as did the Broadway shows. Nonetheless, certain members of the Festival Committee kept complaining, "We are packing them in with *Oklahoma!* and we have to stop for *Aïda*." Thus, the fight for good opera continued year after year, again and again and again. But Robertson and Abravanel persistently stuck together and prevailed.[2]

With the Summer Festival operas having opened the way, the next logical step for the University of Utah and Utah Symphony was to form a University of Utah Opera Company, which, with the added cooperation of the University Theater Department, henceforth presented one or two operas annually in Kingsbury Hall during the academic year. These modest but well-executed productions likely helped prepare the public for opera, and thus laid the foundation for what would become Opera West.

An exciting dimension to these productions was added when Willam F. Christensen came to choreograph the ballets for the Sum-mer Festivals, which, in fact, marked the beginning of ballet's pheno-menal story in Utah.

In all of these collaborations between the University of Utah and the Utah Symphony, it is important to note that Robertson de-liberately kept a low profile, and worked behind the scenes. He always maintained good relations with the media, but preferred to have the spotlight focused on the Symphony and Abravanel so as not

---

[2]Dr. C. Lowell Lees, head of the University Theater Department, directed the staging for these productions. He along with Abravanel and Christensen formed a publicity-garnering triumvirate.

to dilute the impact of any publicity coming their way. But as Abravanel has stated, "He was constantly there, moving very quietly, and always in the right direction."

Nonetheless, despite the high calibre of music and the great beauty and excitement that these Symphony-University presentations brought to the community, there was trouble from the very beginning, with unceasing complaints leveled at Robertson and Abravanel from both the University Music faculty and Utah Symphony members.

As for the University, it was the choral teachers who were among the first to voice their displeasure. With Robertson's arrival, they suddenly had had to abandon their customary programs and devote their energies to teaching students the big choral-orchestral works, all chosen not by them but by Abravanel. Naturally, they felt somewhat displaced, and perhaps were a bit jealous that something more glamorous and dramatic had taken over. In fact, according to Lowell Durham, the aforementioned *Missa Solemnis* venture "almost killed the [whole] choral program." These established choral directors—feeling they were being swept along in a great current—did not like where they were being taken, and a true tug of war developed between them and Abravanel, with Robertson "in the middle, trying to quiet things down."

Discontent spread. Other Music Department faculty also began to show their resentment to the Symphony on campus, complaining that everything in the department was subjected to the Symphony's needs. And it was indeed true that whenever a dispute arose, Robertson inevitably seemed to give first priority to the Symphony and its players.

Then, problems developed regarding those few full-time faculty members who also played in the Symphony. Those on staff but not in the Symphony did not hide their envy for those faculty in the Symphony, who appeared to be drawing double wages. In this matter, even the University administration protested, for President Olpin did not want his faculty members devoting precious time and energies to the Symphony while on full-time salary at his institution. Indeed, one of Robertson's first duties as head of the Music Department had been to negotiate very deftly with the administration so that these members could remain as full-time faculty on somewhat reduced wages and still play in the Symphony. To add to the dilemma, the Symphony's principal players newly named to the University faculty were annoyed that their appointments were not full time, for they felt neglected, being without the security of tenure and steady salary.

Furthermore, among all Symphony players there was general dissatisfaction with the facilities. Although but one year previous, no one had known from one day to the next where rehearsal would be, everyone was now complaining: acoustics were bad; parking was impossible; the rehearsal hall was either too hot or too cold; there were no lockers available for them to store their instruments, and so on, and on, and on.

As if this were not enough, even among the students themselves a severe morale problem developed when some of the younger Symphony players who were also enrolled at the University refused to participate in University music programs. This situation finally became so acute that Robertson and Abravanel were forced to put their heads together and resolve the matter, which they did.

In sum, very few musicians looked beyond their own private domains, and sadly, after the Music Department moved into the closer quarters of Music Hall, the continual bickerings only worsened. In his stubborn defense of this Symphony-University affiliation, even Robertson's reputation was suffering, as this letter shows:

> I certainly enjoyed my visit with you. . . . [It] was not at all like I had anticipated. . . . Before coming to see you I was warned that I would find you very short and snappy and strongly opinionated. In reality you were very easy to reach and pleasant to talk to. As a serious student naturally you have acquired opinions, but many of these opinions you have also proven to be correct and are entitled to them.

How could Robertson withstand this stress day after day, year in and year out? Fortunately, he did not stand alone in his commitment to the Symphony-University collaboration. Certain faculty members served as constant buffers for Robertson; Abravanel was an energetic, steadfast ally; and Robertson's own tenacious inner strength must have been a decisive factor.

Some have averred that Robertson could turn a deaf ear, remain isolated at work in his studio, and simply disregard the all-pervasive bewailing. But facts do not support this opinion. He listened and truly did work to help the malcontents solve their problems. Though he never gave in, only occasionally would he vent his feelings in anger.

There was too much at stake. He was absolutely convinced of the ultimate good of this unique alliance, not only for the two institutions directly involved, but for the region as a whole. His basic reasons can be seen in these following notes, also penned by him:

> A good book—music, etc., makes one feel better—able to go on, noble.
> Earth-creeping mind should look up to the sky of poetry.
> Virtue doth all things excel.

Robertson's unshakable conviction that this affiliation was an enormous asset for everybody kept it unquestioned. And in retrospect, everyone involved had to admit that so long as Robertson, a strong man with imagination, was at the head, no Music Department or Symphony project was ever hindered by the presence of the Utah Symphony on campus.

But was such wholehearted commitment justified? Were the advantages sufficiently great to counteract the general upset and trouble?

On the Symphony's side of the ledger, the benefits were, as Abravanel states, "enormous, enormous." During those early, very uncertain years, the group gained a stability it had never before known. Many Symphony players could now expect to enhance their earnings by performances with the chamber ensembles and various orchestra concerts sponsored by the Music Department. And those who attained faculty status, though neither salaried nor tenured, achieved a certain academic prestige, and since credit was now given for private lessons—something never before allowed—they were able to attract more students.

However, without doubt, the fact that the Utah Symphony now had a regular rehearsal hall—something they otherwise would not have had for many years—proved to be the most significant and stabilizing help of all. Although their first hall in the barracks was horrible, still it was a place to meet every day. And later, when the move was made to Music Hall, it was, as Abravanel fervently claimed, "a seventh heaven."

Moreover, not only did this "Home on Campus" give the Symphony much needed stability. It also saved their budget, for during their stay at the University, the group always rehearsed free of charge, never paying so much as one penny. This alone brought them through those lean, doubtful times. As Abravanel has reiterated, "What this arrangement did for the Symphony, and for the Symphony players, is invaluable."

As for the University of Utah, it, too, profited greatly from its affiliation with the Symphony. This professional organization inevitably became the foundation not only for symphonic music, but for chamber music, opera, and ballet as well—all of which were coming from the University at this time. And thereby the University itself became a center for most musical activities of the area, and the general standard of performance rose to a level heretofore unknown.

The greatest advantages of the Symphony's tie to the Music Department went directly to the students, "who," as one faculty member said, "were blessed because of it." With a "Conservatory Faculty" suddenly on hand for the first time in University history, these youngsters could get the finest professional instruction from first-rate instrumentalists on any instrument they wished. Moreover, with all Symphony rehearsals open to them, they could easily observe professionals at work, not to mention the fact that they were daily hearing the greatest music performed right there on campus. Everyone within listening distance—instrumentalist, vocalist, composer, layman— was constantly and inevitably exposed to the best of the best. All of this could have been nothing other than a great boon and mind-opener to any student, not just aspiring musicians.

In addition, all music students were encouraged to attend specific rehearsals when certain compositions under study in their classes were being prepared, and they were also required to buy season tickets to the regular Symphony subscription concerts in the Tabernacle.

To help these students, Abravanel—much against the wishes of his board—succeeded in getting them special, low-priced student tickets. While a few collegians did object to this extra dose of classical music, most regarded these projects as "a great and exciting time to hear all the good music that was happening." Indeed, after ten or fifteen years, more than one-third of the Symphony audience was composed of youth from fifteen to twenty-three years of age, a fact that deeply impressed the visiting artists, who always looked up at the large student section in amazement. Many students stayed on to become regular subscribers to the Symphony concerts, which shows the wisdom and farsightedness of such pioneering.

These many Symphony-University ventures soon gained nationwide attention. And because it had a professional orchestra on campus, the University of Utah Music Department soon became the envy of academic institutions throughout the land.

From Robertson's personal point of view, by bringing the Symphony and University together and by giving this struggling organization a real home, he felt that at last he was helping establish a stable Utah Symphony where local music students—who, for so many years, had had to go elsewhere to earn a living—could now hope to have a chance for employment in Utah. This, for him, marked the fulfillment of that dream he had voiced so very many years ago.

In summary, the benefits for all concerned cannot be denied. Everyone around—Symphony members, University students and faculty, the Opera, Ballet, Chamber Music organizations, and most importantly, the general public—all profited in ways both tangible and intangible. And, in light of the foregoing, it should once again be stated that Robertson and Abravanel, those two intrepid leaders, set all these projects in motion and kept them going on budgets as lean and precarious as any ever imposed. But they succeeded.

This remarkable affiliation lasted only because two men stubbornly and definitively committed themselves to bringing it about and making it work. Is it any wonder that, in the process, they became steadfast friends?

Chapter Sixteen

EVER COMPOSING AND
LANDMARK UTAH PREMIERES

As the reader will remember, during Abravanel's first season at the helm of the Utah Symphony, he had performed not one, but two of the Utahn's works: the *Punch and Judy Overture* and *Trilogy*. The following season (1948-1949) with Robertson now in Salt Lake City, the Maestro featured yet another opus, the *Prelude, Scherzo, and Ricercare*. The reader will also remember that this work was actually an orchestration of the *Organ Sonata* composed during Robertson's year in Europe. However, as Abravanel averred, unlike the other "very popular organ transcriptions of the day that were always very thick and loud, the Robertson score was like chamber music, very delicate and lean." When one prominent New Yorker, who happened to be visiting Salt Lake City, heard the Symphony's performance of this work, he termed it "an anachronism." But, as Abravanel would later recall, "little did he realize that very soon such titles would be 'the latest,' that every composer worth his salt would be writing a 'Ricercare,' or whatever."

Thus far, Abravanel had been presenting earlier Robertson works written before his move to Salt Lake City, and many devotees wondered if the gifted composer would still find time and energy for his composing in face of all the problems besetting him as head of the University of Utah Music Department. Indeed, he did find the time and energy, for he never could have stopped composing even had he wished. Melodies were always charging through his mind, and one big composition after another constantly occupied him. Once, when asked, "How does a great composer find time away from routine duties to write such prodigious works?" he quietly replied, "He just works longer than most people." Then he went on to explain that throughout his career, he had averaged not more, many times less, than six hours of sleep, and when working on a major composition, he usually wrote uninterruptedly from after dinner until 2:00 A.M. each night. Then, offering a rare comment about his private life, he pensively added:

> I have my compensation (not monetary) for regular overtime hours, but the ones I feel sorry for are my family. They have no vacations with me, but have learned how to use their time profitably, and I'm thankful for that.

During these first years in Salt Lake City, the composition that claimed Robertson's greatest attention was the _Concerto for Violin and Orchestra_. Loving the violin as he did, the Utahn had been thinking about such a concerto for many years. Preliminary sketches date from at least 1935, soon after his return from Europe; and very soon after the successful performances of his _Quintet_, musicians acquainted with his work began encouraging him to write "a big piece for solo violin." Although other large compositions were also claiming his attention during these years, he never abandoned his ideas for the _Violin Concerto_, and about 1940, began really serious work on it.

Word about the _Concerto_ reached many violinists of national and international renown, and one can trace Robertson's halting progress in his replies to their inquiries about it. In 1945 he wrote:

> My _Violin Concerto_ is mostly in the mental stage at present. I have, however, completed the slow movement.

And again in 1946:

> Since last summer I have had little or no time to work on my _Violin Concerto_. However, I hope to get it ready before too long.

Then, as early as 1948, just after the _Trilogy_'s great triumph, he was obliged to tell Hungarian virtuoso, Josef Szigeti—who had written to ask for a copy of the _Concerto_—that the announcement of its completion was premature:

> Two movements are practically composed and the last one is quite fully sketched. . . . I am greatly honored in having you

write about the *Violin Concerto* and shall endeavor to complete it at the very earliest moment.

In this same letter, Robertson explained that he had had "to put the *Concerto* aside in order to compose a commissioned work of large proportions," this being the *Oratorio from the Book of Mormon.* Later that same year, and now established in Salt Lake City, Robertson wrote in response to another request:

> I am working diligently on my *Violin Concerto.* . . . The final movement is in quite a disorganized state at present, so I cannot predict when it will be finished.

These were the months when Robertson would come home from his work at the University, take his violin to the basement, and spend the entire evening playing and re-playing different passages, trying out his ideas, casting some aside while developing others as he literally compelled this work to its conclusion. Having been a remarkable violinist all his life, he knew as well as anyone the instrument's possibilities as well as its limitations; and in this work, he seemed to be testing the violin as much as himself.

The determined composer received additional impetus to finish the *Concerto* when, in response to President Olpin's announcement that a Utah Symphony concert was to be the centerpiece for the University of Utah 1950 Centennial Celebration, Abravanel proposed a premiere of the Robertson *Violin Concerto.* The Maestro had long been aware of this composition, which, as he always said, "had so much to speak for it."

Robertson forthwith promised to have it ready, and with the *Concerto* virtually completed, he set about getting all the intricate parts copied for the many performers involved. In October 1949, he sent a score to Utah Symphony concertmaster, Tibor Zelig, whom Abravanel had chosen to play the demanding solo part. Zelig immediately replied:

> My sincerest congratulations! Your *Concerto* is not only beautiful music but very violinistic too, which will make my task so much more grateful.

A few weeks later, Robertson wrote to a longtime close friend:

I have now completed the *Violin Concerto*. I believe it is my best work to date.

A few years later, in referring to the *Violin Concerto*, Robertson would write more about his lifelong love for the violin, telling how as a young man he had felt destined to become a violin virtuoso, and of his hard work to reach this goal, concluding:

> My success in writing has gradually turned me from the role of the performer to that of the composer, but there will always remain that early devotion to the enchanting sound of the violin.
> It has long been my hope that I could leave the instrument something that would recapture in a more permanent way some of the things I have felt for it. The completion of the *Concerto* is in many ways a fulfillment of that desire.

In the *Violin Concerto*, as in earlier works, Robertson used Ute Indian melodies interwoven with his own. So skillfully did he blend these two distinct musical traditions that one critic would later comment on the remarkable "homogeneity of feeling" throughout the work, and how this merging of both the Indian themes and Robertson's own ideas created "a distinctive American lyricism evocative of Western spaces."

With performers going into rehearsal for the premiere, excitement steadily mounted. The composer, tensely listening to every note from his post in the back of the hall, quietly jotted down suggestions and corrections; soloist Zelig and Symphony members concentrated on mastering the technical and musical difficulties of the new-sounding, unfamiliar score; Maestro Abravanel, who from the beginning had championed the work through various tortuous negotiations, kept reminding his musicians:

> This is a completely beautiful, but untested and unknown work. If we don't give it an honest performance, people will blame not us, but the composer, and that would be unjust to everyone.

And so, on February 27, 1950, in a Kingsbury Hall concert marking the first night of week-long activities commemorating the Centennial of the University of Utah's Founding, Leroy Robertson's *Concerto for Violin and Orchestra* received its first performance. Hailed for its "inspired greatness," its "Mozartian classicism and purity that seemed to pervade the refreshing originality of the modern idiom," it left, as one critic wrote, "the indelible mark of lasting beauty and artistic worth." The slow movement, a "Larghetto," stood out as "the true jewel of the work, . . . [as] unqualifiedly one of the most beautiful slow movements in all concerto literature."

A few weeks after the exciting premiere, the same performers repeated the *Concerto* on a nationwide CBS Standard Hour broadcast.

Even after leaving his post as Utah Symphony concertmaster, Tibor Zelig kept the Robertson *Concerto* in his repertoire. Other musicians as well immediately expressed interest in performing and promoting the work. Nathan Milstein, who had attended one of the early rehearsals, requested a copy. Much to Robertson's disappointment, however, although this great Russian virtuoso repeatedly spoke of it to others, he never seemed to be in a position to perform it himself. Yehudi Menuhin also asked for a copy, saying: "The whole work impresses me as one of the most worthy contributions any American has made to the concerto literature." But again, nothing further developed at this time.

To return to the University of Utah Centennial Celebration: the day after the premiere of the *Violin Concerto*, still another completely new Robertson work concluded the great convocation commemorating the University's actual Founder's Day. Entitled "Motet on a Traditional Theme," and written for chorus and small orchestra, it brought the entire program to a brilliant and dignified conclusion. This composition, popularly known as "All Creatures of Our God and King," soon became a favorite among prominent choral directors throughout the nation, notably because of Peter Wilhousky, who "plugged it" at various choral festivals. Within a year it was published and distributed internationally.

However, although Leroy Robertson had long since achieved recognition as a composer both at home and abroad, and although musicians throughout the country were becoming increasingly aware and approving of how Robertson and Abravanel were bringing great music to the entire West, many local citizens complained. They objected to Abravanel's continuing performances of Robertson works, which indeed had become almost an annual event. And as if to imply that these performances were based on mere politics, they would caustically remark to the Maestro, "Oh, you and Robertson." Ironically, this displeasure came from both ends of the spectrum. One clique complained that this Utahn was "much too modern," and that what he wrote "was not music," while others—newly enamored of the twelve-tone system and other forms of atonality—condemned his music as being "too old-fashioned."

Cosmopolitan Abravanel always reminded these faultfinders that he was not alone in his appreciation and respect for Robertson's compositions; that this composer, deliberately isolated in his Utah mountains and following his intuition—matured, to be sure, by long study—had developed his own individual style; and that he was writing music that was "a darn sight better" and with much more content and genuine invention than many other contemporaries then being touted in America and Europe. Abravanel, loyal to his convictions, would later add:

> This is the way I felt from the beginning. Otherwise I would not have played his works again and again and again and again. I liked them right away.

For his part, it is true that Leroy Robertson, isolated in the West from much of the nation's musical activities, did feel that his work was rejected, or at best, neglected. And he naturally wished that his works had more performances by the great organizations back East. Nonetheless, Robertson had deliberately chosen to stay in Utah, and his first allegiance and appreciation always remained with the Utah Symphony, whose continued existence he had committed himself to secure; and with its Maestro, Maurice Abravanel, whose musicianship he had admired from the beginning, whose experience he respected, and whose friendship he truly enjoyed.

Therefore, despite the ongoing local objections, Robertson continued to compose, and Abravanel continued to perform his works. Thus came about in 1953 one of the most exciting and significant premieres ever heard in the entire West, that of Robertson's *Oratorio from the Book of Mormon.*

Abravanel had actually become acquainted with the *Oratorio* during his first meeting with the Utah composer years before when Robertson was yet at BYU. At that time, Robertson, still regretting the Church's rejection of it for their 1947 Centennial, had simply put it aside, for he had no compelling reason to finish it. But he did fleetingly show it to the newly arrived Abravanel, explaining that it might possibly be staged as a pageant. Through the intervening years, though Robertson was occupied with his other compositions, the Maestro kept urging his friend to complete the work:

> You must finish it. This is very beautiful music you have there already. You must finish it, and it will be played.

Year after year, however, Robertson did very little with it, perhaps because of his original disappointment, but also because he was so involved with developing the University of Utah Music Department, teaching full time, and writing other compositions. Finally, Abravanel insisted:

> Look, Leroy, you must finish it. Try very hard [to get] the Tabernacle Choir to sing it, but if they won't, we will do it with our [University] choirs and choruses.

Thus goaded and encouraged, the meditative composer once again picked up the score, and after five long years proceeded to write the final pages with unsurpassed speed and concentration. At this time, he also explained his delay:

> There was no point in writing [completing] it until we had the resources to produce it. This work is not a work of mine alone. Its realization [can be] brought about only because people have seen fit to support our schools and universities and organizations, where we could teach our people how to produce works of this magnitude.

It truly can be said that had Abravanel not persevered as he did, Leroy Robertson might never have finished the *Oratorio*. As Naomi would later declare, "Without you, Maurice, it would still be in the piano bench."

Preparing a work of such dimensions was indeed a mammoth undertaking, and initiating such a project did involve some risk politically and financially. In both scope and content the *Oratorio from the*

Book of Mormon is a work of titanic proportion, requiring highly trained soloists, two large choruses, a children's chorus, and full symphony orchestra. The autograph score alone covers 170 folio pages, not to mention the separate vocal-piano scores, chorus, and orchestra parts. No wonder Robertson spent every available moment just getting all those notes on paper. Completing his gigantic task within three months, he got all scores and parts ready "just under the wire." Lastly, in a gesture evidencing his highest love and respect, he dedicated this magnum opus to his beloved wife, Naomi.

Concerning the subject matter, Robertson described the *Oratorio* as:

> . . . a fresh, new American approach to the greatest, age-old story every told . . . wherein he [Robertson] hoped to crystallize the powerful event concerning the prediction, the birth, ministry, death and resurrection of Jesus Christ, as contained in the Book of Mormon, at a high level of art which would give it a degree of permanence as a work.

He was also careful to point out that although the text was based on Mormon scripture, he had fashioned lyrics that anyone could accept.

Regarding the music, he specifically stated that some parts were "deceptively naïve." And in describing the orchestral "Pastorale," which sets the mood for the birth of Christ, he once wrote, "the rapidly moving middle section . . . is like a soft wind over the desert."

When asked to give judgment on this work, already being called a masterpiece, the modest composer responded, "I have never written anything with which I was fully satisfied. I doubt that any artist does."

Abravanel scheduled the premiere for mid-February 1953, and as soon as the announcement of the performance appeared, there was spontaneous and immediate reaction, both positive and negative. Some non-Mormon friends of the Symphony—who had never objected to the choral-orchestral presentations of Catholic or Jewish religious works—furiously accused Abravanel of "selling out to the Church," and sarcastically queried, "A Book of Mormon *Oratorio*?" The general public, however, looked forward to this event. Nationally known music magazines and Eastern publications began reporting on the unusual work, one of the few classical oratorios of the twentieth century. Local news media remarked in advance upon its epic stature, and noted the significance of this "important first" that was soon to occur "in the great domed structure on Temple Square." Civic groups honored the composer, with the Salt Lake City Chamber of Commerce giving him a special Citizenship Award for his contribution to the culture of the community, and the Sons of the Utah Pioneers electing him to their Hall of Fame.

Excitement continued to run high. All seats were sold out long before the premiere, and after the first Tabernacle dress rehearsal, the soloists, the three hundred choristers, and the eighty-six Symphony members rose in a body to give Robertson a fifteen-minute ovation.

When the night of the premiere finally arrived, the Tabernacle swiftly filled. Braving a snowstorm, an audience of 6,000 soon jammed the famous building. Many distinguished citizens were in attendance, including high LDS Church dignitaries and government officials on the local, state, and national level. At Robertson's special request, invitations had been sent both to the mayor of his old home town, Fountain Green, and the bishop of the Fountain Green Ward. In Salt Lake City, his neighbors wrote, "Your ward leaders plan to sit in a body and listen and appreciate and clap and clap."

Both the composition and performance more than met all expectations. The vibrant opening measures seemed to charge the air with electricity, and as the final chorus of the soaring "Gloria Patri" brought the *Oratorio* to its brilliant conclusion, the audience jumped to its feet with shouts of "Bravo, Bravo, Bravo!" The rousing ovation lasted some twenty-five minutes as composer, conductor, singers, and orchestra members acknowledged the applause.

The two evenings following, as the performance was repeated at BYU in Provo, and then again in the Salt Lake Tabernacle, the reception was the same. In fact, the *Oratorio* proved so popular, that within less than seven weeks, it was presented six times, with concerts in nearby Ogden, a broadcast over KSL radio, and yet another performance in the Tabernacle at LDS Conference time. Also, a local company made and sold commercial recordings of the work.

The Utah Symphony received an unexpected bonus due to the *Oratorio*'s popularity. With all of the concerts sold out, and the halls filled for each performance, enough funds were generated through ticket sales to bring the Symphony "out of the red," and place it on sound financial footing for awhile. By early March, Robertson was able to write, "I am happy to say the proceeds from these concerts will clear up the deficit of the Symphony for this year." Indeed, so unusual was this turn of events that one New York newspaper ran the story under the headline, "Sacred Work Saves Symphony."

In face of such unprecedented and repeated successes, it was only natural for some people to assume that Robertson was also "cashing in," and after a few weeks, an acquaintance said to him with some envy, "You surely must be getting rich from all this." Robertson laughingly but sardonically replied, "Do you know what I got? A printer's bill of $600, for reproducing the parts." Nor did Robertson ever receive or want a penny from the gate receipts. He was pleased that his work could help the Symphony.

Through these exciting weeks critics praised both the composition and performers:

> It seemed Mr. Abravanel, orchestra and chorus were all spiritually inspired to bring forth all they could of the "out of this world" feeling which you [Robertson] have captured in this composition.

> . . . That we have a man in our midst who possesses the vision and artistic stature of Mr. Abravanel to perform such a composition is a significant sign that we are indeed favored. . . . Not many cities can boast the possession of both a great composer and a great conductor.

The *Oratorio* itself they described as "monumental, historic"; "undoubtedly one of the finest [works] ever to be presented in recent times"; "one of the musical masterpieces of the twentieth century."

However, as with the *Trilogy*, it was the reaction of the general public that likely touched Robertson the most. Not since the triumph of *Trilogy*, had so many letters poured in. Church dignitaries, government officials, fellow musicians, University of Utah colleagues, former students, friends and strangers from across the state wrote to express their deep feelings. They spoke of being "enthralled," "flooded with an experience that was more than music and poetry alone"; of being "impressed and inspired to tears"; they told of "majesty," "prophetic amazement," "reverence," and even "sacred communion." They described the *Oratorio* as being universal and timeless, stating:

> ... Leroy Robertson belongs ... to all the Christian world and there is no boundary to the joy and pleasure he has brought to all lovers of music everywhere.

Others—close friends and a few Symphony members—penned notes of simple thanks and gratitude for one who would devote so much of his life to a work of this kind:

> Three or four times in one's life one gets thrilled to the center of the soul.... I was lifted up beyond anything I can describe—The effect will never wear off and the vibration will last through eternity.

> I somehow caught and never lost that vision that keeps one going.

> As you stood accepting the approval of the audience, many [thought], "There is the man whose creation tonight made flow our tears of sheer joy and rapture." ... Having created a masterpiece that will live long after you, it's an enigma that you are a humble man, but you are doubly admired for that.

And humble he was. Self-effacing and remembering his early life, he graciously acknowledged those who had helped him along the way. At the premiere, when Robertson spied his Fountain Green guests, he excused himself from important officials, "came down and spent time with them [the Fountain Green people], just as equally as with any of the other Church and government dignitaries." Later, as he personally answered each letter, he would add a friendly note of recognition. To an old family friend, he wrote, "I remember how proud my father was of his friendship with you"; and to one of his first music teachers, "I shall always remember the lessons you taught me in Fountain Green"; and to the general manager of a Salt Lake City newspaper, "The presentations of this work could have been as much of a failure as they were a success had it not been for your generous and wholehearted support." To a longtime friend he penned, "It seems to have touched the hearts of the people far beyond my expectations." And in tribute to the performers, he added, "I am sure a great amount of its success is due to the outstanding interpretation given to it by Maurice Abravanel and those working under his magnetic direction."

The Maestro simply responded: "For me, the *Book of Mormon Oratorio* is a very inspired work, a very beautiful work . . . which I love, I love all my life."

During these exciting weeks, Robertson had occasion to thank the Sons of the Utah Pioneers for their signal honor to him. Because, during this address, he eloquently reaffirmed some of his lifelong beliefs, it is well to note a few of his remarks:

> Many realistic souls asked me . . . [why I kept on composing], especially when my eyes gave out . . . the only answer I knew was that I felt it had to be done. . . . When things have to be done, an individual and a people must see to it that they are done.
>
> We often think of the pioneers as drivers of oxen or pullers and pushers of handcarts. Surely, we cannot minimize their physical efforts, but these things were of little importance compared with the great spiritual power which carried them forward. . . .
>
> With our unique spiritual heritage and our talent at hand, it is entirely possible for this people to develop a modern Renaissance in the arts which could reflect to our everlasting glory.
>
> It is to be hoped that our materialistic gains will be properly used to support our artistic and spiritual endeavors in order to bring about the fulfillment of Joseph Smith's prophetic visions. In fact this transcends a hope. It is our obligation and duty to see to it that these ideals are projected from the tops of our mountains to the world.

As a result of numerous requests, Abravanel again performed the monumental *Oratorio* in 1954 and 1955 in concerts coinciding with the annual April General Conference of the LDS Church. One performance, a benefit for the Tabernacle Choir, was also given in May 1955. No one seemed to tire of the work, with critics maintaining that it "became a more glorious experience with each hearing."

However, after the May 1955 presentation, the *Oratorio from the Book of Mormon* would not be performed again for another six years. Needless to say, its composer would not be idle. Already he was well into another big work, the *Concerto for Violoncello and Orchestra.*

Chapter Seventeen

A LONG-HELD DREAM COME TRUE

ALTHOUGH primarily involved with the local music scene during his early years in Salt Lake City, Leroy Robertson still maintained contact with musicians and other friends beyond Utah, largely through correspondence. Each November in commemoration of the *Trilogy* award, he wrote to thank and report to its sponsor, Henry H. Reichhold. His first anniversary letter is typical:

> A year has now passed since the momentous announcement of the Reichhold award. From the standpoint of outside recognition it has been a tremendous thing for me, and inwardly, I have been able to go on in composition to my satisfaction.

Performers from coast to coast were constantly asking him to compose something especially for them: "a piano piece"; "a viola piece . . . so needed in the literature, especially by a composer who knows about the instrument"; and, even "a piece for band." Conductors were requesting scores of his orchestra works, of whom one of the most colorful and persistent was Leopold Stokowski, then conductor of the Philadelphia Orchestra. Mr. Stokowski asked to see three works in particular: the *Overture to Punch and Judy*, *Trilogy*, and the *Prelude, Scherzo, and Ricercare*. After studying them all, he wrote:

> I have made full permanent notes for future performance possibilities . . . [and] am finding appropriate places for these compositions as quickly as possible.

However, citing "limited rehearsals and other difficult conditions," the flamboyant conductor made no definitive promises. Upon leaving the Philadelphia Orchestra, Stokowski continued to write about his hopes for including Robertson's music on some of his projected tours, but somehow he never did.

Not only performers, but composers as well kept in touch with the Utahn. Roy Harris, who had first met Robertson in Colorado, requested scores to Robertson's chamber works and other piano solo music for his gifted wife, Johana, to perform. Colleague Burnett C. Tuthill, who had first become acquainted with Robertson when the *Quintet* was published, sent some of his own scores, which Robertson would later program at the University of Utah. John Vincent of UCLA penned:

> You are so modest that you said nothing of your own compositions and successes. I am hungry for news.

Ernst Toch, who a few years earlier had been Robertson's mentor at USC, asked about Robertson's ongoing work, and then made a statement very typical of a creative, committed composer:

> I am deeply engrossed writing, so I am O.K.

Good friend Arthur Shepherd continued to write on occasion, as did Ernest Bloch.

On both the local and national levels, institutions also continued to honor him. His 1950 election to ASCAP (the American Society of Composers, Authors, and Publishers) brought him special congratulations not only from its president, Otto A. Harbach, but also from founding charter member, Harold Orlob. Regarding Robertson's joining ASCAP, noted New York composer, Robert Russell Bennett, stated:

> Oh yes, I am quite familiar with Robertson's works and I admire them; in my opinion, his compositions are among the few American works free from the banal.

One of Robertson's most challenging honors came in 1953 when the Composers Council of UCLA invited him to head up that year's series of Schoenberg Lectures and Seminars. Held annually as a memorial to the great Austrian composer, these series featured four leading contemporary composers each year, and with such luminaries as Darius Milhaud, Luigi Dallapiccola, Leon Kirchner, and Alexander Tcherepine having been so honored the previous year, Robertson was indeed joining a prestigious group. Taking an unusual week's vacation from the University of Utah in mid-November, he went to UCLA, and within three days, as "Visiting Schoenberg Professor," he taught two intensive composition seminars and delivered an impressive public lecture.

This speech, entitled "Music in an Age of Multiplicity," stands as one of Robertson's most profound and cogent statements about the essential qualities of music and the composer's role in the new Atomic Age, which was then but eight years old. He began by challenging the prevailing theories that championed objectivity in art and scorned emotion:

> In art we are in a period of multiple types of expression . . . [and] in an age when objectivism is the model, it is difficult to raise a voice for anything that transcends the realm of logic.

Then, with extraordinary erudition, he argued that music, though dependent on logic, is, nonetheless, "an aesthetic and spiritual language."

In developing this thesis, Robertson interspersed his remarks with numerous quotations from psychologists, philosophers, poets, and critics, and cited pertinent musical examples as well. But perhaps he was most eloquent when he described vivid personal experiences, telling of the land and people whence he came; the lifelong feelings of spirituality, mystery, and human warmth they had instilled in him; and how music awakens these same emotions:

> After the winter months in the Utah mountains, we look forward to the coming of April and the song of the meadow lark. There is something fresh and rejuvenating about this magic call of the bird.
> There are many passages in music which impress me in the same manner. . . .
> Most of us, I believe, can recall experiences in which our lives have been identified with the mystery of the unknown.
> I remember in my youth how, one evening, I stood fixed on the bank of a willow-lined creek looking at the summer moon in its crescent form sinking behind the shadowed bulk of the old west mountain which helped to rim our narrow valley. . . .
> At another time, I am reminded of how we took our benches out on the "boards" (scrubbed slabs) of my childhood home and sat there quietly conversing together or silently meditating in the stillness of the long twilight. . . .

> I am convinced that we must encourage the conception of an art which is permeated with the warmth of human understanding and friendship.

Then, proposing that art is integral to life, that culture is basic, not incidental, that we need nourishment for the soul as well as for the body, he suggested:

> We must continue our search for a way to integrate art with the totality of experience. . . . It will be necessary for us to learn how to use the tremendous amount of energy bequeathed to us by the Atomic Age to promote the well-being of humanity—not destroy it. But culture must reciprocate. It cannot lag, and art must point the way.

Envisioning a day when art and artists would indeed have assumed this necessary function, he continued:

> The Age of Multiplicity . . . will [then] become a revitalized Age of Unity [where] the eternal values of the logical expression of the spiritual, beautiful, and good, will operate in a fullness of purpose beyond anything ever realized.

Offering specific guidelines for determining what makes truly great art, Robertson then cited one of his favorite authors, the Greek rhetor, Longinus:

> Genius does not merely persuade an audience, but lifts it to ecstasy. . . . That is truly effective which comes with such mighty and irresistible force as to overpower the hearer. . . . Excellence of style is the concomitant of a great soul. . . .
> What is rightly great will bear close examination, attracts us with an irresistible fascination, and imprints itself deeply in our memories. Consider a passage fully and genuinely excellent only when it pleases all [types of] men in all ages.

Lastly, in a beautiful summary, Robertson alluded to that burning inspiration within all artists:

> As a touchstone for our composers and as a concluding thought, I am led to the following [Stephen Spender] poem. . . . :
> "I think continually of those who were great,
> Who, from the womb, remembered the soul's history
> Through corridors of light where the hours are suns
> Endless and singing. Whose lovely ambition
> Was that their lips, still touched with fire,

Should tell of the Spirit clothed from head to foot in song.

. . . .

"... who in their lives fought for life,
Who were at their hearts the fire's centre.
Born of the sun they traveled towards the sun
And left the vivid air signed with their honor."

Robertson then expressed this final wish, which, in a sense, reflected his whole life's work:

Regardless of our varied styles and ideas I hope we may aspire to this company. Thank you.

On November 20, 1953, just two days after brilliantly presenting the Schoenberg Seminars and Lecture, Leroy Robertson made a most unprecedented transition. Appearing crosstown at USC, this acclaimed composer-professor once again became a student. Unpretentiously sitting before his examining committee, he took and successfully passed the oral (and final) exam for his Ph.D. And thus that dream so doggedly pursued for more than two decades became reality. At last, he had earned his doctorate, one of very few internationally known composers to do so.[1]

After completing his master's degree in 1932, and already during his studies in Europe, he had set his sights on this goal; and for the next twenty-two years, he was to overcome untold obstacles before reaching it. Early on, he discovered that his biggest ongoing problem would be to get enough credit "on the books" at a qualified university, and as a full-time professor at BYU, he simply could not get time off to spend the required residency at any of those faraway and rare institutions then granting the degree.

In 1935, in desperation, he had even asked his former Berlin mentor, Dr. Hugo Leichtentritt—then at Harvard—about fulfilling the classwork requirements by correspondence. For both Leichten-

---

[1]Although the degree was granted to Robertson upon his passing of the final oral exams, it was not conferred in an official public ceremony until January 1954. Robertson was not present for this occasion.

tritt and Harvard this was, of course, impossible. The reader will remember his 1936 summer studies at USC with Arnold Schoenberg; and then again—after a ten-year hiatus—how in 1946 he resumed his USC classwork, which he had to cut short due to the pressures of finishing his *Oratorio*. Plans for continuing his USC studies the following year turned to "airy nothing" when the BYU administration refused to extend his leave. Meanwhile, in an effort to amass more credits, he enrolled in a few graduate classes at BYU, even though he was carrying an extraordinarily heavy teaching load. Eventually this determined man would complete his credits at USC by commuting between Salt Lake City and Los Angeles.

After moving to the University of Utah, he felt even more compelled to "get that degree out of the way," an undertaking that his new colleagues considered "very courageous," for—as the reader will remember—he was inundated with problems of expanding the Music Department, teaching the entire graduate music program, and settling the Utah Symphony into its new home on campus. Furthermore, he had reached an apex in his academic career, so, "Why," everyone wondered, "why did he want or need this doctorate?"

Robertson felt some pressure because from the beginning of President Olpin's tenure, this recently appointed president had demanded that all departments offer the Ph.D. as soon as possible, and Robertson already had a number of candidates lining up for their degrees. Thus the following anecdote likely explains one of Robertson's reasons for going on as he did.

One day, a fellow faculty member in the Music Department, seeing what he was putting himself through to get the Ph.D., asked, "Why are you doing this? You're already a famous composer; you're internationally known; you're at the top of your profession. Why are you killing yourself just to get this degree?" Robertson simply replied, "I feel I don't have the right to take people along a path I haven't travelled myself."

As it turned out, his insistence upon having such firsthand experience proved to be right. At this time, the Ph.D. in Music was still relatively new, and as one of the pioneers, Robertson would have to help set some of the standards.

But, during those years just previous to completing his doctorate, and as a candidate preparing his final exams, Robertson was very anxious, more so than many because he was much older than most. With Composition as his major subject, he elected to take a supplementary exam in English to fulfill USC's requirements for a secondary subject. Encouraged and guided by his University of Utah colleague, English Professor Dr. Harold Folland, he instituted an intensive reading program on his own.

These were the months dragging into years when the good composer sat each night in the midst of his family, concentrating on his studies, making notes more about literature, criticism, history, and philosophy than about music. As his wife, son, and daughters tiptoed around him, he memorized and analyzed so intently that nothing could have disturbed him. But occasionally, his face would light up with a new idea, and then he would discuss it with whichever family member happened to be nearby. In early 1952, he wrote to good friend, Walter Kramer:

> When I pass another examination I hope to complete the requirements for my Ph.D. I suppose my learning has interfered too long with my education.

By journeying to USC on weekends and during breaks in the school year, Robertson finally amassed the necessary credits and passed the usual set of "prelim" exams required of all doctoral candidates. The dissertation, which usually remains as the biggest hurdle for any such candidate, presented no problem to Leroy Robertson. He merely offered the Guidance Committee his most recent compositions, namely, the *Concerto for Violin and Orchestra* and the *Oratorio from the Book of Mormon*. Interestingly enough, the Committee opted for the *Oratorio*, which, even before his final oral exam, had not only been performed many times, but had also been recorded. This fact greatly impressed the Committee member representing the Graduate School.

At last the big day arrived, and on that November afternoon when Leroy Robertson came before the Examining Committee for his final oral exam, he passed with no trouble; some even said he passed with brilliance. Three days later, Robertson received this letter from Raymond Morehead, chairman of the USC Music Department:

> Your visit to us made a great impression on me. I liked the depth, richness, transparency of your music and was glad to note that you personally exemplified the qualities of your compositions. Your modesty, sincerity, and simplicity recalled the true values of life. . . . I, for one, will take every opportunity to hear more of your compositions.

On that same day, Max Krone, Dean of the Institute of Arts, also took time to pen a note:

> Dear Leroy
> I was so sorry to miss your final examination Friday for I did want to see you finish up in a blaze of glory after all these years.
> . . .
> Anyhow, congratulations on getting the degree completed. You certainly deserve the distinction and we are proud to have you as an alumnus of the University.

Robertson immediately responded:

> I want you to know that I deeply appreciate the wonderful support and encouragement you have given me in my work since we first met in 1946.

After this momentous week in California, Robertson simply caught the next train and came back home to Utah, where once again he became immersed in the daily routine. There was no fanfare, and so quietly did he resume his work that there was no public announcement of his extraordinary November achievements until the following spring, and then, almost by accident. However, Robertson did cherish his degree, and always lifted his head a bit higher when he was addressed as "Dr. Robertson."

A few weeks after his return from California, indeed, in early December of that eventful year, Leroy Robertson took on another unusual responsibility, one closely related to the Utah Symphony but not directly related to music.

For some months Utah Symphony principal 'cellist, Joseph Wetzels, had been dying of cancer. Unmarried and with his immediate family living in Belgium, he was virtually alone. Because he could not bear the thought of going to a hospital—which to him was always so *anonyme* (impersonal)—Symphony members, students, and other close friends daily brought him food, ran his errands, and kept him company as best they could, all the time watching him grow ever weaker and less able to care for himself. Inevitably the day came when Wetzels could no longer get out of bed, and at that moment, Leroy Robertson, who had been monitoring from the sidelines, stepped into the picture.

Having assured himself that he would not be endangering the health of his family, Robertson brought the stricken man into his own home, gave him a room, meals, companionship and solace. From his sickbed, Wetzels gratefully murmured, "I was a stranger, and ye took me in."

Caring for this guest automatically became a family affair. Because Naomi was at home the most, she bore the brunt of the daily work. But, before and after school, each child regularly helped out with some task or other. For his part, Leroy constantly visited with the weakening man, took care of his personal needs, and always assured him that he would not be alone.

Within ten days, late one night and just as the Christmas Season was shifting into high gear, Joseph Wetzels died. He died at peace among friends and with dignity. And as the Robertsons watched the funeral directors carry his still body from their warm home into the snowy darkness, they too were at peace, though sobered by the nearness and mystery of death. That year they celebrated Christmas with profound thoughtfulness and love.

Chapter Eighteen

PILGRIMAGE TO GREECE

DURING the 1950s Leroy Robertson was continually receiving news about performances of his works not only in the United States but also abroad. The *String Quartet* was being played from Los Angeles to New York, while the *American Serenade* was being heard in music festivals from Edinburgh to Rome; the *Two Concert Etudes for Piano* were being performed in South America, Europe, and even South Africa; and the *Quintet for Piano and Strings* drew added acclaim at the Tenth Anniversary of the Institute of Contemporary Music held in Hartford, Connecticut. The ever popular *Overture to Punch and Judy* was attracting its share of attention as well, for nationwide broadcasts and noncommercial recordings by both the Los Angeles Philharmonic and NBC Orchestra aroused ongoing interest in this work. Conductors, especially those in the East, were requesting scores and parts from the composer, and performing this charming *Overture* with great success.

Nevertheless, the dedicated musician had to focus his main attention on the University duties of teaching, instigating new programs, and overseeing recently established ones, with composing largely delegated as usual to his spare time.

In early 1955, however, Robertson decided to tackle a very distinguished composing project, and accepted a commission which would give rise to one of his most important orchestral compositions. The National Federation of Music Clubs had approached him in January about writing a work to be played as a Salute to Greece on the Voice of America program. The venture was subsequently taken over and sponsored by the Knights of Thermopylae, a unique organization comprised of Greek citizens from throughout the world, and headquartered in America. The Knights, also known as the "Phalanx," were planning a ceremonious summer excursion to their homeland to establish an International Memorial Park at the historic battlefield of Thermopylae, where, in 480 B.C., a valiant phalanx of 300 Spartans led by King Leonidas, perished to the last man defending Greece against Xerxes and his invading Persians. Many official celebrations and trips throughout the Peloponnesus were to take place, and the highlight of the whole affair was to be a concert by the Athens Symphony featuring the premiere of Robertson's composition, which he would come to dedicate to "Thermopylae and its heroes."

Robertson did indeed regard this work as his personal salutation to Greece, a country whose thought and art he had long studied and admired. Even some ten years earlier he had written:

> Greeks based art on life, achieved high seriousness, largeness of utterancy, exquisite design and workmanship. . . . [Let] your standard then be Greece.

Guided by such ideals, as he had been for decades, he was now fervently seeking to incorporate them in this very memorable composition, which he decided should be a "Passacaglia"—a strict musical form whose very structure would demand the explicit thinking and expression he so revered in Greek art and literature.

With the concert scheduled for early July, Robertson had no time to lose. In less than four months he had not only to compose the entire work, but also get the score and orchestra parts copied, printed, and shipped overseas to the performers in Greece in time for rehearsals. Once again, his wife and children found him sitting all evening long in his favorite chair midst their constant comings and goings, where with large manuscript paper spread across his knee and pencil in hand, he wrote with uncommon speed. In mid-April he took time to pen this brief note to a former student:

> Since February I have been in the isolation ward composing and scoring a *Passacaglia for Orchestra*. . . . It is quite an ambitious work of theme and twenty-five variations. Some of the variations have inclined to grow into little symphonic movements on their own so I have been quite occupied in herding them into their various pens and stalls and keeping them there.

This work, as no other, would show Robertson's purely technical skills as a composer. Indeed, it would come to impress Maestro Abravanel as a brainchild built on mathematics and "cerebral counterpoint." But for Leroy Robertson it was much more than that. As he quickly and deftly composed, he did feel driven by "a divine gift . . . and natural rage passing the reach of common reason."

Upon completing his *Passacaglia*, with its dedication to Thermopylae, he wrote to the Knights:

> Inasmuch as Greek art is eternal in its influence upon the world, I have attempted in this composition to pay tribute to this great aesthetic contribution of Hellas. Indeed, without the sustaining inspiration of the Greek conception of beauty, our human race might have degenerated into savagery long ago. I must say that I have not felt the inspiration of the muse in the creation of a work as I have felt it in this one.

Having finished the work in record time, he was able to get everything ready well in advance of the July concert.

The Utah composer was of course invited to participate in the Knights' excursion to Greece, which was scheduled to begin in late June, with festivities to last for at least six weeks. Robertson keenly anticipated the trip, for he had long wished to visit this ancient country and see for himself its many wonders. Therefore, he quickly made all necessary travel arrangements for himself and Naomi.

Other Utahns who would play prominent roles in these events were sculptor Avard Fairbanks, who had been commissioned to create a heroic bronze statue of Lycurgus, ancient Spartan lawgiver; and Christopher E. Athas and his wife, Alice, distinguished members of the Utah Greek community. Another former Utahn to figure prominently in the ceremonies would be Cavendish Cannon, then United States Ambassador to Greece.

Everything was proceeding as planned. Already in late April, official ceremonies began when Robertson and Fairbanks were granted honorary membership in the Knights' Phalanx. Then, suddenly, just days before the group was to depart, an accident befell Naomi that might have changed all of Leroy's plans. His beloved "Bonnie" fell and severely fractured her ankle. Immobilized with a cast to her hip and hospitalized, she could not possibly make the trip. Leroy, deeply worried for his wife, truly felt that he could not leave her. Yet, he was torn. How could he ever shun what was predicted to be one of the most auspicious premieres of one of his greatest compositions?

Naomi well understood her husband and his dilemma. She knew of his concern and love for her, but she realized even more how very much this Athens premiere would mean to him for the rest of his life. Though in great pain, she bitterly hid her own terrible disappointment and stubbornly insisted that he make this pilgrimage to Greece. Thus, racked by his anxiety for Naomi, yet excited about the forthcoming *Passacaglia* performance, Leroy agonizingly decided to go. It would turn out to be the right decision.

In late June, he set sail from New York harbor aboard the newest luxury Greek cruise ship, "Queen Frederika," with the Phalanx and other guests for a twelve-day voyage that would take them across the Atlantic, through the Strait of Gibraltar, over the Mediterranean with stops at Naples and Pompeii, and to their final destination, Piraeus, the famed port of Athens. While Leroy enjoyed this passage in many respects, it cannot be said that he was really at ease. He missed Naomi greatly, talked of her constantly, and kept hoping that she might recover enough to join him before the entire excursion came to an end. He likely worried himself sick, for a persistent staphylococcic ("staph") infection had him daily visiting the ship's physician. As the days passed by, he became increasingly apprehensive. Should he indeed have left Naomi? Would Jim, then fourteen years old, be all right? And as he looked ahead, he wondered, would his *Passacaglia* live up to everyone's expectations?

The prestigious concert, sponsored by the Greek Ministry of Education, was to be given July 6 in the venerated ancient Theater of Herodes Atticus at the foot of the Acropolis, and would take place just three days after the Phalanx' arrival in Greece. Alec Sherman, noted conductor of the London Symphony Orchestra, who had come at the special invitation of the Greek government, would direct the performance. Needless to say, as soon as possible after getting settled in Athens, Robertson conferred with Mr. Sherman and attended the final rehearsals.

It is worth noting that these meetings marked the beginning of Robertson's enduring friendship with Mr. Sherman and his wife, famed concert pianist, Gina Bachauer. Indeed, this relationship also marked the beginning of the Greek-Utah musical connection that later would flower into a Utah Symphony tour of Greece; concerts in Utah with the Utah Symphony by Gina Bachauer and her pupil, Greek Princess Irene; and the International Gina Bachauer Piano Competition.

The big night arrived. The huge Herodes Atticus filled to capacity with invited guests, among whom were members of the Greek Parliament and Cabinet, American Embassy officials, and other notable dignitaries. Then everyone stood, for, to cap it all, the entire royal family, King Paul, Queen Frederika, and their three children, took their places in the Royal Box located on the front row. The concert began. First came a number by Gluck, and then, the long-awaited and much publicized *Passacaglia*. As its solemn theme, first announced in the lower register of the orchestra, continuously interwove its way through the entire composition to emerge in a brilliant climax, it held the whole audience spellbound. At the last chord, spontaneous, enthusiastic and sustained applause broke out.

A letter to Naomi from Mrs. Avard Fairbanks describes the occasion:

> . . . Your husband was truly very successful last night. . . . His music was superb—the applause wonderful, and as usual he went over big doing everything *just* right. The Queen beckoned him to come to her after he took the hand of the conductor and first violinist [concertmaster]—he bowed to great applause—twice or three times and the Queen kept on beckoning; then he went to the Queen—kissed her hand with a . . . [slight] bow—then took the King's hand—then the young (16 yrs) Crown Prince of Sparta, then the older princess, then the younger princess, and it was just perfect. . . . He is bringing much goodwill, honors and love to our country.

The following day, Athenian critics gave unstinting praise:

> *Passacaglia* is the work of an inspired and erudite musician who elaborates his themes on a sound basis of classical development.

> Robertson's work is worthy of recognition, not only because he is internationally known, but because he is an artist and composer of the highest caliber—possessing the creative ability to express what he feels in his heart and soul. . . . It is a timely salute and we are most appreciative and grateful to Leroy Robertson for his expression and tribute. Music has no boundaries and we welcome with open arms this beautiful gesture of friendship and goodwill—our lives have been enriched by this experience here this evening.

After such success, Robertson, now somewhat more relaxed, heartily joined in the many festivities: trips to the great battlefields of Thermopylae and Marathon; to Epidauros, Delphi, and Sparta, where the Fairbanks statue was unveiled. "Greece is a wonderful country," he wrote home.

In Athens, along with visits to the great National Museum, he spent almost a whole day in the bookshops lining University Street seeking a copy in the original Classical Greek of one of his favorite works, Longinus' essay, "On the Sublime" (*Peri Hypsous*), which had so deeply impressed him since his early doctoral studies at USC. He also made a private trip to the Areopagus (Mars' Hill), and as he stood looking down over the city's ancient agora, he thought of Socrates, Plato, Aristotle, the Apostle Paul, and others who had taught at this venerable site. And he could not help but muse, with a slight smile, "All these great master-teachers, and not one had a Degree in Education." In addition, he was present with other members of the group at a very impressive official ceremony in which the Utah State flag was given to the King of Greece, while the Greek flag was in turn given to the Utahns to bring back to Utah Governor J. Bracken Lee as a personal gift from the King.

Of all Robertson's experiences in Greece, however, the one that he would later recount most often was the visit he made with the Athases to the home of Chris' sister in Lavídhi, the remote mountain village of their birth. The house was plain, lacking many modern conveniences, but immaculately clean, with freshly scrubbed floors and newly whitewashed walls. As Leroy accepted the warm hospitality of this kind lady, he could not help but recall his own simple boyhood home and loving family life in Fountain Green, a similarity that struck a very vibrant chord.

And, almost as an extra bonus, while travelling through the Greek countryside, he listened and notated many folk melodies, some of which he would later use in his own compositions.

After about ten days on the Greek mainland, Robertson left his fellow voyagers and flew to Rhodes "in order to see the wonderful islands of the Aegean and to get a rest from all the activities in Athens." At this point he did indeed need a bit of solitude. In the comparative quiet of this beautiful island, Robertson, now allowed to go at his own pace, once again began to feel "more like himself." He visited the ancient sites and marveled at the "Harbor of Saint Paul," where, by Rhodesian tradition, this remarkable apostle stopped on his way to Rome. Above all, however, Robertson set about composing, and here, he wrote—or at least sketched out—part of one of his largest works, a long-projected *Concerto for Piano and Orchestra*, no doubt inspired by his recent experiences on the Grecian mainland and by his newly formed friendship to Gina Bachauer and Alec Sherman.

Following these few peaceful days in Rhodes, Robertson returned to Athens. But, ever concerned for Naomi, he decided to cut his trip short and almost immediately left by plane for America. Not feeling able to make the long flight nonstop, he did, however, arrange for a brief layover in Rome, that other great Mediterranean city of antiquity. Here, he took time to visit a few of the usual tourist attractions, but musician that he was, the highlight for him was hearing an outdoor opera performance at the famous Baths of Caracalla. Then, vowing to come back to the lands of the Mediterranean—next time with his family—he flew directly home, arriving in Salt Lake City in late July, with exciting tales to tell and suitcases laden with gifts.

He found Naomi home from the hospital, but confined to a wheelchair. It would be many months before she could again walk unaided.

* * * * *

As for the *Passacaglia*, it would go on to become one of Leroy Robertson's most widely performed orchestral works. In December of that same year, just five months after Athens, it had its American premiere with Maurice Abravanel and the Utah Symphony. Their curiosity aroused by all the extensive and dramatic European publicity, Utahns keenly awaited the December concert.

Before this Utah performance, some of Robertson's Music Department colleagues invited the composer to explain the *Passacaglia* to a few of their students, which he was very glad to do. For the more advanced theory students, he brought scores, and came "like a parent showing off his favorite child." For two full hours, he enthusiastically pointed out the various techniques employed in its composition. At one point, after having exhibited how the work contained nearly every contrapuntal device imaginable, he stopped, smiled, and said, with that Sanpete drawl he reserved for special occasions, "Here, they all thought I'd 'shot my wad,' but now, watch this. . . ." Then, reverting to his scholarly demeanor, he continued for at least another half hour showing the wonders of this masterwork to his enchanted audience. On another day, in discussing the *Passacaglia* with the students of Music I—that non-technical course open to all University students—he did bring a score, but rather than present any technical analysis, he talked about the work's background and its links to Greece. The Music I teacher, however, did ask Robertson to tell the students what general techniques they should listen for in the music, whereupon the composer paused a few seconds, and with a twinkle in his eye that normally appeared only when he had an interesting story to tell, he said, "Well, it goes up and it goes down."

The following year, Robertson's longtime friend, composer Arthur Shepherd, requested a *Passacaglia* score not only for his own interest, but also in order to get it to George Szell, music director and conductor of the Cleveland Orchestra. As soon as possible, Robertson dispatched a copy, and upon receiving it, Shepherd replied:

> I have had great enjoyment reading through this composition. I find it a veritable "tour de force" in contrapuntal ingenuity, and I suspect that it is much more than that! . . . I have the impression that this *Passacaglia* represents an artistic achievement of a high order.

In this same letter Shepherd noted that he would personally place the score on George Szell's table, *"where it will be under his nose."*

Arthur Shepherd was as good as his word, and in late January 1956, Szell wrote to Robertson thanking him for the score, saying that he was attracted to it and hoped for "an early opportunity to perform it." Soon thereafter, during a chance meeting at a Cleveland concert, Szell passed this note to Shepherd, who sent it on to Robertson:

> Received score of *Passacaglia* by Leroi Robertson. Remarkable piece. Thank you.

Some years later Robertson would get word from George Szell that he had indeed programmed the *Passacaglia* for the forthcoming subscription season of the Cleveland Orchestra, a performance Leroy Robertson was eagerly hoping to hear. But, unfortunately this great conductor would die before the concert could take place.

The *Passacaglia* nonetheless continued its steady course.

Four years after its premiere, Maestro Abravanel conducted another performance of the work with the Utah Symphony, and then immediately took it to Germany for a momentous performance with the Berlin Philharmonic Orchestra. After highly praising Abravanel for his gifted conducting, the Berlin critic wrote:

> The most convincing number of the evening was Leroy Robertson's *Passacaglia*, a work that draws strong, soul-searching effects from this oft time-tested variation form. . . . With a rich contrapuntal display and gripping variety of invention, a line is firmly drawn from its very beginning to the festive finale. . . . The craftsmanship is balanced by a very strong personal element.

In May of this same year, the *Passacaglia* was chosen by the International Rostrum of Composers, headquartered in Paris, as "the best American symphony work of 1959." The judges had selected it from a tape made during the recent Utah Symphony performance and submitted to the Rostrum by Professor Keith Engar of KUED-TV. Engar reported afterwards that of all the American entries, the *Passacaglia* "generated the most enthusiasm." This honor subsequently led to performances—both in concert and broadcast—throughout Europe, Israel, Australia, and the United States.

For Leroy Robertson a very exciting series of performances took place in April 1960, when the Philadelphia Orchestra, conducted by

Eugene Ormandy, played the *Passacaglia* in three regular subscription season concerts in Philadelphia, and then again in their regular Carnegie Hall series in New York. Nine months previous, Ormandy had already asked Robertson to come east for these performances as well as for the final rehearsal. As Mr. Ormandy's secretary wrote, "He [Ormandy] would like you to take a well-deserved bow."

Robertson, elated at the thought of hearing this involved composition in the hands of such virtuoso players, made arrangements to go. In fact, he arrived one day early, having been greatly impressed by his first trip on a Turbo-jet—at that time the latest and fastest commercial plane flying. Upon his arrival, as he walked the streets of downtown Philadelphia, he got quite a lift when he saw the billboards:

> I wish you could see the big posters out in front of the Academy of Music announcing the first performance in Phil[adelphia] of the *Passacaglia*.

Next morning, as requested, he attended the final rehearsal, and later reported:

> I am glad I came, especially for the rehearsal because it [the *Passacaglia*] was going a little too fast and everyone was a bit bewildered. . . . We all had some doubts—except one—that was Kincaid—he told me from the start how much he liked playing the work and what a great work it was—and did he play it![1]

That afternoon, at the premiere concert, which was also broadcast, all doubts about the work were laid to rest. As Robertson wrote that evening, the *Passacaglia* received "a wonderful performance in a thrilling program." The Utahn, portrayed by the announcer as "a tall, scholarly, shy gentleman," went onstage to acknowledge the warm reception, obviously very pleased.

Robertson again describes the event:

> The audience applauded and cheered for it. . . . Ormandy told me before[hand] not to expect much of a reaction from the audience since the Friday afternoon group never gets excited—but

---

[1] William M. Kincaid was first flutist of the Philadelphia Orchestra and ranked among the foremost performers of the twentieth century.

they did this time. . . . You just can't imagine how marvelous those complicated variations sounded.

The Philadelphia press was also enthusiastic:

> The work is full of drama and urgency and emerges as a piece of workmanship mature and well-knit. . . . There are passages that are properly epic in quality.

After the Carnegie Hall performance, many of New York City's leading publications gave favorable reviews as well:

> Robertson's commemorating the Battle of Thermopylae in a classical framework not only echoed his purpose but provided a medium for solid craftsmanship. Perhaps this helps convey a likeness of his music to a commemorative ode in poetry. Certainly the atmosphere is there.

> There is much heroic action and classical strength to this music. The *Passacaglia* was given a sweeping and sonorous performance. I can't imagine Leonidas and his 300 Spartan warriors being celebrated by a better orchestra.

> The *Passacaglia* pays its debt to the theme which Bach employs in his monumental *Passacaglia in C minor*. As Robertson progresses, however, he gives his music imaginative treatment in the contemporary spirit. At the work's climax and conclusion the ear knows that a twentieth century composer has not merely spoken but has managed to say something fresh and pertinent within the confines of the "Passacaglia" structure.

Eugene Ormandy liked the *Passacaglia* so much that early on he had expressed to Robertson a possibility of recording it if costs could be defrayed. And the day following these April performances, the Philadelphia Orchestra Manager telegraphed Robertson (now returned to Utah) to ask if he could raise $2600 for the project. Ormandy himself had already been able to secure a much larger sum from an Episcopalian clergyman and hoped that Robertson might find similar support in the LDS community. Robertson, who did not have such money personally available, did try to solicit aid for the recording from local and national organizations, but sadly his efforts came to naught. What would have been a most beautiful and landmark recording was never made.

The Utah composer naturally felt bitterly disappointed. But his *Passacaglia*, now accepted for publication by Galaxy, was still enjoying worldwide success. And, as usual, this composer would be going on to other projects.

Chapter Nineteen

FOR LOVE OF COUNTRY, CHOIR, AND 'CELLO

WHILE the excitement of the composition and performances of the *Passacaglia* brought much joy to Leroy Robertson, all this fervor did come right in the midst of many other important activities ongoing and overlapping in his life, both within and without Utah.

One of these projects—of major proportions and long duration—concerned the *Music in America Series of Recordings*, conceived and championed by his friend, Dr. Karl Krueger, whom the reader will remember as the renowned conductor who had premiered Robertson's prizewinning *Trilogy* with the Detroit Symphony. The Utah composer's involvement with the *Music in America Series* had inauspiciously begun in January 1950, when Dr. Krueger sent him a letter and two brochures telling of the American Arts Orchestra, an organization newly formed by Dr. Krueger, which was to be "characteristically American," i.e., it would concentrate on performing the works of American composers. In his letter, Dr. Krueger asked Robertson for suggestions and help, and a few months later, invited the Utahn to become a charter member of the sponsoring society. Robertson, very interested in such an enterprise, accepted at once.

Ever since their first meeting in Detroit, the two musicians had developed a close relationship, for they shared common ideals and dreams regarding American music, its promise and importance in the world. But thousands of miles always seemed to separate them. As Krueger had once written to his Utah friend, "It would be such a treat to me to sit down and chat with you." In response, and commenting on Dr. Krueger's new orchestra venture, Robertson wrote:

> I believe we are in agreement that what America needs . . . is a new dynamic force, not materialistic, but a force which represents the true spiritual and cultural concepts of our great nation.

After an initial series of broadcasts with the American Arts Orchestra, Dr. Krueger decided to expand his project and make a series of recordings of American music from its beginnings to the present day. For, although certain individual American composers had gained some recognition, even as late as 1950, no one had ever yet compiled a comprehensive "History of American Music," and Dr. Krueger hoped these recordings would help fill that gap. He was able to interest other visionaries in his idea, and immediately named Dr. Carleton Sprague Smith and Leroy Robertson as coeditors of this ambitious project.

In accepting this task, the Utahn learned that not only his composing but also his scholastic talents would come into play. Indeed, he was soon told that he would "be at the service of the government for its information services abroad." This was no small deal.

His first assignment was "to make a concise treatment of American music, 1800-1900, aimed at the laymen as well as professionals." When the announcement appeared that Leroy Robertson could write about music as well as compose it, the news both surprised and delighted his friends in the music world everywhere.

This voluminous recording venture would continue for at least fifteen years. However, it was often difficult to keep it funded, and at one point Dr. Krueger confided to his staunch Utah ally:

> . . . It seems almost impossible to interest individuals (to the extent of their pocketbooks) in the fate of American compositions, and it is obvious that members of the clique which is hostile to any real representation of American music, except that belonging to their own circle, have their people in key positions of every foundation that concerns itself with music; in any case, this has been my experience.

But Dr. Krueger later consoled himself (and Robertson, who agreed):

> I have long since ceased being bothered by the various shoddy cliques; it is my conviction that they inevitably will fail of their purpose. Our all-important job is to make the compositions *known*; after that is achieved, I feel that events will properly shape themselves.

Eventually, in order to obtain wider financial support and better secure his undertaking, Dr. Krueger organized the Society for the Preservation of the American Musical Heritage, and named Robertson to the advisory board. Interestingly enough, so well did Dr. Krueger know the Utahn that he included Robertson even before consulting him. Now restructured, the project survived, and the completed archive of recordings finally came to include significant American compositions from Colonial times through the mid-twentieth century.

Over the years, Leroy Robertson continually contributed to the series in many different ways. His composing skills came into play when he was asked to write full and independent piano parts for two sets of sonatas by Colonial composers Raynor Taylor and Giovanni Gualdo, who—as was typical for this period—had merely indicated a "figured bass," i.e., terse mathematical notations for the bass line. Obviously, creating such piano parts is a tour de force for any composer because one must observe the limits and style set by another while still expressing one's own individuality. Dr. Krueger well recognized this fact as he encouraged Robertson:

> I understand completely that you cannot "put a time tag on the creative process." Don't let that worry you. I'm grateful that *you* are doing this important piece of work for us, for I love these [Taylor] *Sonatas.*

Upon receiving the completed Taylor *Sonata* scores within a few months, Dr. Krueger again wrote:

> Permit me to congratulate you upon the really superb piece of work you did. . . . It is just the kind of thing I had hoped for; you have made real duos of these pieces. . . . I am most grateful to you.

As for the Gualdo works, Dr. Krueger wrote:

> I am struck, first, by your always sure sense of style—your superlative craftsmanship I have come to take for granted—and second, by the high inspiration you bring to bear on a task which lesser men would discharge, at best, in a routine manner.

With the release of these *Sonatas*, other musicians across the land became interested in playing them, especially the Taylor-Robertson ones. However, Robertson had generously presented his original manuscripts to Dr. Krueger as a personal gift, and to date, there are very few copies extant.

Whereas he used his composing talents for the *Sonatas*, Robertson also became an editor and writer when Dr. Krueger requested that he edit certain choral anthems of Colonial composers William Billings and Daniel Read, and write the program notes for the record jackets. As Dr. Krueger averred:

> I not only know your competence in this area but also your ability to place these composers in proper perspective.

Next, in addition to his composing, editing, and writing program notes, Robertson was asked to get performers and supervise the recording for two of the series albums, which naturally presented problems of a completely different nature. The first album was to be a diverse selection of choral works dating from Colonial times through the twentieth century, and would contain—along with a work by Colonial composer Charles Theodore Pachelbel—some Mormon hymnody, and three excerpts from Robertson's *Oratorio from the Book of Mormon*. For these performances, Robertson recruited the University of Utah Chorus and Orchestra, as well as noted Tabernacle organist, Alexander Schreiner. When this album was completed, Dr. Krueger wrote, "I consider it one of our best issues." The second album to be made under Robertson's supervision contained the aforementioned anthems of Billings and Read. Upon receiving these pieces, all edited, recorded, and complete with Robertson's program notes, Dr. Krueger simply wrote, "They are just right."

This series also included two original compositions by Leroy Robertson: his widely performed *String Quartet in E minor* and the popular *American Serenade*. At Dr. Krueger's request, Robertson went to Chicago where the Weicher Quartet was preparing these numbers for recording, and where the recordings were to be made. However, much to the composer's disappointment, although he was able to attend the rehearsals, a schedule change prevented him from being at the recording session. Nonetheless, all went well, and Dr. Krueger soon wrote:

The Quartet and I all felt it was a real privilege to have a part in bringing these works to a wider public.

Dr. Krueger subsequently inquired about recording Robertson's prizewinning *Quintet*, but nothing further developed in this regard.

The *Music in America Series of Recordings* did enjoy steadily growing success. Already in 1961, Dr. Krueger would report that the recordings were being broadcast in New York, throughout California, and from there to other western outlets. Two years later he would announce that the Society had been invited to broadcast for thirteen weeks over the Network of the National Education Television and Radio Foundation (now known as PBS), "the tops among such organizations." At this point, it is likely worth noting that these recordings were never intended for commercial sales, but were always distributed to educational institutions, noncommercial radio stations, and to members of the Society, who paid dues to help finance the project.

Some years later, with the series completed, Dr. Krueger would further report:

> *All* the Society's recordings are to found in virtually all leading educational institutions in this country [U.S.A.], as well as in the University of Amsterdam and the British Archive of Sound; beyond that they are in the foremost public libraries and radio stations of the nation, and in the collections of untold numbers of private music lovers, throughout the world—from Tokyo to South Africa to Stockholm to the most unlikely places.

For his part, Leroy Robertson was always happy to contribute to this vast and lengthy enterprise. Moreover, his recognition of its ultimate importance and his respect for Dr. Karl Krueger were such that he could never accept a penny for his efforts. Many years later, in retrospect, Dr. Krueger would spontaneously write:

> Your father [Leroy Robertson] was the most understanding and steadfast friend and supporter of this Society it ever had. As a human being, he was among the noblest and most generous that I have been privileged to have encountered during a long lifetime. Because I so respected him as a man and musician, what he gave me by way of encouragement had particular force.

*   *   *   *   *

Another series of commissions requiring Leroy Robertson's time and talents during these same years involved the Salt Lake Mormon Tabernacle Choir, which in the late 1950s began a number of successful recordings with the Philadelphia Orchestra, Eugene Ormandy conducting. Since the Choir had long been singing Robertson's shorter choral works—both on their tours and broadcasts—and since his ability to write for chorus and large orchestra had been well demonstrated in the *Oratorio from the Book of Mormon*, it was only logical that Choir director Richard P. Condie and Choir manager Lester Hewlett should choose him to arrange many pieces for these special recordings.

The composer's first assignment was to make a setting to the well-known Mormon hymn, "Come, Come, Ye Saints," a work that came to be scheduled not only for recording but also for performances in Philadelphia and New York during the fall of 1958. Robertson took this task very much to heart, for this hymn had long been a part of his own Mormon pioneer heritage, and he had previously set it many times. But now he at last felt free to exploit the full resources of a great professional orchestra and choir, something not possible heretofore.

He once explained how the somber introduction of this new arrangement—beginning in the low strings and rising through the orchestra—was meant to depict the stirring of the pioneers as they arose every morning at first light to round up their animals and prepare them for the long day's journey ahead. And indeed, with each verse, he somehow caught the tragedy and triumph of the difficult trek made by his forebears.

At the invitation of the Choir and Mr. Ormandy, Robertson travelled east for the various concerts and recording sessions. "Come, Come, Ye Saints" went very well as did the other scheduled numbers. But, after the final recording session, the production crew discovered that they yet needed four more minutes of music to fill out the album. Robertson, seeing his chance, unobtrusively showed Mr. Ormandy a score of his now renowned setting to the Lord's Prayer, which he "just happened to have" in his briefcase. Mr. Ormandy liked the piece at once, decided that it fit their needs perfectly, and recorded it on the spot, after only one "read-through." The Utahn soon received this note from Mr. Ormandy's secretary:

> Mr. Ormandy asked me to send you his congratulations on the recording of your "Come, Come, Ye Saints" and "The Lord's Prayer.". . . They are wonderful.

Thus had begun Leroy Robertson's pleasant association with Eugene Ormandy and the Philadelphia Orchestra.

Interestingly enough, when the entire album was finally issued, it was entitled *The Lord's Prayer*, and would eventually earn for the Choir its first "Gold Record," which meant that 1,000,000 copies had been sold. Meanwhile, the spin-off record from this album—featuring "The Battle Hymn of the Republic" and "The Lord's Prayer" on the flip side—became so popular that the Choir received a Grammy Award for it. For many years, the quiet composer would listen somewhat bemused as he heard his sacred anthem blasting forth on juke boxes in all the cafes and diners around and about.

However, whereas "The Lord's Prayer" was greeted with enthusiasm by everyone, his somewhat untraditional setting of "Come, Come, Ye Saints" produced some negative reactions among a few high Mormon dignitaries. Indeed, the Utah composer was told that one very influential Church official had remarked, "Robertson really let us down this time."

Fortunately, this assessment was not general. Soon, notes like the following began to arrive from across the country:

> Both my wife and I have found spiritual strength in our recording of "Come [Come] Ye Saints." This is music that must make glad the heart of God. Thank you.

Through the years Robertson would be able to report that this work was being widely performed by orchestra and choruses not only throughout the United States but also abroad. Galaxy soon published it, but with the unusual proviso that Robertson retain the copyright and that the LDS Church be allowed to perform and use it without asking the customary permission.

Robertson's next number specially arranged for the Tabernacle Choir and Philadelphia Orchestra was the Israeli National anthem,

"Hatikva," which was to be included in an album featuring the national anthems of many countries worldwide. Because of the interest already elicited in Israel by Robertson's *Passacaglia*, and with his own awakening interest in Israeli music, this Utah composer was a logical choice for the politically sensitive task. In this regard, one very ticklish problem facing Robertson was getting the original Hebrew translated into an English text that would accurately express the meaning as well as fit the melody and be "singable." For this task, he enlisted the aid of University of Utah professor, Louis C. Zucker, a noted and highly respected Hebraist.

With the text in hand, the Utah composer opted to give this anthem a setting somewhat different from its traditional jiggy folk-dance character in that he had it move at a slower tempo. This, he felt, would give the anthem a dignity and dimension more befitting the subject. Although a few local Jewish traditionalists protested, Robertson, guided by his innate musical and poetic sense, did not change his original concept. Nonetheless, he could not help but wonder how this arrangement would be received by the world at large.

Robertson completed the score in early spring 1962, and again at the Choir management's and Mr. Ormandy's request, he once more journeyed east for a May recording in Philadelphia. After the first read-through with the Choir and Orchestra, everyone applauded, much to Robertson's relief, and Mr. Ormandy smilingly remarked, "You have made a friend of every Jew in the Orchestra." And in fact, as soon as the album was released, Robertson's setting of "Hatikva" was hailed not only by the Jewish communities in America but also in Israel. It was subsequently published by Carl Fischer, Inc.

Other Robertson works to be chosen by the Choir and Mr. Ormandy for recording were "Old Things Are Done Away," that deceptively simple little piece from the *Oratorio from the Book of Mormon*, and his arrangement of Stephen Foster's "Beautiful Dreamer."

Then, in the midst of these recordings with the Philadelphia Orchestra, the Choir was asked to make a Christmas album with the New York Philharmonic, Leonard Bernstein conducting. Robertson was again commissioned to make some arrangements, this time, four favorite Christmas carols. Realizing that, as with the Philadelphia

Orchestra, he would be writing for some of the greatest symphony performers in the world, Robertson created brilliant instrumental parts, rich in sound and variety of color. One does not hear his setting of "O Come, All Ye Faithful" without feeling "joyful and triumphant," while, on the other hand, his "O Little Town of Bethlehem" is full of the quiet desert solitude which Robertson himself had known as a lad. The completed album, recorded in the Salt Lake Tabernacle, September 1963, would have enormous success almost before it was issued. Already in October, noted composer Cyril Jenkins wrote to Robertson:

> At the moment I am finalizing arrangements for them [Robertson's four Christmas carol settings] to be broadcast over the BBC Network for overseas broadcasts with Canada, South Africa, Australia, and New Zealand.

So brilliant were these Robertson arrangements that they would often be chosen for reissue in other subsequent Christmas albums.

Apart from numbers arranged for choir and orchestra, Robertson also made special settings to be recorded by the Choir with the great organ in the Salt Lake Tabernacle. These included five Civil War songs, three Stephen Foster songs, and the choral setting, "O Lord Most Holy," adapted from César Franck's "Panis Angelicus." Another of Robertson's original anthems, "O Brother Man," became part of yet a different Choir album.

It has sometimes been asked if all these choral settings actually represent original work on Robertson's part. In answer, he once commented:

> . . . They probably are [to be] classified as arrangements. However, they are published and recorded and in a sense are extended and original compositions.

In any event, it is clear that here—as in his writing for the *Music in America Series*—Robertson exhibited a deep sensitivity for the thinking of other composers and a consummate skill in adapting to the musical styles of other times and lands, all, however, while imprinting a bit of his own personality and taste. Like any poet, he did, after all, create things "which otherwise could not have come into existence."

It is worth noting further that whenever a Robertson work was to be recorded, the Choir leaders would ask him to attend the recording session. Usually the sound engineers would invite him to sit with them in the recording booth, for his keen ear could quickly identify the trouble spots and suggest a solution. Since this saved a lot of valuable time, everyone involved appreciated his presence, and even asked him to critique numbers other than his own.

At Choir manager Lester Hewlett's invitation, Robertson also accompanied the group on many of their tours, particularly if they were performing some of his works—as they often were. Occasionally, Naomi would join him. Truth to tell, his dear wife's first airplane trip was on the Choir's Northwest Tour in August 1962, an experience she had been dreading, but one that completely converted her to the idea of flying.

Beyond performing and recording many of Robertson's choral works, the Choir directors also presented and discussed them at various choral clinics held throughout the country. Thus, there is no gainsaying that although Leroy Robertson was never officially connected to the Salt Lake Mormon Tabernacle Choir, his contributions to their program were significant and long-lasting.

*   *   *   *   *

Even though deeply involved with the aforenamed projects concerning the *Music in America Series* and the Tabernacle Choir, Leroy Robertson always had new compositions crowding through his mind, of which one of the largest and most persistent at this time was the *Concerto for Violoncello and Orchestra*.

As with the violin, Robertson had loved the sound of the 'cello since childhood.[1] But only decades later, when he heard famed 'cellist Zara Nelsova present a concert in Provo, did he first seriously consider writing a concerto for this noble instrument. Interestingly enough, while still completing the *Violin Concerto*, he had begun to

---

[1] As has been mentioned, Leroy, as a little boy, had spent hours playing and replaying on his Uncle Jim's "talking machine" a 'cello recording of Schumann's "Träumerei," entranced and marvelling at its beauty.

think about composing such a work for 'cello, and already in early 1951, he wrote to his 'cellist daughter Marian—then studying in France—that he was sketching the first movement of the *'Cello Concerto*. When she returned home a few months later, he did indeed have the first pencil-draft pages ready for her to see.

Although Leroy Robertson did not himself play the 'cello, his thorough knowledge of the violin gave him an edge in composing brilliantly for all the string instruments. As for the 'cello, through Marian's playing as well as his own perusal of the literature, he had become well acquainted with the possibilities and resources of the instrument. And, as a further check on his writing, he often had this daughter "try out" many of the passages in order to test his ideas. As for the orchestra, he composed this work differently from any orchestral piece he had done heretofore in that, like Mozart, he put the entire score directly on paper without first drafting a sketch (i.e., a sort of piano reduction) of the orchestra parts.

Even before the *Concerto* was finished, many 'cellists had their eye on this composition, and upon its completion in 1954 they expressed their interest in and hope for playing it.

With this provocative work, Robertson succeeded in creating a *'Cello Concerto* that was "marvelously written for solo instrument and orchestra, . . . extremely difficult but . . . still 'cellistic, not impossible to play"; a piece "for both orchestra and soloist, with an interesting interplay of the two." Harmonically it was significantly different from previous compositions.

When Robertson showed this *Concerto* to Maestro Abravanel, the two musicians, after some consideration, opted to ask none other than Zara Nelsova to perform the solo part, that very lady whose playing so many years before had first inspired it. This superb artist —hailed as "one of the greatest 'cellists of all times"—accepted their invitation, and after studying the score, graciously wrote to the composer:

> I am very much looking forward to playing the *Concerto*. It is a wonderful work and I feel it will be tremendously effective.

Abravanel scheduled the premiere for mid-November 1956. Upon arriving a few days ahead of time to consult in person with the composer and conductor, Miss Nelsova confirmed her enthusiasm for the work:

> . . . In this new composition, Dr. Robertson has written for us the first major ['cello] concerto to appear in a long time, . . . full of wonderful moments and beautiful music. The slow movement is simply exquisite. . . . This is a work that will be performed a lot, not discarded like so many that seem to have been written for one premier playing. It is an important work in the 'cello repertoire—a real 'cello piece.

In order to have the peace and freedom necessary to practice without interruption, Miss Nelsova stayed at the Holladay home of Leroy's younger sister, Wanda, now a professor in the University's Education Department. After intense stints with the 'cello, the visiting artist did enjoy taking time off to walk in the crisp November air at the foot of nearby Mount Olympus.

Preparing the performance of such an extensive and completely new and never-before-heard work took much effort for all concerned. The soloist was mastering a tremendously challenging part; orchestra members were reading their own complicated parts for the very first time; the conductor had to interpret and hold everything together; and in the background, the composer, critically hearing his brainchild come to life, was intently listening so as to forestall possible difficulties and correct any inadvertent mistakes that may have crept in.

Rehearsals went well, however, and the November premiere was splendorous. After the concert, enthusiasm ran high. Miss Nelsova was praised for her "impeccable technique, sound musicianship, . . . [and] more than that, an understanding heart [that] brought warmth and life to the work." For his part, Abravanel was hailed for "his faith in Robertson compositions and . . . his ability to bring them from manuscript to listener." But it was the *Concerto* itself that grabbed the lion's share of attention:

> A monumental addition to the 'cello literature . . . the new *Concerto* is certainly the most important 'cello work to be penned in decades and must rank with Bloch's *Schelomo* as one of the two greatest 'cello concerti of the twentieth century.

It is a large, broad work of the same dimensions as the *Trilogy*, and the overall formal plan is well conceived and beautifully carried out. . . . As usual, the Robertson craftsmanship finds the work compact and economical. . . . It contains lovely thematic materials . . . [that] rank with Robertson's best.

Sadly, however, predictions about the future popularity of the *'Cello Concerto* did not come true. After the auspicious premiere, it was never again given a performance with orchestra. Despite her continued efforts, Miss Nelsova was unable to interest other conductors in the work, nor did Abravanel ever reprogram it. The work was to remain silent in the archives, waiting to be given a new voice some other day.

* * * * *

Two other Robertson works from this period deserve mention: the string orchestra version of his *American Serenade* and the *Alleluia and Chorale for Band and Chorus*.

To no one's surprise, long before the *'Cello Concerto*'s premiere, the Utahn had been working on various new compositions. And in February 1957—just three months after that impressive November concert—his *American Serenade*, in its new string orchestra setting, was premiered by Abravanel and the Utah Symphony string section.

Some ten years earlier, the original quartet version with string bass added had been played by an ensemble at Eastman School of Music, Carl Fuerstner directing, and at that time, composer Howard Hanson, in attendance, called it "very good." However, Robertson knew that if the *Serenade* were to be really viable as a string orchestra piece, vital changes had to be made in all the parts. Finally, thanks to a commission from philanthropist Morris Rosenblatt, Robertson was able to make the necessary revisions and prepare the rewritten 1957 score and parts.

This broader orchestra form seemed to magnify the folk qualities of the work. The first movement, "Caprice," described as "buoyant, light and cheerful," was likened to "a summer breeze in our mountain pines," while the second movement, that mysterious and nostalgic "Nocturne," evoked "all the romance to be found under western skies." The finale, "Dance," infectious and reminiscent of a real hoedown, displayed "unusual brilliance and intensity." But concerning its innate popular appeal and romanticism, Robertson astutely remarked:

> [This] romantic appeal by the same token makes it the despair of the esoteric snobs who are appointed among themselves to be arbiters of current taste.

The performance itself elicited a standing ovation, which visibly pleased the composer. Although Abravanel never programmed it again, other conductors gladly took it into their repertoire.

The other new work of this period, the *Alleluia and Chorale for Band and Chorus*, is significant because it is the only piece Robertson specifically composed for band. Written in 1959 and dedicated to the University of Utah Concert Band, it was premiered by this organization and the University of Utah Chorus, Forrest Stoll conducting, in May 1959, as part of the University commencement festivities. Much appreciated as a new addition to the concert band literature, it received subsequent performances by other nearby university bands and choruses. And, after it was listed in a 1962 catalogue of band compositions, band directors from afar began to ask Robertson for the score and parts. This work has remained unpublished, however.

During these years, Robertson compositions continued to be heard not only locally, but also nationally and internationally. By the end of the 1950s, the composer could report performances of his works throughout the Western Hemisphere, Europe, Australia, and even Japan.

Further honor came to him in early 1959 when the National Federation of Music Clubs presented him with their National Presidential Award for his outstanding work in music circles. On this occasion, the Federation President stated, "Nobody has done more to further American music than Dr. Leroy J. Robertson." It was a tribute that certainly described this quiet man's goals and purposes in life.

15   Maurice Abravanel (left) and Robertson looking over a new Robertson score,
Barracks Rehearsal Hall, University of Utah, 1957.
Photo reprinted by permission of the *Deseret News*.

16 *Left:* Robertson (left) and
Utah Governor George D. Clyde
singing a few bars from the
Oratorio from the Book of Mormon,
Salt Lake City, 1961.
Photo reprinted by permission
of the *Deseret News*.

17 *Below:* Chorus member's
eyeview of Abravanel conducting a
performance of the *Oratorio from
the Book of Mormon*, Salt Lake
Tabernacle, 1961.
Photo reprinted by permission
of the *Deseret News*

18 Montage of sketches rapidly notated by Robertson on the nearest scrap
of paper at hand.   Clockwise from top: IRS envelope, 1945;
envelope from Michigan Governor and Mrs. George Romney, 1967,
"Michael's Song" from *Pegeen*; desk memo pad, ca. 1955.

19   Robertson writing at chalkboard,
Music Hall Office, University of Utah, ca. 1958.

20   Site of the *Passacaglia* premiere, Athens, Greece, 1955.
Lower left: the Herodes Atticus Theater at the foot
of the Acropolis, with the Parthenon above.

21   Eugene Ormandy (left)
and Robertson
studying the *Passacaglia* score,
Philadelphia, 1960.

22   Gina Bachauer and Robertson,
Salt Lake City, 1965.
Good friends meet again.
Photo reprinted by permission
of the *Deseret News*.

23 Grant Johannesen, ca. 1966.
Photo by Martin Zwick.

24 Tossy Spivakovsky, ca. 1961.

25 Karl Krueger, ca. 1950.

26 Zara Nelsova, ca. 1956.

27   Robertson, Music Building Office, University of Utah, ca. 1965.

PART IV

BEYOND THE VALLEY OF THE GREAT SALT LAKE

Chapter Twenty

SUCCESSES AND SORROWS

FOR Leroy Robertson the 1960s began well. Twelve years had passed since his coming to Salt Lake City, and on a personal level there had been some significant changes. His children, now grown, were striking out on their own, leaving Leroy and Naomi as the only steady residents in the "White House on 1400 East." They kept in touch by on and off visits, with Leroy always making at least one weekly phone call to any child out of town. Soon grandchildren would enlarge the family circle and often come calling, much to the delight of their loving grandparents.

However, in many ways, life remained the same. A deep part of the composer still hearkened to earlier days in Sanpete and Utah Counties, and he maintained contact with his relatives and lifelong friends, as did they with him. In fact, he even purchased an acre of land at the foot of Mount Timpanogos, and when possible, would return to Utah Valley to tramp over his fields, enjoy the view, and plan the home he intended to build there for himself and Naomi.

Nonetheless, Robertson's interests were now firmly centered in Salt Lake, his work at the University and his composing.

These were the years that spawned his writing for the Tabernacle Choir and Dr. Karl Krueger's *Music in America* series of recordings. The *Piano Concerto* was well on its way to completion, and he was also committing himself to composing many anthems specifically for the LDS Church. On a somewhat different note, he was more directly involved with the children of the Salt Lake City schools, for, as part of their regular curriculum, they were studying his *Punch and Judy Overture*, and he would talk to various groups about this work.

It was midsummer, 1960, when a quite unexpected letter arrived from the Cleveland Institute of Music. This noted conservatory was seeking a new director and asked Robertson if he would be interested in the position. What an ideal situation for this composer in faraway Utah. In Cleveland, he would have direct access to the Cleveland Orchestra, and equally important, from a base in Cleveland— situated as it is between the great music centers of the Midwest and the East Coast—he would no longer be so musically isolated. And, as a sentimental capstone, the Utahn could never forget that his beloved mentor, Ernest Bloch, had been the first director of this venerable institution.

The overall picture attracted Robertson so much that he did indeed journey to Cleveland to make his own firsthand observations. He liked the city, its bustle and excitement, its proximity to Lake Erie. He liked the people, the Institute, and of course, he loved hearing the Cleveland Orchestra. He imagined himself and Naomi settling there and having the children come to visit. But, after much heartrending deliberation, he ultimately decided to remain in Utah —just as he had so many years before when his prizewinning *Trilogy* brought him offers from across America, including Canada and Mexico.

No one knows his exact reasons for this decision. Perhaps, now at nearly age sixty-four and soon to face retirement, he did not wish to lose his University pension as he had upon leaving BYU. Perhaps he just did not want to start over as teacher and administrator of a new program at another school, even such a great one as the Cleveland Institute. Perhaps his deep love for Utah and its mountains, deserts, and people, overshadowed all. At any rate, Robertson quietly went on with his work in Utah as if nothing had happened, and very few people even knew about this episode in his life.

The year 1961 brought the recording of two major Robertson compositions: the *Oratorio from the Book of Mormon* and the *Concerto for Violin and Orchestra*, both with Abravanel and the Utah Symphony under the prestigious Vanguard label.

After a hiatus of some half-dozen years, the much acclaimed *Oratorio*—now recognized as the most outstanding religious work yet written in the Western Hemisphere—was to be heard in concert once again, this time in April at the time of the Annual LDS General Conference; and the recording would be made directly afterward. The concert performance held the audience spellbound, and as before, the *Oratorio* brought the listeners to their feet at its conclusion. Among the thousands to attend that concert, one very special person was Leroy's aged Uncle Will Adams, who sweetly stated to his daughter, Ruth, that he "had never had such a thrill in his whole life . . . his whole body felt the praise and honor given," and in tender recognition of what dedicated labor such a composition had demanded, Ruth later wrote to Leroy:

> To know that Dad has a wonderful nephew who studied, and was willing to pay the high price in all other ways, to have the ability . . . to express himself, is indeed an inspiration.

After the concert, the big job at hand was the recording, which was scheduled to be made within the week. This would take place at the University of Utah Music Building in the hall usually reserved for Utah Symphony rehearsals and school concerts. Never before used for recording, these facilities can at best be termed challenging. Imagination and improvisation, tinged with much goodwill, had to come to the fore. As Vanguard's technicians set up their many microphones, testing and "taking a level" on each one, these experienced experts determined that a certain resonance was lacking. No problem! They merely strung a special cable up one flight of stairs and into the Mens' Restroom, where they had discovered the sound needed. After posting a large "Out of Order" sign on the door, they were ready to begin. Fortunately, no one trespassed. Despite these rather precarious conditions, the recording sessions proceeded normally, with no unusual delays, and Vanguard had the *Oratorio* ready for release by Christmas.

As the recording made its way across the country, Leroy Robertson's *Oratorio from the Book of Mormon* received its first national, then international exposure. Critics from coast to coast featured it in their reviews, all of which reflected the widening impact of this work, hitherto kept pretty much within Utah and the Mormon community. They congratulated Vanguard for its enterprise and skill, and the performers for their brilliance. Without exception, the *Oratorio* itself, which suddenly interested both Mormons and non-Mormons, drew the most commentary, being described as:

> ... a sweeping work ... one of the more inspired contemporary liturgical compositions; surprisingly big, powerfully dramatic; majestic and melodious; a ... stirring work of grand design.

Of the composer they wrote:

> Leroy Robertson is a western composer of considerable artistic stature who is not as well known in this part of the country [the East Coast] as he should be. ... Some of this composer's music has been acridly modern, but here he reverts to a style that is occasionally reminiscent of Mendelssohn but is more often infused with the passionate intensity of Ernest Bloch.

The entire endeavor, i.e., the quality of the composition, performance and recording, caught nearly everyone off-guard. As one critic candidly admitted:

> On the face of it, this immense *Oratorio* out of Utah might seem the sort of music for outsiders to avoid. ... [But] I found I really didn't mind it a bit, though all my intellectual sense kept saying I should.
> Indeed, the fervently musical performance by these dedicated Utah people suggests a good comparison, architecturally and stylistically: the music somehow reminds one of the famous Mormon Temple itself, out in Salt Lake City. That sturdy shrine is nominally a monument to early American architectural naivete, but even so it manages to convey an astonishing quality of strength, dedicated workmanship and community togetherness. Impressive even if you've just flown in from Notre Dame or Chartres the day before. So it is with this *Oratorio*. Interesting.

Very soon after the recording's release, Robertson began receiving numerous requests for copies of the score and parts, especially from non-Mormons across the country and abroad. However, with the advanced techniques of photo- and computerized copying then nonexistent, duplicates remained scarce and expensive to make. Robertson was therefore often forced to reply: "As soon as I can get enough money together to pay for some more photostats, I'll get a score in your hands."

A few ambitious musicians beyond Utah wished to mount performances in their own regions, but Robertson did not really encourage them. Ever frank, he described the project as "a monumental undertaking . . . [that] requires a lot of work to prepare." Such proposed performances never did materialize during the composer's lifetime. But, he would yet hear his *Oratorio* on the local scene twice more. One month after the 1961 April revival and recording, Abravanel and his same devoted troops presented it at a benefit concert for the Tabernacle Choir, and seven years later, the BYU choruses and Utah Symphony would perform it in Provo.

It is interesting to note that almost from the beginning, three choral pieces from the *Oratorio* did take on lives of their own, and were often performed, recorded, and published independently throughout the years. And the peaceful "Pastorale" for orchestra became a favorite of Abravanel, who frequently played it both as a regularly programmed work, or a tradition-breaking encore.

The second major Robertson composition to be recorded in 1961 was his *Concerto for Violin and Orchestra*, which again brought national and international attention to Utah. Once more, the Utah Symphony, Abravanel conducting, and Vanguard combined their resources, while Russian violin virtuoso, Tossy Spivakovsky—hailed by many as "one of the greatest artists of all time"—joined the group to play the demanding solo part.

Spivakovsky had seen the score sometime in the late 1950s, nearly a decade after its premiere, and immediately had become its ardent champion. However, as he studied the work and became better acquainted with it, he cautiously and courageously advised a small change in the first movement. His letter to Robertson about this is a masterpiece in tact:

> I recognize, of course, the audacity in suggesting any changes, even a such a minor one, to the composer. But I do hope you will find a performer's point of view worth some consideration, although I am absolutely opposed, in principal [sic], to change one iota in a manuscript.
>
> I am looking forward very much to playing your beautiful work.

Robertson, who himself had always been a bit dissatisfied with the *Concerto*'s overall construction, responded at once, making even more changes than the violinist had proposed. Intensive rewriting during 1960-1961 brought the composition to its final form. Of his *Violin Concerto* Robertson then wrote:

> The music, like that of all my more important works, projects the spirit of the Utah landscape with its inspiration of varied colors from desert to mountains.

Spivakovsky first performed the *Concerto* in late fall, 1961, with Abravanel and the Utah Symphony, just before the Vanguard recording session. Touted as a Utah-Russia collaboration, the entire venture took on added excitement, coming as it did in the midst of the Cold War. There were at least two sold-out concerts that electrified the audiences. In its new and final version, the *Violin Concerto*, with its "cruel, audacious and wonderful demands upon the solo instrument," was applauded as "a tribute to Utah quite as much as those more palpably on view every day." It even impressed a few public officials. New Salt Lake City Commissioner, Con Harrison, wrote:

> Equally as thrilling as the election . . . was the performance of your *Violin Concerto*. . . . I have known it to be a magnificent work, but I guess many of us just didn't realize how truly magnificent it is.

Not only local friends, but New York musicians as well sent congratulations:

> I am so pleased that Spivakovsky has put it [the *Violin Concerto*] in his books—as the saying goes. . . . This means your *Concerto* will attain immortality.

As with the *Oratorio*, the recording sessions were held in the University of Utah's Music Building, with virtually the same conditions and facilities. Again, despite the improvised cable-laying and unpredictable acoustics, the recording proceeded on schedule, and the album was released within eight months. This was no mean feat, for along with Robertson's *Concerto*, they also recorded Stravinsky's *Concerto for Violin and Orchestra*.

Like the *Oratorio*, it pleased critics crosscountry:

[The Robertson *Violin Concerto*] is honest if modest music with a lyricism that expresses real emotion and from which a sweet and dignified personality emerges. In these days it is a pleasure to hear something new, or relatively so, that is neither forced or doctrinaire. Robertson's *Concerto* fits Spivakovsky like a glove and Abravanel's accompaniment appears to be sympathetic and expert.

The two twentieth century works by composers 14 years apart in age and half a world apart at birth . . . are outstanding examples of modern music.

[Robertson's *Concerto*] spins with the exact precision of a jeweled watch. Not a note is out of place, and the musical line is always strong and infectious.

One tribute that must have touched Robertson very deeply came from Harrison Keller, his violin teacher from so many years before at the New England Conservatory:

I have played it [the *Concerto* recording] many times, each hearing revealed new beauties. . . . To have had some small part in inspiring your great gift is gratifying and I will quote from a letter to me by Leopold Auer in 1915, his English not perfect—"I am glad too having be able to provoke in your soul the sacred fire of noble art." This is, of course, the essence of great teaching.

Through the years Spivakovsky championed Robertson's *Concerto* with conductors throughout the United States, but for some reason, they were not interested. Other violinists as well admired the work, terming it a masterpiece, but few cared to tackle it. As Eugene Ormandy would later write to Robertson:

[Your *Violin Concerto*] is a fine work, without any doubt. The question is, who would want to learn a new concerto?"

So, despite the recording being broadcast regularly, and despite the score and parts being published and placed for wide distribution, the Robertson *Concerto for Violin and Orchestra* would not become a popular item during the composer's lifetime.

*　*　*　*　*

As of early spring, 1962, Leroy Robertson's general tide of success began to ebb, and he started to face problems somewhat more pressing and worrisome than composing or performances of his compositions. What was to become a turning point suddenly forced its way into his life. He was now sixty-five years old, the usual age of mandatory retirement for department heads at the state-owned University of Utah. The years had indeed gone by, but as one colleague remarked, "[Robertson] didn't seem to change really, nor did *he* feel that he had changed." True, he no longer was pencil-slim as in his early years, but with hair still naturally coal black, face wrinkle-free, and eyes sparkling, he did not show his age. Most important, that clear mind remained as searching and active as ever.

Robertson had been fervently hoping that an exception to the University's retirement rule would be made in his case—as had been done for some other department heads—for he wished to solidify programs still being developed. But sadly, he sensed that changes were afoot. Already, the year previous, he had been told that the administration no longer wished him to teach full time and direct the Music Department every quarter as he had done since coming to the University. And there can be no dispute that his strong, stubborn ways had not always suited those used to "government by committee and consensus." As another department head had once almost enviously remarked, "Robertson has the reputation of being quite autocratic, but then, how else can one keep all those maverick musicians pulling in the same direction?"

Moreover, through the years, many of his unique accomplishments in the community and University had not become generally known. As Lowell Durham wrote to the University administration:

> Prof. Robertson is not one to toot any horn but that of Artistic and Educational Excellence.

In another letter to his mentor, Durham recalled what had been achieved:

> We have fought many common battles since then [Robertson's arrival at the University of Utah] and I shall always regard my "Robertson years" as the most rewarding; for I have seen you, almost single-handedly (with an assist from Maurice and a few others) transform the music scene by your dogged determination to insist on quality, your uncanny grasp of the overall situation, your high ideals, and your personal warmth and understanding.

No matter. It was a grievous surprise when in mid-March, with no official consultation or warning, the dedicated composer-teacher-administrator opened the morning newspaper to see his photograph splashed across the page alongside the headline: "Robertson to retire from U Music Post." Here, for the first time, he also learned that his successor had been named. Within days, however, in a kinder and more official way, he received some pleasant news. Though retiring him as head of the Music Department, the University of Utah had appointed him its Composer-in-Residence. He would still be teaching his beloved students and keep that prized office-studio with its expansive view westward to the Great Salt Lake .

With the almost simultaneous announcements of his retirement and new appointment as Composer-in-Residence, letters of thanks and appreciation began to arrive from colleagues, former students, and friends. At a special luncheon given for him by the Utah Symphony Guild, Robertson took the opportunity to explain why he had chosen not to leave his mountain homeland. He truly believed in Utah's great cultural potential, and then, with an eye to the future, he earnestly concluded:

> Americans were quite concerned over the first sputnik sent into space. However, Russia has been sending up cultural sputniks for centuries. I think it's about time America got into the cultural race too.

Robertson may have sometimes wondered later on if he would not have been happier in completely leaving the University at this point. For, in no time, he would sadly perceive that few of his innovative programs could ever remain as he had envisioned. As longtime colleague and faculty member Louis W. Booth stated:

> You have worked hard and with an uncompromising idealism that has at once been a thorn in our sides and a great blessing . . . it will seem quite strange to have a new aspect to look forward to. . . . You will undoubtedly see us floundering. This I can see already.

Indeed, many projects instituted and developed by him were soon to disappear, of which one of the most dramatic and immediate was the Utah Symphony's Home on Campus. Although this residency had created constant problems, Robertson's unwavering belief in the advantages of having a professional symphony at the University had made their stay unquestioned. But almost immediately after his leaving as head, the Music Department faculty decided against their remaining. With Robertson at the head, "it went smoothly. [Afterwards] it was a fight," Abravanel would later comment.

Other programs which Robertson had to see end were the outdoor Summer Festivals, the Kingsbury Hall operas, and the Contemporary Music Concerts. Also, the curriculum he had built, which indeed had brought the Music Department in accord with national standards, was jettisoned.

But, while to the world, Leroy Robertson may have been retired, in his heart he could not stop. He did not even seem to slow down. A former BYU colleague summed up the composer's feelings:

> Dear Roy,
>   It just can't be possible that you are knocking at the 65 door! And retirement! Immoral—you'll never retire until the Big Call comes. . . . Don't retire.

At once Robertson wistfully replied:

> Thanks for your good note. . . . In a day when there is so much double-talk, hypocrisy and perversion it is good to be reminded of the decency and fairness of friends such as you. . . . I wish I could retire for awhile, but I seem to be getting deeper into it all the time.

Indeed, such was the case. Many still sought his services. He was yet heavily involved with the *Music in America Series* and Tabernacle Choir projects; the Ford Foundation asked him to nominate candidates for their "Program for Concert Soloists"; students—even from abroad—were requesting permission to study with him at the University, where he was still teaching and consistently preparing many Ph.D. candidates. In addition, just three months after leaving as head of the Music Department, he would be called to serve as chairman of the LDS General Music Committee, a position he would greatly strengthen. He would also be travelling to hear and supervise performances of his music.

Of course, he never stopped composing. Works—both large and

not so large—date from this period. For example, there were many songs soon to be both published and recorded.

One of these larger works derives from the summer of 1963 when Arizona State University President, G. Homer Durham, commissioned him to write a special orchestra piece to celebrate the opening of their Grady Gammage Auditorium, the last large building designed by architect Frank Lloyd Wright. In his commission, President Durham proposed that, "should it strike his favor," Robertson might write an overture which would incorporate and conclude with Arizona State's "Alma Mater." Robertson not only followed this suggestion, but also named the overture *Saguaro*, in honor of that University's Saguaro cactus emblem.

The festive occasion—which would feature the Phoenix Symphony and Metropolitan Opera star Eileen Farrell in two concerts—was scheduled for fall, 1964. Leroy and Naomi decided to attend, for in addition to hearing the premiere of his *Saguaro Overture*, they could visit with his brother, Doyle, who had been residing in Phoenix with his family for some years.

The trip did turn out to be a very happy interlude. The concerts themselves created much excitement and were attended by leading public officials, including the Governor of Arizona as well as recently widowed Mrs. Frank Lloyd Wright. There were many social affairs; and Leroy and Naomi were very glad to visit once again with their friends, President and Mrs. Durham. But, through all the public honors, Leroy was most happy to be with Doyle and his family. He even arranged for his kin to have special reserved seats at the concert next to Mrs. Wright, and was as proud to have the dignitaries meet them as he was to have them meet the dignitaries.

Arizona State University took the *Saguaro Overture* to heart. Just six months after its premiere, it was again featured at that University's Charter Day Convocation.

Meanwhile, Abravanel would also program *Saguaro* many times in early 1965. The work also became popular for a while with a few university orchestras as well, and according to reports, the audiences always received it extremely well, with "enthusiastic and prolonged applause."

But though kept very busy, in many ways Robertson did not find these years "all beer and skittles." Even before his leaving as Music Department head, bothersome health problems had begun to surface. His eyesight, which had troubled him since his youth, was steadily growing worse. And diabetes, likely present for some time, would soon be diagnosed. He confided to friends in the East of a distressful summer, and at the same time wrote to one of his daughters:

> I wish I were not so lazy. . . . I must get the onion skins of the [*Passacaglia*] parts to Galaxy for their reproduction. Also I must orchestrate the extension of the 3rd movement of the *Violin Concerto* and fix the parts. Ten years ago I looked forward to doing work of this kind, but now all I feel like doing is to sit in the old chair in the corner with my feet on the [foot]stool and wish everything was done.

But then, he unpretentiously continued:

> I wrote a number for chorus Thursday and one on Friday. The one on Friday I did from 4 to 6 P.M. It needs a little editing.

Despite these health vexations, Leroy never really slackened his pace, and he fully expected to remain at the University of Utah as a teacher for many, many years to come. He had in fact been told that he could keep "as complete a schedule as [he] would want to carry."

However, in late 1964 the picture changed. President Olpin's successor, James C. Fletcher, for reasons unknown to Robertson, arbitrarily determined that Robertson should not only definitively retire from all graduate teaching, but also should no longer be Composer-in-Residence. True, Robertson was then sixty-eight years old—the standard cut-off age—but the University had long allowed a number of its distinguished faculty to supervise and teach some graduate students well beyond this age.

When Robertson's students got word of the pending decision, they formed themselves into a committee, and formally petitioned the administration to keep "their professor." Nor did this decision sit well with many in the community at large. As one prominent citizen wrote:

> He [Lowell Durham] informed me, much to my disappointment, that this would be your last year at the University of Utah. I sincerely believe the University will lose one of its few priceless pillars.

For his part, this dedicated teacher, primarily concerned that his current students earn their degrees without undue complication, asked to stay on until those then working under his direction should finish.

But, all to no avail. The word was irrevocable. Leroy Robertson would no longer teach and would be removed from every committee of those students whose work he had been directing—even the ones about to get their degrees. Furthermore, as of July 1, 1965, Ned Rorem would replace him as Composer-in-Residence.

However, the administration was not completely heartless. For, although they had decisively severed Robertson from the Music Department, they did not absolutely dismiss their noted composer and teacher. In fact, the University created a new position especially for him, naming him as their first Distinguished Research Professor, a post hitherto unknown at the institution and subsequently to be held by other great University of Utah mentors.

It was significant that this first Research Professorship go to a man from Fine Arts, and the honor was rightly deemed a personal tribute to the composer. But then, Leroy Robertson was no stranger to the University's Research Committee. For many years, by performances and publications of his scores, he had tangibly shown what must go into a creative work and had thereby extended the usual idea of research.

At this time, the Music Department itself honored their former head by devoting one full concert to Robertson compositions during their Seventeenth Annual Chamber Music Festival. BYU as well nominated him for their David O. McKay Humanities Award.

Robertson did, of course, appreciate these signal honors. However, nothing would ever compensate for the loss of his University students. He felt crushed. As one student later remarked:

> It was as if a light was being extinguished . . . not that he had enjoyed the power, but he felt helpless . . . [about] helping his students.

From his earliest years, Robertson had always delighted in teaching others, and he literally thrived on his students' work and input. He loved to see what they were doing and show them what he was doing, and when they were so abruptly taken from him, he did indeed lose a great part of his life. The University administration may have thought they were favoring him by giving him more time to compose, but, in Leroy Robertson's case, this reasoning proved to be very wrong.

At this personally difficult time, one of the most heart-warming expressions came to him from the University of Utah student body officers:

> On behalf of the Associated Students [we] would like to join the administration and faculty in commending you for the outstanding service given to the University of Utah during the past 17 years.
> One of the hardships an institution of higher education faces is losing high quality professors. When the loss occurs, as has happened, all that can be said is thank you for your fine service, and [that] your work, and effort is appreciated.

Robertson immediately responded:

> I appreciate the expressions conveyed in your kind letter. . . .
> During my association with the University, I have always found the students to be farsighted, cooperative and a source of inspiration.

Not only did this venerable teacher-composer lose his students. He also had to depart his beloved studio. One can only imagine the heartache as he removed his files and scores to a small room in the old George Thomas Library, with no piano and only a small desk—no place for composing.

Furthermore, Robertson was soon to discover that any correspondence addressed to him at the Music Department would simply be filed away or misplaced. On one occasion, when he went in search of a missing pension check, he found it covered with dust on top of the Music Department general mailbox. Across the front, and over his clearly inscribed name, someone had scrawled, "Unknown at this address."

Small wonder he felt betrayed, and could only ask "Why?" Perhaps, as Abravanel would later comment: "The time comes when people don't realize what we have done and simply want a change."

*   *   *   *   *

Through this discouraging and critical period, Leroy Robertson certainly had no intention of leading a sedentary life. As he stated:

> I like association with other people. I think something might happen if I did not continue my work. I'll be in something or other.

Interestingly enough, and in a sort of ironic twist, one of his most immediate projects was to compose a special number for the University of Utah in appreciation of the Distinguished Research Professorship awarded him; and thus in late June, just before stepping aside as Composer-in-Residence, he completed his *University of Utah Festival Overture*. A truly festive, fresh, and joyous overture—based on four University of Utah campus songs, with the University's "Alma Mater" appearing at the end "in a climactic manner with the organ"—it much belies the age and sadness of its composer.

Heralded by advance press fanfare, the *Festival Overture* was premiered by the Utah Symphony, Abravanel conducting, on Thanksgiving Eve, 1965. Well received by everyone, it elicited kudos for its "sweet, singing, and powerful clarity." As one writer remarked, after noting the skill and elegance of the composing:

> It is an extraordinary feat to incorporate "I Am a Utah Man, Sir" into anything, but Dr. Robertson does it nicely and with wit.

Both the Utah Symphony and University of Utah Symphony would later play the *Festival Overture* a few times, with one auspicious performance taking place at the dedication ceremonies of the newly constructed Marriott Library. Nonetheless, it was not widely nor often heard, and remained unpublished.

However, other Robertson works were frequently played. Most of these performances were recordings broadcast throughout the USA, Canada, Europe, and Australia, while some requests for scores and news of "live" performances came from Texas and Illinois.

During these years, activities other than composing also captured Robertson's interest. His work had caught the attention of noted psychologist, Calvin W. Taylor, whose own research dealt with the creative mind, and who, in 1965, founded the Institute for Behavioral Research in Creativity. Dr. Taylor at once enlisted Robertson's support, and named him an Institute Trustee. Robertson, in turn, did enjoy giving lectures and participating in seminars and symposiums, where he spoke of his personal experiences not only as a composer but also as a teacher creating in the classroom with his students.

Another organization soon to take Robertson's time and attention was the Utah Institute of Fine Arts, of which he became a member by special appointment from Governor Calvin L. Rampton.

Then, in early spring, 1966, new doors for college teaching suddenly seemed to open which interested Robertson greatly, for he had sorely missed his youthful students. In late March, he and Naomi journeyed to Hawaii, partly on vacation and partly on assignment from the LDS Church. He naturally visited the Church College in Laie, met with various faculty officials, and heard a few student performances. As guests of friends at Laie, far away from the bustle of Honolulu, he and Naomi enjoyed strolling along the uncrowded beaches and the generally relaxed pace of living. He loved the gentleness of the people, which, he noticed, showed itself everywhere—even in their playing of classical music.

Robertson's visit must have pleased the Church College officials as well, for soon after his return to the mainland, President Owen J. Cook invited him to come teach "for a year or two or as long as you would like to stay." As incentive, the invitation continued:

> It is a quiet place. Composers should find adequate inspiration here.

This particular composer, greatly attracted by the whole idea, promptly accepted President Cook's offer, and even suggested that he could begin teaching in early 1967. But, inexplicably and in a strange about-face, Cook vaguely responded by citing budgetary restrictions, and promising further correspondence when he had "more definite word on finance." For a while, the perplexed yet hopeful composer stood by, expecting some definitive news, but nothing further ever developed. Just one more dashed hope to absorb.

Not surprisingly however, Leroy Robertson kept up his courage by composing. As he wrote to good friend, Dr. Karl Krueger:

> During the past two months I have had many discouraging, and disappointing days. In spite of this I am happily occupied in the composition of a new *Piano Concerto*. I began it a month ago [March] and it should be completed by the end of May.

Truth to tell, Robertson had been thinking about this *Concerto* since 1950, but only five years later, immediately upon his return from Greece and inspired by his friendship with Gina Bachauer, did he compose the work. In fact, to honor that memorable trip to the Mediterranean, he even incorporated into it a Greek folk melody that had particularly intrigued him. In the main, however, the 1955 manuscript was an extended version of the original 1950 sketches, which he now condensed and scored in final form. With an extraordinary sense of timing and direction, this mature and experienced composer deftly trimmed his material to the bone. No superfluous note could remain. In this vein, he one day remarked—with the saddest and most wistful look:

> I have just cut from the slow movement nineteen measures of the most beautiful music I have ever written. It wasn't going anywhere.

While composing, he himself would play over and over the various solo passages with a depth of sound and transcendence unmatched by anyone that expressed something far more than just the notes. He loved that *Piano Concerto*, and completed it in less than six months.

As solo performers of this new work, Robertson originally had two pianists in mind, Gina Bachauer and renowned Utahn Grant Johannesen.[1] The latter "got the nod," and Abravanel set the premiere for late fall, 1966.

---

[1]For reasons unknown, Gina Bachauer would not see the *Concerto* until Naomi sent her a copy some four years after Robertson's death.

Once again, preparing the soloist's and orchestral scores for so large and complicated a work was no easy task. For example, merely copying the florid solo part required much effort, and at one point, in an effort to save time, Robertson decided to paste this part—which had already been transcribed separately for the soloist's score—into the orchestra score instead of recopying it. Alas, when the orchestra score was printed up, no staff to hold the notes appeared in the piano part. Near tragedy was averted when a dedicated employee at the printing company offered to take a pen and ruler and carefully draw in by hand all the missing staff lines, some 175 pages worth.

The music reached Mr. Johannesen one movement at a time. By the spring of 1966 he had received the entire *Concerto* and was "beginning to delve into the delights of the work." In August he wrote:

> I just want to tell you how much I am enjoying the work on your *Concerto*. Next week my accompanist will be ready to attack the orchestra part [transcribed for a second piano].

Three months later, the last day of November, the Robertson *Concerto for Piano and Orchestra* was premiered.[2] That night all of northern Utah was blanketed in dense fog thicker than anyone could remember. Still, the Tabernacle gradually filled. In a tense atmosphere brought on by both the weather and the excitement of a first performance, the audience raptly listened to every note. Johannesen and the Robertson *Piano Concerto*, which "centerpieced" the evening, proved their worth. Indeed, the magic transition of the eloquent slow movement to the "Finale" held everyone breathless.

At its conclusion, there was a long standing ovation (twelve minutes according to newspaper accounts). However, this time, for a change, the critics did not share the audience enthusiasm. One writer suggested that Robertson write a different "Finale"—and this

---

[2]The *Piano Concerto* actually received its first public reading a few days earlier in a special school concert at East High School, Johannesen's alma mater. The enraptured students gave the performance a long, standing ovation.

despite the fact that Robertson himself felt that at last he had succeeded in composing a last movement that matched or "topped" the others. Crosstown, another intrepid reporter complained:

> The Nov 31 [*sic*!] Utah Symphony Orchestra concert may be one that . . . regrettably, serious music lovers would rather forget . . . [for afterwards] they went home in cars surrounded by gloom, oblivious of the fog.

Artist that he was, Robertson never did depend on critics to tell him what he did (or did not) achieve. But in face of such negative reaction to the *Piano Concerto*, the composer did appreciate these comments by local sports writer, Hack Miller, who, Robertson often maintained, gave one of the most insightful music critiques he had ever read:

> Pardon me for meddling in music, but I've watched football coaches for some 32 years program their pigskinnery, chalk their charts, invent their innovations, but I've always wanted to know how a genius like Dr. Leroy Robertson comes up with the *Piano Concerto* . . . played Wednesday. When we get Johannesen, Robertson and Abravanel's Utah Symphony on the offense, who can defend against it? . . .
>
> But it isn't the final program that intrigues me as much as how in thunder Dr. Robertson, for instance, can keep all his plays straight. Maybe his tackles run into his guards a little and sometimes the quarterback misses the option, but I notice they do two things well, start and stop together.
>
> I can't imagine the chalk work that would go into their skull drills. And they don't have the advantage of game films to play for their day's progress. . . .
>
> As we shook hands with . . . Dr. Leroy Robertson, we thought that in the centuries to come how great might be the occasion of his debut with his *Piano Concerto*. . . .
>
> Maybe it's a little like football after all. Knute Rockne fame didn't get the high fix until long after the wizards at writing had worked over his words.
>
> At the grand old age of 70, this great composer might never really know how much he has contributed to the culture of mankind.

Leroy Robertson would never again hear his *Piano Concerto*. But after the final score was finally published some three years later, he did send a copy to Dr. Karl Krueger. Following the same general theme as Hack Miller, Dr. Krueger responded:

> I consider the *[Piano] Concerto* a very brilliant piece of work.
> . . . I was particularly intrigued by the rhythmic imagination of
> the first movement; and the little cadenza is a beauty. But my
> favorite movement is the Second. I have always been struck by
> your God-given gift of melody. . . . The last movement is a gem!
> The whole is superbly planned. . . . My hearty congratulations.
> You have given us so much of beauty in your early life, and it is
> deeply gratifying to me to see you continue with undiminished
> power.

And continue he did. Age alone would never affect this man's
ever-present creativity.

Chapter Twenty-One

FOR LOVE OF CHURCH[1]

AT this point in the narrative, we shall, for a moment, go back to 1962, just four years before the premiere of the *Piano Concerto*, and just as Robertson was preparing to step down as head of the University of Utah Music Department.

One day, while he was working in his office, the phone rang, and at the other end of the line sounded a familiar voice. It was Hugh B. Brown, Second Counselor in the First Presidency of the LDS Church. Getting right to the point, President Brown asked Robertson to become chairman of the General Church Music Committee, which at the moment had only an interim leader.[2] Caught by surprise; realizing that this position would entail guiding the music program for the entire Church—fast becoming worldwide; and remembering that he would still be teaching many graduate students at the University, the conscientious composer-professor replied that he would first "have to check his schedule." In response, President Brown merely chuckled, "Roy, we're not used to hearing 'No.'" Needless to say, "Roy" accepted the assignment then and there.

Thus, in September 1962, Leroy Robertson was formally ap-

---

[1]Rather than scatter Robertson's musical activities for the LDS Church throughout the foregoing chapters, the author felt this facet of his life would be more meaningful if these various events were concentrated in one chapter. Some incidents previously mentioned will be more fully discussed here. The author wishes to reiterate that complete documentation can be found in the companion manuscript mentioned in the Preface.

[2]At this time David O. McKay was President of the Church. However, all three members of the First Presidency are called "President."

pointed chairman of the Church General Music Committee (hereafter referred to as GMC).

A devout Mormon, Robertson had always served the Church through the years, often in positions not involving music. During his early years at BYU, he had taught a class of Religion that consistently attracted large numbers of students because of its "thought-provoking and deep spirituality;" and in the various local wards where he lived, he often taught a priesthood class.

Not surprisingly however, Leroy Robertson gave his largest and likely most enduring Church service as a musician. Wherever he found himself—Fountain Green, Boston, Berlin—he could regularly be heard playing his violin in the diverse Church services; and, if no one else was available, he readily sat at the piano or organ to accompany the hymn-singing. Indeed, it was as a violin-toting lad that he first caught the attention of Apostle Melvin J. Ballard in that chance meeting which made such a lasting impression on both the youth and this high-ranking General Authority. Elder Ballard henceforth kept his eye on the young musician, encouraging him to compose for the Church. For his part, Robertson always responded to the older man's requests for music.

For example, very soon after Elder Ballard became chairman of the newly formed GMC, he sent out a call for anthems "by home composers that would be as useful and high class as possible." The anthems were to be published in a very limited collection with but one composition per composer accepted. Elder Ballard himself wrote directly to Robertson, then in Boston, asking him to compose an anthem for this competition. It was significant for young Robertson that his Christmas anthem, "Behold, a Star Appeareth" not only was accepted for publication, but also won first prize.

Another ongoing project of the GMC during these early years was the compilation of the 1927 hymnal, to which Robertson was also asked to contribute, and which marks the first of many LDS hymnbooks to contain works by Leroy Robertson. Of the four hymns chosen to appear therein, two deserve comment. One, "I'm a Pilgrim, I'm a Stranger," was first written as a composition assignment for one of Robertson's classes at the New England Conservatory. Another, "Beware a Fiend in Angel Form," became the subject of an amusing anecdote often recounted by its composer. It seems that one day, a BYU colleague remarked to him, "There's only one hymn in the whole LDS hymnody about Evil, and that was written by Leroy Robertson." Actually, this piece, set to a text by LDS Church historian, Orson F. Whitney, is a warning against the trickery of Satan. Nonetheless, although the other Robertson hymns became well established in the LDS musical tradition, "Beware a Fiend . . ." never appeared in subsequent publications.

In 1930, three years after the publication of this 1927 hymnal, another, quite different project placed new Robertson works of a more gigantic scale before the LDS people. To commemorate the Centennial of its founding, the Church staged a monumental sacred pageant, "The Message of the Ages," in the Salt Lake Tabernacle; and Robertson, as a member of the pageant committee, wrote much of the music. He composed a trumpet fanfare and the "dispensation music"—passages used at the beginning of each tableau to unify the whole production—and also helped choose and integrate all the other musical numbers. Scoring every piece for full orchestra, he created a work that came to be praised as a masterpiece.

This pageant, which began April 6 and continued for some thirty nights with approximately 200,000 people in attendance, proved to be the outstanding feature of the Centennial Celebration. Robertson, however, was not present at any of these performances. For, after carefully preparing the score and parts, and after checking out initial rehearsals, already begun in February, he left in early March for his San Francisco studies with Ernest Bloch. Nonetheless, though Robertson was absent from the pageant, the music he wrote for it made him known to a wide segment of the populace who had hitherto never before heard his name. It further served to confirm his talent to the General Authorities. Clearly, he was steadily becoming recognized as an outstanding musician in the Church.

During the 1930s Leroy Robertson came ever more to the fore as an important Church musician thanks to the frequent Salt Lake City performances of the BYU Symphony Orchestra. Sometimes they played in the Tabernacle, sometimes in the Assembly Hall. And when they appeared with choruses—either BYU groups or the Tabernacle Choir—Robertson and his performers presented for the first time in Utah many choral-orchestral masterpieces as they had been originally written, i.e., for orchestra, not organ accompaniment.

A landmark collaboration between the Church and Robertson's BYU Symphony Orchestra would occur in the mid-1940s, when, at the request of President J. Reuben Clark, Jr., they appeared with him in a series of Sunday night broadcasts.[3] Aired over Radio KSL, these programs consisted of a sermon by President Clark, preceded and followed by suitable pieces from the classical orchestral repertoire.

Indeed, it was at about this time that President Clark proposed to Robertson that he organize and direct a Church-sponsored volunteer orchestra, which, among other things, would perform on a regular basis during the time-honored weekly CBS broadcasts of the Tabernacle Choir. Sadly, however, this wonderful proposal never became reality, and for many reasons. Robertson was absolutely unable to convince President Clark that in order for any orchestra to present such frequent and ongoing programs, the Church would need at least a core of paid professionals.[4] The experienced musician politely but persistently tried to explain to this venerable Church leader that, unlike the Tabernacle Choir which could excuse a few singers now and then due to its size, every orchestra member would be needed at all rehearsals and performances; and further, in addition to the scheduled rehearsals and performances, these players would have to practice many, many hours in private so as to have the music adequately prepared. In sum, the orchestra members would have to devote so much of their time to this assignment that they could only maintain part-time jobs elsewhere in earning their living. Also, yet another quite different problem to be faced was the fact that all national radio

---

[3]At this time, J. Reuben Clark, Jr., was First Counselor in the First Presidency of the Church.

[4]Robertson had good historic precedent for taking this position. Already in the early 1860s Brigham Young himself had regular wages paid to the orchestra players of the Salt Lake Theatre.

networks required instrumentalists to be members of the Musicians Union (as indeed were Tabernacle organists Frank W. Asper and Alexander Schreiner), so CBS would have demanded that the orchestra players be "union" as well. Of course, such reasoning flew directly in the face of the long-standing LDS policy of strictly volunteer service by all. Thus, hopes for a professional, or perhaps semiprofessional Church orchestra remained unfulfilled.

It is worth noting that Robertson's resolute stand about forming a Church orchestra did not in any way diminish President Clark's respect for Leroy Robertson, nor Robertson's appreciation for President Clark.

Indeed, it was President Clark who brought Robertson's *Oratorio from the Book of Mormon* to the attention of the other two members of the First Presidency, and who spearheaded their commissioning him to finish this work for the Church's 1947 Centennial Celebration of the Mormons' arrival in the Salt Lake Valley. Although Robertson's commission was subsequently aborted, the initial news of this assignment encouraged other musicians in the Church. As one colleague wrote:

> I feel to rejoice that at last the recognition has come. . . . Each time the Brethren show their generosity and keen interest in music means the advancement of the idealism for which we are striving.

Leroy Robertson's first extended official calling for Churchwide service had already come in 1938 with his appointment to membership in the GMC. This assignment necessitated monthly committee meetings which, for some ten years, meant journeys from Provo to Salt Lake City, and many hours of concentrated homework outside the scheduled gatherings. A few months after Robertson's appointment to the Committee and following the death of its first chairman, Apostle Melvin J. Ballard, the GMC was reorganized, with Robertson named Second Assistant in early October 1939. A few years later, in February 1943, he became First Assistant.

Among the myriad tasks confronting the GMC during these years, the compilation of a new LDS hymnal proved to be the largest and lengthiest. Faced with the need of providing for a constantly growing Church membership, the General Authorities felt that such a volume should be prepared to replace both the 1927 hymnbook and the venerable *Deseret Sunday School Songs*. In making this assignment to the GMC, the authorities proposed that it be a one-year project, but Committee member Alexander Schreiner courageously opined that such a work would take at least ten years, and would "be all the better for it."

The GMC at once began to review material from many sources, eventually selecting standard works from both the LDS and other Christian traditions. In addition, they sought to include new hymns from the then current crop of LDS composers, young and old.

The Committee naturally had to scrutinize each text to affirm its suitability to LDS tenets, and the rules to be observed in this regard were very strict. For example, one evening, as Robertson sat at home, poring over and editing the numerous texts submitted, he respectfully, but somewhat bemusedly, observed, "It's interesting that some women's names are acceptable to the Church and others aren't. We Mormons can sing about 'Grace' all we want, but not about 'Mary.'"[5]

As to the music, the GMC generally favored chorale-like melodies of great dignity, and tended to reject the old revivalistic hymn tunes that had been so prevalent in nineteenth- and early twentieth-century America.

Robertson himself was assigned to set some ten texts, which, in addition to two pieces kept from the 1927 hymnal, made a total of twelve Robertson hymns which would appear in the volume then being prepared.

When composing his hymns, Robertson unwaveringly adhered to the ancient Christian definition of a hymn as being a "*Song of Praise to the Lord.*" He further explained that "Good hymns are written in the language of prayer, praise, faith, and self-commitment, and as such, they become a vital part of religious worship."

---

[5]Robertson was merely making a gentle allusion to the fact that Mariolatry (worship of the Virgin Mary) is not an LDS tenet.

As Alexander Schreiner had predicted, work on the new hymnal progressed slowly. Each Committee member conscientiously critiqued every contribution. And just as Robertson kept an eagle eye on every note written, so did his colleagues—sometimes to the composer's discomfiture. For example, one day after a GMC meeting, he came home "absolutely fit to be tied" because a few members had found what they perceived to be a technical error in some of his writing. However, in typical fashion, rather than arguing further at the moment, he methodically began to collect evidence justifying his position. And to assure its complete accuracy, he even assigned one of his BYU graduate students to write a master's thesis analyzing how Bach, the undisputed master of chorale-writing, had resolved this particular problem. The resultant study inevitably proved Robertson right, as well he knew it would. Needless to say, the vindicated composer gladly presented copies of the completed thesis, replete with its exhaustive analyses, to those Committee members needing them.

Not only each member of the GMC, but the General Authorities as well, had to approve all hymnbook materials, and these high Church officials did take their time to examine the proposed volume. As one Committee member wrote:

> The Brethren have asked that we include all verses of the older standardized hymns in our new book. The Hymn Book is still in their office (the First Presidency) and we have no idea when they will return it to us. I suppose we must exercise patience but it takes a lot of it.

At last, in 1948, after ten full years of arduous labor, the long-awaited hymnal came off the press. Simply entitled *Hymns—The Church of Jesus Christ of Latter-day Saints*, it was described as the "latest and probably most complete [hymn book] yet made for general use among the Latter-day Saints." Encouraging its wide use, and noting that this hymnal was planned for all adult gatherings of the Church, the General Authorities expressed the hope that these hymns would provide a means for teaching "faith, devotion, prayer, and other principles of the restored gospel"; and they urged all directors, choristers and organists to keep this purpose in mind when planning their music.

Reaction to the new hymnal was immediate, strong, and mixed. Many applauded its high tone of dignity and worship; but, others, who had grown up singing the swinging, march-like tunes of the *Deseret Sunday School Songs*, missed the old standbys of their childhood and youth. One very high General Authority would even exclaim later that in a hymnal he wanted tunes he could sing "while milking the cows." Thus, within two years, a new edition appeared, which, though basically the same as the 1948 volume, did drop some of the newly added hymns in favor of a few old revivalistic standards that had formerly been omitted. Interestingly enough, Robertson's own efforts to perfect this hymnal would continue for many years to come.

In addition to preparing the new hymnbook, the GMC had many other Church music projects. Robertson's special assignments involved instrumental and ensemble music, although his advice and input were sought for all the various programs being developed. His influence spread, and Church leaders from far and near, musician and non-musician, did not hesitate to seek his help. As one high authority wrote:

> Your fine spirit of cooperation, your unselfish attitude and your humility have made it a joy to be associated with you.

And in this manner, Leroy Robertson loyally labored for music in the Church until that eventful 1962 phone call from President Brown which led to his appointment as chairman of the GMC. That same firm hand which had built first-class music departments at two universities now set out to guide the overall music program of the Latter-day Saints.[6]

Due to his international stature as a composer as well as his high

---

[6]At this point it is important to note that the Mormon Tabernacle Choir has always remained entirely independent from the GMC in operation, organization, and programming. Prominent musicians connected with the Choir have, however, served on the GMC. In alphabetical order, one may cite, among others who served during Robertson's chairmanship: Frank Asper, Richard P. Condie, J. Spencer Cornwall, Robert Cundick, Roy M. Darley, Alexander Schreiner, and Jay Welch.

national profile as teacher and administrator, this appointment generated much positive reaction. At home he was praised as "a highly trained musician who can be counted on to encourage and give practical leadership. . .," while, from overseas, Church members wrote of their delight: "[The GMC] needed someone of your calibre in this position." Colleague Alexander Schreiner would later describe him as "a wonderfully wise chairman and a very kind chairman."

These qualities in Robertson's character can perhaps best be seen in excerpts from letters exchanged between him and former student Crawford Gates, who had become a member of the GMC just before Robertson assumed the chairmanship. From Crawford we read:

> . . . you were kind enough to let me glimpse at what you felt might be my contribution to the Church through music, and gave me some keynotes from your own experience as to how I might overcome and triumph in my own soul over any adversities that might come. . . . If I live up to what you have felt me capable, it will be in part due to the fact that you also gave me some invaluable tools to achieve what may lie potentially within me. . . . I admire and respect your genuine spirituality. I recall our first conversation in 1946 when you said, "We want you to be a product of the Church."

With a bit of realistic self-criticism, Robertson would later write to Crawford:

> I was going to compliment you on . . . [your] fine contribution at the close of the [GMC] meeting, but I saw a traffic cop going up the street so I hastened to get to my car to put in another penny before the meter showed a violation. This is a glaring indication of being pennywise and pound-foolish. . . .
> I have always admired your talent and the things you have done and are doing with it. But more than this I have held in greater esteem and appreciation the fact that you are a person of high moral character. There is a passage in scripture which says Seek ye first the Kingdom of God and all other things shall be added. I have felt that you have sought the Kingdom first rather than the other things.

During Robertson's tenure as chairman, GMC meetings took place in a modest two-room suite on the upper floor of a Salt Lake City bank building located at State Street and First South. One afternoon as he left this office, Robertson observed that the bank building—recently placed under another ownership—boasted a different sign displaying its new name. He dryly wrote:

> You see I am located in a different bank which is at least something—especially since the one bank evaporated and the other came down and surrounded me. I suppose that is like taking on a new body except for size.

At this time the GMC consisted of eleven members, including Robertson, with Carol H. Cannon serving as executive secretary. In addition, all the various auxiliaries—i.e., the Sunday School, the Children's Primary, the MIA (Mutual Improvement Association, a group for youth), and the Relief Society (the women's organization)—had music representatives who worked closely with the GMC. Under the direction of the First Presidency, the GMC was immediately responsible to three advisors chosen from the Quorum of the Twelve Apostles. Robertson cogently delineated their role and position:

> The General Music Committee is an advisory committee and we do not seek any authority. Please know that we are eager to be prudent as well as helpful, and to serve the Church to the best of our ability.

The GMC's role was to enunciate guiding principles, to advise and inform. Their basic responsibilities—which had long been in place—were to set music policies, and correlate the music forces, or, in other words, "unify the efforts of all who are engaged in music assignments." They also had to "examine and approve all publications, manuscripts and recordings relative to Church music."

To further delineate their work, Robertson forthwith enunciated three main objectives: (1) to see that local Church music groups were organized and functioning; (2) to define standards for appropriate repertoire and performance; and (3) to expand and intensify the Church music education program. However, Leroy Robertson's deepest concern—and this no doubt underlay all others—was to emphasize the importance of music, which he saw as "a vital force in building and sustaining the morale of the Church and identified with all activities of the Saints," and which, for him, was a sacred, integral part of LDS religious services.

These aspirations, though slow to be realized, came to be sensed by the people at large. As one Church member wrote:

> The membership of the Church should be most grateful that there are men of your artistic stature who are willing to devote the time necessary to maintain the true relationship between music and worship in the Church.

Concerning the objectives for repertoire and performance, the GMC made a concerted effort to upgrade the general quality of both. The 1948/1950 hymnal remained the guide for hymn-singing. And to encourage more extensive use of all the hymns—especially after a survey showed that many new hymns were being neglected in favor of a few old favorites—the GMC compiled and circulated a list of "recommended but little used hymns." As further incentive to acquaint the congregations with a larger variety of hymns, a "Hymn of the Month" project was instituted, wherein, during Sunday School hymn-practice period, the people would regularly learn a different hymn. And, with an eye to the future, another program was introduced in Junior Sunday School advising that the children learn one different LDS hymn each year.

Concerning special musical numbers for Church services, the GMC also wished to acquaint the people with usable compositions of the greatest composers, all while utterly discouraging "love songs, popular ballads and theatrical numbers." A "Preliminary recommended anthem list" soon followed, wherein works by such masters as Bach, Handel, Haydn, etc., predominated. While wholeheartedly approving every selection listed, pragmatic Robertson could not refrain from privately noting, "Genl. Authority will put them [Church choirs and soloists] back on hymns."

Already, in the mid-1960s it had become apparent that there would soon be need for a new hymnbook, and as the GMC began soliciting contributions for it, Robertson reiterated his basic criterion "that the great doctrines of the gospel should be expressed with worthy, noble words set to music that intensifies and glorifies the meaning of the doctrines expressed."

In their search for both new hymns and special musical numbers, the GMC again sought out works being written by contemporary LDS composers, untrained as well as trained. As these new compositions poured in, members of the GMC, and Robertson in particular, examined each piece. One observer wrote:

> Unless one would sit in the office of Dr. Leroy J. Robertson . . . or the office of Mrs. Carol H. Cannon, one would never believe how many original compositions are submitted with the hope that the Music Committee will accept them.

In holding to his announced standards, Robertson did not hesitate to explain why the GMC rejected certain works:

> We feel that the songs you mention . . . are quite commercial, sectarian and foreign to the spirit of the gospel.

While the GMC was ultimately responsible for the music program in all LDS gatherings, it was sacrament meeting that concerned Robertson above all others. Regarding this most sacred of LDS services open to the general public, he eloquently expressed his own deep feelings:

> The worship of our Heavenly Father should be at the center of our Sacrament meeting service, and it must never be worship for the sake of maintaining activity. If it is, the worship becomes secondary and activity the primary objective. The Lord should be worshipped for His own sake, not for what He will do for us.

For sacrament meeting, the ward choir had long been established as the official singing group, and, with this in mind, Robertson resolutely determined to have a good choir in every ward. His fervent support for such a choir was likely a holdover from his Fountain Green childhood, where this corps, with its regular Thursday evening rehearsals and Sunday performances, provided the chief musical activity for the whole community. As usual, his vision remained very practical. He calculated that there was room for about four thousand ward choirs, and in his efforts to multiply them throughout the Church, he received full backing of the three GMC advisors from the Quorum of the Twelve, who plainly stated:

> Note that the [Ward] Choir is not an adjunct that is variable or optional. It is a part of the regular program. It is a permanent organization.

As an added encouragement to activate ward choirs, Stake Choir Festivals were organized, in which the ward groups could perform both separately and together on a regular basis. A letter from Robertson shows how he personally involved himself in these activities:

> Now I must set up a program of Church numbers for Stake Festival Concerts to be given next year [1968-1969] with directions for performing the same. That must be ready before June 12 [three days hence] so I can assign members of the committee the job of writing up the details.

Along with fostering the development of ward choirs and the Stake Choir Festivals, Robertson also concerned himself with another series of festivals then being initiated by the MIA for Church youth. These were the Young Artists Festivals, organized to give musically gifted and well-trained Church youth a chance to perform, and they immediately caught Robertson's imagination. He, as well as others, felt that such festivals had "the potential of becoming a great cultural and spiritual event which could parallel our [youth] sports program."

That Robertson would have such interest in this program is not surprising, for this caring father, grandfather, and longtime teacher had always delighted in helping young people. In fact, once during an interview, when asked about his attitude toward youth:

> His eyes brightened and a charming smile crept across his lips. He answered, "Very positive; yes, very positive. Where youth is concerned, I am most optimistic. With the training received on the campuses of our universities along with the guidance of the Church auxiliaries, our young people are prepared for the complex problems of society."

Then sensing that much yet lay ahead for Robertson, the same interview concluded:

> . . . this quiet gentleman is still working on many vibrant projects. . . . May he bless us for many years with his God-given gift.

It was during these years that Robertson turned his "God-given gift" to composing specifically for Church youth some of his most beautiful anthems. He wanted the young people to have music of great quality that was within their grasp and not too difficult to sing.

At this same time Robertson was also writing anthems and other shorter songs for the Church as a whole. Just one look at the first draft of these manuscripts evidences the inspiration and facility with which he composed. It was as if he had the whole piece in mind before ever setting a note on paper. Two complete anthems, "Song of Praise" and "Song of Prayer"—both neatly and surely notated on their onion-skin manuscript paper pasted over the pages of an *MIA Music Supplement 1967-68*—have no changes whatever, except for one note later inked in as a possible alternative. In another number, "Blessed the Bread . . . ," only one word differs in the final publication from Robertson's original penciled editings of the text, while the entire melodic line—rapidly dashed off—shows but two measures (seven notes) that he ultimately changed.

One of these short pieces, "The Lord Bless Thee," has an interesting origin. As a brown tattered manuscript, it was sent to Robertson by President David O. McKay, who himself had received it from a Church member then living in West Pakistan. Along with the manuscript came a letter:

> This music was found in the attic of an old house near Joliet, Illinois . . . and I thought that maybe the song might have been written by one of the brethren in the early days of the Church.

After some research, Robertson determined that both the words and music were originally entitled "Aaronic Benediction." In deciphering and editing the almost unreadable pages, Robertson gave the hymn what others have termed "a greatly improved harmonization and rhythmic scoring."

As noted, along with their efforts to upgrade the repertoire of Church music, the GMC was also concerned over the quality of musical performance. In this regard, one specific problem to be tackled by Robertson and his colleagues involved the use of musical instruments in LDS services. Long-standing policy had designated the organ as the accepted instrument of the Church, with the piano permitted occasionally for accompanying the choir. Orchestral instruments —especially brass and percussion—were to be used sparingly. Refining and further defining this policy became an ongoing problem.

As one who had spent his life playing violin in Church services and composing for all instruments, Robertson knew better than most what special beauty and variety each instrument could bring. Therefore, he was inclined to be open-minded and flexible about which instruments could be used. What he held to be more important than the instrument per se was that "the literature performed be of high quality and the performers capable." However, he did stand firmly against using any electronic devices or amplification since this distorted any instrument's true sound.

Thanks to Robertson and a few other Committee members, the earlier restrictions against orchestral instruments were eventually relaxed, and the GMC announced that musical numbers in sacrament meeting should be determined not by the instrument, but by "whether they be spiritually uplifting rather than merely entertaining." Significantly, in this same announcement, they added, "The fact that no text accompanies these compositions should not bar them as spiritually uplifting." Robertson cogently developed this idea in his response to a Church musician who had inquired about what music was acceptable for sacrament meeting:

> I consider an established masterpiece in art or music as being "sacred." In music there are many "masterpieces" of this kind.
> If instrumental music is used in a sacramental service it should be of a devotional nature. . . .
> I judge by your letter that you are a musician of ability and good taste and I feel you will be able to select . . music which will be fitting for this sacred occasion.

To help expand this policy, and in order to provide instrumentalists with repertoire acceptable in Church services, Robertson himself arranged some thirty standard LDS hymns for instruments, published as *Hymns from the Crossroads*. This *Instrumental Hymnal*, as Robertson subtitled it, opened Church doors to a wide variety of instruments and even gave the hymns a fresh, new color. As he always did when using Church material, Robertson had sought permission from the First Presidency to make these settings, permission they readily granted with the proviso that "the arrangements will not in any way alter the original character of the hymns."

Interestingly enough, although Robertson was relaxed in his attitude about the use of orchestral instruments in Church, he took an adamant stand against electronic organs, which were increasingly being placed in ward chapels, a tendency which, at this time, was not supported by the First Presidency. Feeling deeply that pipe organs, because of their unique tone quality, "have been, and will continue to be the standard ones for playing devotional music," Robertson did not shy away from expressing his concerns:

> We view with alarm the trend of the past few years and the present policy to install only electronic organs in all ward chapels and many stake houses and to build chapels that will accommodate only these kinds of instruments.

Of course, financing always loomed as a basic problem, and in answer to complaints about the pipe organ's higher purchase price, Robertson countered that "their life span is long and the cost of upkeep relatively small." From England, noted composer-organist Cyril Jenkins confirmed this fact, describing the Church's apparent preference for electronic organs as "serious and vicious," and lamenting that "only a few of the [Church's electronic] organs are now playable and it seems such a tragedy that it [this preference for electronic organs] should be allowed to continue."

So opposed was Robertson to electronic organs that for congregations unable to afford a pipe organ he proposed:

> a fine Italian reed organ for smaller wards. . . . Otherwise a $3200 Steinway piano for small and some medium size wards would be better than an electronic organ.

To be sure, Robertson's staunch arguments in favor of pipe organs had not been well received by everyone, and despite his protestations, installation of electronic organs in wards did provisionally become the official Church policy. Nonetheless, through much persistence, Robertson and his supporters eventually prevailed. But they sensed that their "victory" was only temporary. In 1969, in answer to a query about a pipe organ, Robertson wrote:

> For a time it was almost impossible to get a pipe organ into a ward, but that ban has now been lifted. Now it is possible to get

a modest-sized pipe organ . . . installed in a ward, so whatever happens, fight for some kind of pipe organ installation and keep me informed.

With the Church ever growing and constantly spreading over wider and wider areas, communication between the GMC and the people became an increasingly critical problem. To be effective, the contacts had to go both ways, from headquarters in Salt Lake City to the local music authorities, and vice versa. The GMC of course followed the well-established lines of communication long held in the LDS Church, i.e., from General Authorities to stake leaders, who, in turn, met with ward officials. The procedure is reversed for getting word from local leaders "upwards."

In an effort to get input from local leaders as to their needs, capabilities, and practices, the GMC began sending out many questionnaires and surveys. Robertson keenly felt the necessity of gaining the interest and support of the local priesthood authorities, for it was they, after all, who selected and guided those directly responsible for the local music programs.

In a further effort to obtain firsthand knowledge of these widely scattered music programs, Robertson himself began to travel extensively, especially throughout the USA. He thus became the first GMC chairman to journey literally crosscountry for the sole purpose of instructing fellow-members and learning from them about Church music. He personally conferred with stake and ward authorities; he spoke at stake conferences; and as he listened and taught, he carefully noted basic problems: leadership from the priesthood; advice on repertoire; training courses in music; gaps in communication between the wards and GMC; and the need for follow-up meetings.

Concerning the scope, frequency, and general political climate surrounding these trips of the 1960s, he once dryly wrote:

> We [Naomi and I] are scheduled to go to Portland on Mar. 1st and to Florida on April 12th. Of course we never know for sure until the time comes—but if we should go to Florida we might could arrange to get hijacked into Cuba—That would really cap the bottle. Naturally on a trip of this kind one never un-caps the bottle as far as I know.

In helping local leaders develop their programs, the GMC faced one basic challenge. By and large, Church music programs rested in the hands of people having little or no musical training. At best, some may have had a few piano lessons or studied "voice" a little bit, but, for the most part, those called to serve—though indeed good-hearted and willing—were woefully unprepared as musicians. Furthermore, there seemed to be a general apathy, even distrust, towards the few professional musicians at hand.

As a viable solution, Robertson envisioned a well-organized and extensive program of music education and training for music leaders (especially conductors and organists), with some elementary classes of music theory added. True, for many years the GMC had offered a few classes on a limited scale, but never had they been organized to an extent quite so large and continual as was now being proposed.

Other musicians across the Church supported the idea. As one faithful member opined, "where sincerity alone might fail, a little education could help." Some even offered their assistance in setting up the courses. These people sought technical training in the various music skills. But much more importantly, they hoped to instill in others the ideal of better music in the Church. As one valiant GMC member would later state, "Art cannot really go down. The people have to come up."

Implementing this truly visionary program would prove to be a gigantic task. As to area, the Latter-day Saints were then scattered across the globe. As to numbers, one scholar roughly calculated a standing need for 28,000 organists alone. Obviously, the situation was the same for choristers. Already in 1964, Robertson—thinking of the many youth wanting help—estimated that he had a "student body of over 70,000 young people," which, as he modestly went on to comment, "keeps me fairly well occupied."

Finding suitable teachers became one of the foremost requirements for this project. And therefore, Robertson began seeking out the many highly trained professional musicians in the Church, who could, in turn, teach others. As he explained:

> Experience has demonstrated that there is a definite advantage in having the most qualified musicians within a stake identifying

and associating with all the other musicians in the stake, most of whom will be amateurs. [This association will bring] unity of purpose and companionship.

Amassing such numbers of music leaders, though perhaps difficult for many, presented little problem for Robertson. He had long been well acquainted with the many excellent musicians in the Church then working both in the East and the West. Also, he had kept in touch with former students, themselves now teaching in music departments of major universities throughout the country: from New Jersey and Maine westward to Oregon and California; from Wisconsin and Michigan southward to Arkansas and Louisiana, and most points in between. This seasoned administrator now began to enlist their support. Other GMC members as well spotted promising young talent, which they immediately called to Robertson's attention. In short order, Robertson felt that the Church had assembled a staff of professional musicians—albeit all unpaid—equal to that of any conservatory in the land.

With the training of organists and choristers always looming as the greatest requisite, the GMC set out to offer widespread and ongoing classes in conducting and organ-playing. Preparatory to these courses, and as supplements thereto, the GMC distributed "Notes to Choristers" and "Notes for Organists," each being a set of specific instructions for leading and playing certain anthems and hymns.

To supplement these organ and conducting classes, the GMC proposed that each stake conduct music seminars, with the kind and number to be determined at the stake, not the GMC level. In addition, the GMC offered to set up special workshops for choristers and organists, complete with exams and awards, and—as extra encouragement for outstanding young musicians—the promise of a performance in the Salt Lake Tabernacle.

Then, in an unexpectedly bold effort to get needed facilities, qualified instructors, and regular instruction for ward and stake musicians, Robertson suggested that Music Departments of the Church-owned institutions for higher learning—namely, BYU, Ricks College, and the College of Hawaii—become teaching centers for those called to serve in local music positions.

While the administrations at all three schools reacted favorably, Robertson most thoroughly pursued the idea with BYU officials. Together they worked out a plan wherein the GMC itself would enroll students from its stake and ward programs for classes at BYU in conducting and organ instruction. Sad to say, if anything ever did materialize from this carefully organized and detailed venture, it was short-lived.

Robertson likewise endeavored to find more instructors and instruction in music for Church members outside Utah. He worked closely with the music faculty at Ricks College, and always encouraged ward and stake musicians to enroll in choral and organ classes being taught without charge at the public institutions in their own communities.

However, by far the most dramatic and biggest step forward in this ever-expanding education project came in late 1967 when the GMC learned that beginning in 1968, the Church would add another layer of administration by combining stakes into regions, and would henceforth conduct additional conferences throughout the Church on this new regional level. Seeing this as an opportunity for even more widespread and better organized instruction, Robertson succeeded in getting music placed on the regular agendas of these regional conferences. The plan was for all stake music personnel to meet together, under the direction of a representative from Church headquarters, who could then give personal and direct information from the GMC as to policies, practices, and specific programs being developed. Not surprisingly, Robertson endeavored to have ward as well as stake music leaders in attendance if possible.

As soon as it was announced that regional conferences would include music sessions, interest ran high. Before long Robertson would remark:

> My telephone has been ringing all afternoon about organ lessons, etc.—The phones have been going like crazy.

For these regional music sessions, the GMC prepared detailed outlines of the material to be covered. However, the overall program purposely remained adaptable enough for each regional music representative to make use of his own ideas. One of the GMC's main goals was to help the stake music leaders assume the responsibility for carrying out the teaching programs already in place. And if a stake did not itself have musicians qualified enough to do this, the GMC stood ready to send out the needed instructors, one more step in Robertson's plan to get effective music instruction to the people. The GMC certainly realized that the regional music sessions could not be a "total or final answer to the problem of providing well-trained music leadership to this fast-growing and expanding Church, [but they hoped to] point the right direction."

For all of these regional sessions, either members of the GMC itself or assigned representatives—chosen by Robertson from among the Church's outstanding trained musicians—went out to teach. To add to the "faculty" he had already recruited, Robertson again reached out across the land, and obtained yet even more professionals, ranging from Seattle to Boston to Florida, and, as usual, points in between. One member described this recruitment as "the most promising thing in Church music in 30 years."

Robertson himself taught at conferences in the Salt Lake area. His outline for one of these classes shows the fresh and broad insight he could still bring to an age-old and persistent problem:

> Tempos (for singing)
> (1) Affected by building; size of congregations; singing ability and desire to sing; resonance; reverberation; [time allowed or needed for] recordings (5 min., etc.).
> (2) Good average possible.
> (3) Dignified tempos—have been properly felt by congregations over the years.

He then discussed the rather recent tendency for "hurried hymns," which, though they seem to have more life, are "better as accompaniment, not for singing."

One anecdote illustrates his own feelings about fast tempos for congregational singing. Once, upon leaving a sacrament meeting where one of his own hymns had been sung, he met a member who remarked how good it must be for a composer to hear one of his hymns. Robertson sullenly retorted, "They took it so fast I didn't recognize it."

Through these regional music sessions, the GMC directly contacted members far and wide. After eighteen months, Robertson reported:

> We have been able with the help of outstanding musicians called to this work to cover all the regions of this country (USA), parts of Canada, the British Isles, [Holland,] West Germany, and Switzerland.

Information coming from the various regional representatives of these music sessions showed that the needs and concerns were many, and that worldwide, the problems were the same: organization, quality of performance, and appropriate repertoire. Robertson conscientiously studied these reports and used them as a basis for developing further projects.

To improve the necessary communication between the GMC and local leaders, and to supplement the ongoing classes and regional sessions, the GMC prepared and sent out frequent and regular publications. In addition to these, six new handbooks were to be prepared; films were being presented with great success; and with unusual foresight, Robertson suggested that television be used "on an extended scale in the future."

Also, the GMC had to solve the ever-increasing need for hymnbooks in translation; and by 1968, several standard hymns had been put into ten European languages. Moreover, work was proceeding on getting hymns and certain anthems translated for Chinese-speaking members, as well as people in Vietnam, Thailand, and Lebanon.

Of all these publications, one that especially captivated Robertson, as father and grandfather, was the new children's songbook then in progress. With Robert Cundick, the book's immediate supervisor, Robertson personally examined the many manuscripts submitted and freely offered advice. He encouraged Cundick to seek out the current "new crop" of LDS composers, but was pleased to find any material of musical worth whether it came from the trained or untrained musician. One song about pioneer children who "walked and walked and walked and walked," brought a particularly big smile to his face as he insisted, "We've got to include that one. It is really sweet."

Of course, these new GMC initiatives for upgrading Church music could not proceed untroubled. Whereas many grateful members did express gratitude for Robertson's leadership, others vehemently complained, demanding still more recognition and use of trained musicians, more encouragement for LDS composers, and more direct contact with the GMC, especially Robertson. Some opined that the music program should be put on a status equaling that of the other Church auxiliaries. One disgruntled member—himself a regional representative for some of the music sessions—even complained directly to the advisors from the Quorum of the Twelve, maintaining that, in addition to other failures, the GMC was "about 20 years behind the times [and] isolated from the needs and desires and realities of musical life in the Wards and Stakes."

Though some of these grievances obviously resulted from incomplete knowledge as to the GMC's workload, many did indeed echo Robertson's own concerns, concerns which he hoped to address as he set about planning the second year of music sessions—now lengthened and expanded—at the Churchwide regional conferences.

Then unobtrusively, deep and unexpected changes began to appear. In late 1968, word came to the GMC of a new policy regarding the use of musical instruments. A special committee, appointed by President David O. McKay to make recommendations for general conference music, had established that henceforth the only instrument to be permitted in general conference would be the organ. President McKay, foreseeing that such a policy "might have a far-reaching effect [and be] applied not only to the Tabernacle but to chapels throughout the Church," asked the GMC members for their opinions in this matter. There is no record of the GMC's responses, but one may rightly conjecture that Robertson held to his long-standing feelings about permitting the use of most instruments in Church services provided the music be appropriate and well played.

The new year, 1969, began. Lengthier regional music sessions and other projects were rolling ahead as planned. But, in early March without warning, a bombshell exploded. The First Presidency informed Robertson and the GMC that the aforementioned special committee on general conference music was now to "have its duties expanded to take over the duties that have been carried on in the past by the General Music Committee. . . . This recommendation was approved with the understanding that you brethren who now form the General Music Committee be considered as consulting advisers to this special committee."

Thus, after nearly fifty years, the General Music Committee was, in effect, dissolved.

Even though Robertson himself may have been fighting terrible discouragement at the seeming lack of progress in really improving Church music—or at least at its slow, slow pace—and though he obediently accepted the pronouncement of these most high Church authorities, he truly did not comprehend their decision. Once again —as he had upon his definitive dismissal from the University of Utah Music Department—he could only ask, "Why, why?"

However, for yet a few months, Robertson was called upon to convene the GMC, but for what practical purpose he sadly wondered:

> We (the Genl Mus Com) are due for a meeting at three. I have just made out an agenda—mostly spiritual and vaporous—since we are floating about without any direction at present and unable to do anything about it. Sometime back our committee was changed from an executive committee to a consulting one, to advise another group. . . . They are supposed to direct the performance now, but thus far nothing is being done or recommended, so our outfit is just marking time. . . . I feel that we did have a program set in motion, which, if it could have been followed up and developed, might have done a lot of good, but I fear that all this has now come to an end, and things will revert back, as the Book of Mormon states, to where "The sow goes to her mire and the dog to its vomit."

Then, in a burst of Robertson sarcasm, and for a bit of comic relief, he turned to quite another topic:

> I don't believe [President] Nixon has remade any part of our solar system this week, but he has sold some property in Florida and bought some near Los Angeles on the Pacific. He will likely be flying over the Rockies one of these days, so if you feel a warm holy atmosphere descend . . . that may be the reason.

As he faced this personal crisis, Leroy Robertson, who had never been one to indulge in self-pity, once again did as he had done so many times before. He sought solace in hard work. The new special committee was requesting his suggestions for the music program. Simultaneously, he had to evaluate and respond to the reports constantly arriving from the regional music representatives still "out in the field." Robertson well knew that this information—once tabulated and organized—would be of "considerable value in helping plan the Church music program of the future." As he sent a personal note of thanks to each of these regional music representatives, while hiding his own disappointment, he expressed to them his abiding hopes for a continued development of good music in the Church.

Also, at this time, the Church asked him to arrange music for the recently formed Mormon Youth Symphony. So, in early summer, 1969, he refined for them the instrumentation of his *Instrumental Hymnal*. Then, just six months later in January 1970, he was again requested to write for the Church. This time they wanted him to orchestrate five pieces—four by Evan Stephens and another by Ebenezer Beesley—for a special program being planned to commemorate the 150th anniversary of Joseph Smith's First Vision, which had occurred, as Joseph Smith himself described, "on the morning of a beautiful clear day, early in the spring of eighteen hundred and twenty." With the performance scheduled for early April, Robertson had all scores ready for rehearsals by early February, less than four weeks after the request. Even a cursory study of them reveals his innate genius for setting a text so as to enhance its meaning. That he would spend such effort at this time in his life in behalf of other composers' works evidences not only his extreme facility for orchestration, but even more importantly, his devotion to the Church.

Interestingly enough, the First Presidency still addressed him as "Head of the Music Department."[7] However, to a very few close associates, Robertson quietly spoke of "passing on the torch."

Through it all, he still unwaveringly stood as a champion of

---

[7]Joseph Fielding Smith was now President of the Church.

music and its effects upon the human soul. Though he continually decried the downhill, spirit-debasing trend rapidly developing on the Pop Music scene—both within and without the Church—he chose to emphasize "the other side of the coin." For example, at Christmas time, 1970, he thrilled to a Tabernacle concert given by the BYU Philharmonic and "about 6000 students having no limitation as to creed and color":

> I doubt if there has ever been consummated in America such a worthwhile ethical project. Certainly there was a magnificent example of how to bridge the so-called "generation gap," and identify our young people with an experience of real moral and spiritual value.

Also, true to form, he continued to encourage fresh talent and ideas:

> We should certainly not close our eyes and ears to any worthy work that is not traditional. . . . We've had a whole new dimension given us by the space age, and some might think that it will not affect the music and the arts, but it could. . . . I often feel that the music of the future, and church music with it, may well reflect the life and times of things we find hard to comprehend today.

In summary, aside from the innumerable works he composed for his Church—of which the *Oratorio from the Book of Mormon* may prove to be his most enduring contribution—Leroy Robertson left a legacy of ideals and goals for LDS Music. "Goals that we haven't been able to reach yet; we're still striving," one colleague opined. And he ever stood ready to offer practical advice and hope for all those yet to follow:

> What is important is to get started. Perfection certainly is to be desired, but it generally comes where there is patience and persistence. The thing that counts in music is its power to move for good those who create and perform it and those who listen to it. This experience is not reserved for the "high and mighty" alone. In fact it has often been shown that our Father will look upon all humble, honest and sincere effort with favor, if those engaged in His work will do better than their best under all circumstances.

Chapter Twenty-Two

PEGEEN THEN FINALE

IF ever there was a man who consistently strove "to do better than his best under all circumstances," that man was Leroy Robertson. And his own circumstances were growing increasingly difficult with passing time. The old eye troubles which had surfaced during his Boston years and had constantly plagued him thereafter finally became so severe that he could no longer read or decipher music. For example, one day after laboriously trying to sight-read a piano part that would never before have bothered him, he despaired to Naomi, "I couldn't see the notes." Frequent visits to ophthalmologists and the ever-resultant eye glasses offered but slight, and at best, only temporary relief. Already by midsummer, 1967, he would write:

> I can't enjoy myself any place at present except at home with my eyes closed most of the time.

Yet, it was precisely under these conditions that, undeterred, he undertook one of his most ambitious compositions, an opera, no less. Since the mid-1950s, Robertson had been interested in writing such a work and through the years had been looking for suitable subject matter. Finally, after reading many plays, narrative poems, and stories, he settled upon John Millington Synge's *The Playboy of the Western World*, a bittersweet, three-act comedy. Not only did the story and its colorful characters intrigue him, but its vivid, melodious language enchanted him even more. The words just seemed to "sing" for him, and he delighted in repeating Synge's lines aloud, over and over and over again.

Just as he had done with his *Oratorio*, Robertson first edited and laid out the entire libretto. Also he was beginning to write the music. Some sketches in fact date from at least 1962.

As the work progressed, he realized that it had a lighter and more popular appeal than that of a tragic grand opera. Thus early on, he began to envision it as being suitable for Broadway, though it was somewhat different from the standard musicals then in vogue. Characterizing the opus as a Folk Opera, he chose to name it *Pegeen* (the Irish form of "Peggy") after the heroine, who rapidly became for him the main figure. Later, as he got more and more into the opera, he would smile and muse, "I am certainly getting to like that little Pegeen."

By early 1965 he had completed a piano-vocal score of the first act which he showed to his friend, experienced Broadway composer Harold Orlob, and Orlob, in turn, was enthusiastic enough about the score to show it to another veteran Broadway composer, Otto Harbach. Harbach, feeling that "it represented a unique new musical form which would have excellent possibilities for the stage," even had a New York agent contact Robertson. This agent, however, thought that it might be too operatic for Broadway and asked to see more than just the libretto and first act.

But sadly, at the moment, although he had the music fixed clearly in his mind, Robertson could not see well enough to notate it quickly and continually; and unfortunately, it was much too complicated a work for him to dictate to a scribe—had he been able to find one. Thus, he could send no more of the score just then.

In fact, the afflicted composer could no longer see well enough even to drive his car, and was obliged to go back and forth by bus from home to his GMC office downtown. As he described it, even boarding the bus was difficult:

> My eyes have become quite bad of late. In order to determine the number of my bus I have had to wait until it stopped—then get out in front to see what it was—and afterwards checking with the driver too.

In February 1968, his ophthalmologist quite suddenly determined that he should undergo cataract surgery, an operation which was then much more serious and much less satisfactory than it would later become. It did help that this physician took a deep, personal interest in Robertson's case, appreciating his point of view, his reputation and value to society, which, as the distressed composer observed was "something I have not seen in a long time."

He resolutely put his affairs in order, which meant, among other things, finalizing details for the LDS regional music sessions then being instituted for the first time. How he did it all is hard to imagine.

Although Leroy was hopeful about the outcome, Naomi felt a certain foreboding:

> . . . I have a feeling this [cataract surgery] is the beginning of us really going into "old age" . . . [but] we'll hope for the best.

After the surgery and a five-day hospital stay, he returned home. But for some strange reason, he could not see even from the unoperated eye, and "pretty much just kept his eyes closed." However, by mid-February, he was able to pen a few letters, though in very large script with all the customary apostrophes omitted (which was unusual for this meticulous speller):

> If these lines get mixed up its because I cant see very well. The operation was a success according to the doctor and the patient is alive so that's *good*.

For such an active man, the recuperation, though steady, seemed unbearably slow, and time hung heavy:

> I am glad to see the weeks pass. I'm afraid I'll be a nuisance to myself and everyone else for quite awhile until I can see again. . . . its just a matter of waiting for the sight to adjust and I can't be very patient I guess.

One month after the surgery he dryly chronicled his limited activities, activities so atypical for him:

> I spent the morning eating breakfast, soaking my eye (hot packs) at intervals, sketching some musical ideas, washing the dishes—going to sleep in the brown chair. . . , waking up for the telephone—shaving—another call. . . . So you see . . . [all in all], I am able to put in a tremendous day for a person [who is] blind in one eye and can't see out the other.

But Leroy Robertson simply could not stay home "in the brown chair" for long. With son Jim's help, he was soon going to his GMC office to attend to the many projects at hand and convene the needed GMC meetings. Within weeks he could see well enough to once again ride the bus to work, "cross the streets, go up the elevator, fool around in my office, go down the elevator and walk around town, see the number on the bus, ride it home . . . get back to the house and *read* the slick pages of the *Reader's Digest!*"

Then dismayingly, it suddenly became apparent that he would need similar surgery on the other eye, and much sooner than had been expected. With the second surgery scheduled near the end of June, the composer found he had only twelve days to attend to the unusual amount of paper work that had relentlessly been accumulating. Copies of manuscripts needed to be "cleaned up" and sent to Washington, D.C., for copyright registration; he had to ready the final copy of the *Piano Concerto* for the printer—an intricate manuscript of about 120 pages yet to be mounted; as for the GMC, he had to prepare materials for the upcoming Stake Festival Concerts, and make the many contacts necessary to get the next year's regional music sessions underway around the world.

Through it all, he was truly tired and discouraged. Other composers, lesser known but more favored, were receiving grants to have their works recorded. "Everything bad is getting help now," he protested. Just days before re-entering the hospital, he despaired to a daughter:

> . . . we (you and me) are both very busy—the only difference is—your labors are amounting to something while mine are of no consequence.

The second cataract surgery was pronounced successful, but the healing was much, much slower than anyone had anticipated. Light —especially sunlight—he could not tolerate. Barely able to see with either eye, and largely confined to the house for many weeks, he had to endure his lot:

> I have learned with my eye operations that there is nothing a person can do but wait for things to heal, pain to leave, and vision to return in its own time and way.

Yet, despite everything, he somehow kept up his courage and

managed to pass the time:

> During my months at home between and after operations I have been able to get better only because I could find something to do—regulated work and a cheerful attitude is the best medicine.

Though severely restricted in his activities, and feeling quite dependent because he could no longer drive at all, Robertson nonetheless increased his work schedule. In late summer he was attending meetings and giving interviews for the Creativity Institute, and once again regularly taking the bus to his downtown office.

Further, to the surprise of many and much to his delight, in September, Leroy Robertson returned to the University of Utah Music Department, where he had been asked to teach once again—an invitation he had already accepted in mid-July, "depending on the eyes." He would have two undergraduate courses and serve as consultant to the composition students. He had missed this close association with young people, and was eager to be back among them. When asked why, he answered:

> Perhaps I need rejuvenating, . . . I've always received more from my students than I've given. They're so unspoiled, so fresh in their attitudes. Teaching is the choicest kind of life, and I've missed it.

Then, just before his classes were scheduled to start, he realistically quipped:

> I am going up to the doctors to get a new pair of glasses this afternoon. I hope they work out—otherwise the campus hippies will surely be on my back for teaching false doctrine.

As the venerable composer met his young charges, he took special pains to become personally acquainted with each one. He enjoyed walking with one or another to and from class, casually chatting, learning their backgrounds, interests, and needs. During class, as before, he happily and deftly showed these students—most of them neophytes—how to set up their scores so as to get the most sound from the simplest and fewest notes, his wit as sharp as ever. "This score is like a mountain in labor giving birth to a mouse," he remarked once again as he went to the blackboard and quickly sketched the easiest and richest way to set up the sound. Not one student ever guessed how nearly blind was their "new" professor, though some may have wondered why he always rode the bus.

During these late 1960s and early 1970s, performances of Robertson works continued. Locally, Abravanel programmed earlier compositions that for him had become standbys, such as *Punch and Judy* and the "Pastorale" from the *Oratorio*. Whenever these works were performed at school concerts about the Salt Lake Valley—with *Punch and Judy* being an especial favorite—the composer often managed somehow to be in attendance, both encouraged and nostalgic as he heard and re-heard his beloved masterpieces. Other local organizations as well were programming Robertson choral works, which were consistently growing in popularity.

Perhaps more significantly—for it signaled a trend that would continue many decades—his choral numbers were being widely heard outside the Intermountain Region. The "Lord's Prayer" became especially popular, being the regular sign-off theme of the local radio station even in faraway Machias, Maine, as well as part of the standard repertoire of a Japanese Choir in even farther away Tokyo, Japan.

Robertson works recorded by the Tabernacle Choir—both his original compositions and the orchestra-chorus arrangements—came to be consistent best sellers not only in the United States and Canada, but also throughout Europe, especially Great Britain and Scandinavia, as well as Australia.

Moreover, letters asking about his music came from strangers in distant lands. A librarian from Bremen (then in West Germany) wanted to know when the *Oratorio* would be published. A young paralyzed man from the remote island of Saaremaa, Estonia (then behind the Iron Curtain) wished to have an autographed photo. He wrote:

> I was born and I have grown up at the sea and I love the sea very much. I know everything about your activities. I believe you have well deserved. Your works made a deep impression on me.

And a melancholy letter from a German couple living in Canada queried:

Yes, what will the 70s bring? Sometimes I have a dark feelings
. . . cabin and castle will pass away, but I believe that the plans,
the talents and impressions go with us through the gates of death.
Especially with music.

A few local recognitions were coming to Robertson as well. In
the spring of 1968 (between the two eye surgeries), Brigham Young
University honored him at their commencement with the Franklin
S. Harris Fine Arts Award. For Leroy Robertson this was a beautiful
day because despite his health problems, he did enjoy returning to the
campus of his younger days.

About eighteen months later, another significant honor came to
the composer when an Honorum was created in his name at the University of Utah. Sponsored by his students, former students, and
friends, this Honorum—later to become a Foundation—established a
fund to be used for many purposes, of which the most important to
the composer was the annual scholarship to be given to a deserving
University music student, preferably a composer.

This project—the brainchild of Professor Louis W. Booth—was
announced during the University's Twenty-second Annual Chamber
Music Festival and came as a complete surprise to Robertson as he sat
"quietly in the center of the University Music Hall . . . with his wife
and several members of his family, including some grandchildren."

Letters sent to Robertson at this time from former students
reflect the lasting impact he had had upon them. Though each was
unique, they all expressed gratitude. Excerpts from two are cited:

> I began thinking about my violin and how much joy it has
> brought me, especially since I studied with you during the war
> . . . I lived with my husband's parents . . . and took lessons while
> my husband was overseas. I'll always remember how kind you
> were. I have kept playing through the years and only about a
> year ago helped to start an orchestra in Heber [Utah]. We're still
> struggling along with a small group . . . [but] we have played for
> two school operettas.

> The recollection of our meeting last summer causes me to
> reflect with pride that I may regard myself not only as a former
> student of yours, but a present one. Through your disciplines
> you have led us into the soul of music as few can, and the
> opportunity of thanking you is not to be taken lightly.

Even in these difficult later years, Robertson's concern for his former students remained as deep as ever, much like that of a loving grandfather. One young man, grieving over the loss of his first-born, wrote to this understanding teacher and asked to visit him stating:

> You have helped me through other crises. We love you.

With compassion, Robertson replied:

> We were greatly shocked to learn of the death of your baby. It seems like the passing of our own little ones. . . . When we see our baby [grandson] we are constantly reminded of you and your great loss. . . .
>   It is comforting to know that you have lived to merit the admiration, love and support from your many associates and from your Heavenly father who will care for you and your baby in the veiled interim which will separate you for a short time. . . . Sister Robertson and our family will be happy to see you anytime.

*   *   *   *   *

Despite such honors and close ties, during these last years of the 1960s and beginning 1970s, gone indeed were the challenging days of Leroy Robertson's powerful and active participation on the music scene, whether international, national, or local. With the 1968 classes at the University of Utah, his long public teaching career had ended. With the dissolution of the GMC in 1969, his regular service to the General Music Program of the Church had also come to a close. Rarely seeing any of his former University or Church colleagues, he felt isolated, even bitter at times. Nonetheless he did not stay at home and lament.

About a year after the dissolution of the GMC, the LDS Church moved him to a small, cubbyhole office in one of their downtown buildings, which barely had space for a desk, a chair, and one large filing cabinet. With no piano, no blackboard, no view to speak of, it was an office quite unlike any he had ever known. Yet, every day, this dogged man went by bus to that little room, and day in, day out, he worked on manuscripts, mainly preparing copies of his earlier big compositions for final printing and publication—even though he could no longer see well enough to do the fine transcribing.

In fact, for many decades he had trained and employed several copyists, mostly students able and willing to do such demanding work. With no computer technology then available, each page demanded hours of arduous labor, and there had been literally thousands of pages to be copied over time. Of the many copyists who had helped, two in particular stand out for their meticulous, artistic autography: Norma Lee Belnap (née Madsen), and Henry Maiben. Of course, perfectionist that he was, after each page was copied, Robertson himself proofread every detail, editing, and, if necessary, correcting any inadvertent errors that may have crept in.

During these years, Robertson was very much concerned about getting final, published copies of his scores out into the world. Since the late 1930s, musicians in both America and Europe had often asked for his scores, and requests were still ongoing.

Of all his large scores, the one that most consistently occupied him at this time was the *Trilogy*, a work so large, detailed, and complex that even after thirty years, no final printed copy had yet been made from his original manuscript. Although Henry Maiben had many years previous undertaken the task of making such a copy, the transcribing had gone very slowly and yet remained unfinished. In order to speed things along, Robertson himself was now spending hours every day correcting and mounting the large pages. Sometimes he could not conceal his frustration:

Sunday 3:20 P.M.
I am down in my office . . . its almost time for me to leave the *Trilogy* mess I'm in and go home. On the way I will stop [at the grocery store] for a cabbage head, etc. . . . My head feels like a cabbage right now so maybe I can pass that off to mother for the real thing.

And again:

I have become involved in finishing up the last half dozen pages of the *Trilogy* and once at it and in it I have been afraid to quit for fear, as Henry's mother said, it would take another twenty years to complete the job.
My eyes have been real obliging so I have been able to do the manuscript as well as ever and I have really saved time in not waiting on copyists.

At last, after more than twenty years work, this final score —unbelievable in its beauty—was ready for the printer, and in early fall, 1970, Robertson at last got a copyright for *Trilogy*, his "Wayward Child" of the late 1930s. With this masterwork now printed, Robertson finally had enough copies on hand to send to all those requesting the score. He could not help but remark:

> It seems rather ironic that the *Trilogy* should be among the last [of my compositions] to be released, but it has been because the others have just pushed it aside.

With printed copies now available for immediate and widespread distribution, Robertson also had high hopes of getting the work recorded. Abravanel wished to record it with the Utah Symphony, and Vox Records was equally interested in the project. But, as had been the case so many times before, funding became a problem. Once again, *Trilogy*'s very size created a stumbling block. Due to the extra players and rehearsal time it required, the additional monies could not be found. *Trilogy* seemed destined to remain with its composer, unheard and unrecorded. Yet another disappointment to absorb.

* * * * *

Often, after spending those long hours poring over his scores, Robertson would relax in mid-afternoon by writing letters. They show how he coped with his ever present fatigue and growing health problems. Although they contain touches of bitter sarcasm, behind the words one can sense that old Sanpete humor:

> 3:15 not A.M.
> This piece of paper has been *lying around* on my desk all day so I am going to put it to some other use—what follows will be of a truthful nature if that is within my power. This time of day I am so drowsy and vacant that there is plenty of room for truthful ideas to enter if not exit . . . without effort and strain.
>
> I think I should join Mike [an eight-month-old grandson] in his sleeping every afternoon. [But I should really] find a way to stay awake long enough to get caught up with all my requirements and enjoy more of the daylight hours, etc.—especially now that one should be saving them for a wise and noble purpose instead of yawning and wasting away . . . without being able to live to the full and enjoy and appreciate all the important things that

[President] Nixon is doing for mankind in general and me in particular according to everything I am hearing over the air and reading in the papers which seem to be loaded with pleasurable propaganda to be enjoyed now if possible, otherwise in the near and far distant future.

As the foregoing hints, the composer would amuse himself from time to time by taking potshots at both the media and the Washington scene:

3:00 P.M.

I am quite confused about national issues but since there are others in Washington as mixed up as I am I shall let them enlighten the country when they are able—since they seem to be in reverse, they may help things out best by backing into the ocean.

. . . should I add a little more fertilizer to the state of the national messages which are coming so fast now [that they are] more or less a 'mess' minus the 'ages.'. . .

I have nothing to report on the national scene except that the bull is growing daily into an enormous animal.

Now and again, the then-current President, Richard Nixon, whom Robertson dubbed "the Whittier windmill," seemed a fair target:

The Whittier windmill is not pumping today as far as I know —but since I have not yet read the Sunday funnies I cannot say for sure whether the pump is in action or not—it likely pumps hot air regardless, so you can count on that.

I stayed home yesterday and was fit to be tied by night—I was in a mood to preach and wave my arms like you-know-who, but I knew it would not help the tax bill for the middle class so I kept my silence and sat in the chair with my feet on the [foot]stool.

As a final "P.S.," he once added:

I have lost track of Nixon. I hope he hasn't.

Although Robertson himself was unwilling to recognize—much less admit it—the years were, as Naomi wrote on their forty-third wedding anniversary, "passing very fast." Over time, many dear colleagues had passed away, which Leroy had seemed to take in stride. But finally, when he learned of the death of Cleveland Orchestra's

George Szell, he was somehow jolted into facing his own mortality. Remembering also Arnold Schoenberg, Ernest Bloch and other close colleagues now gone, he could only remark in anguish, "All my friends are dying."

During the late 1960s, as circumstances made him ever more isolated from his former colleagues, he sought and found solace in his family. He went on outings with his brothers and sisters; and as a caring father, he showed constant concern for his children—now grown and gone from home—being ever mindful of their problems and successes. However, it was now the grandchildren who were bringing him his happiest moments. As son Jim would later write:

> Dad always had a special place in his heart for babies, and when the grandchildren began to come on the scene, the entertainment of days past was reborn. To watch [this] grandpa around his [little ones] would almost bring tears to your eyes. In public, it was almost embarrassing the way he would try different ways to amuse . . . and keep them happy—and then one became aware of the deep love he was unashamedly expressing—and the climate suddenly changed to *very* proud.

From youngest to oldest, each child brought him special joy:

> I never saw anything so cute as Michael when he came crawling out of the bedroom toward us.
>
> David writes some stunning little letters. His spelling puts the Eng. language to shame for its fonetic faults.
>
> I have not found a more apt little student on the violin in a long time [referring to granddaughter Kaye].

And day after day, with one grandchild or another sitting on his lap and at his feet, he would spin out wonderful, spellbinding stories invented on the spot, much as he had done for his own little children in earlier years, and much as his own beloved "Grandpaw Robertson" had done so very long ago for all the children of Fountain Green.

Needless to say, the closest companion of all was Naomi, with whom he now shared life's simple pleasures, such as helping her find some spring garden plants, and "going out for noodles," one of their long-standing traditions. And when she was feeling "the winter blues," he would leave his office earlier than usual, and come home to try and do whatever he could to lift her spirits:

> 3 P.M.
> I am going home and take mother out some place to eat. . . . She doesn't want to leave the house . . . [but] perhaps a change out in the weather will snap her out of her ailments.

Thus, as the 1970s rolled in, Leroy Robertson's life became very private and plain. Every day he went by bus to his downtown office, where he continued editing his large scores—especially the *Trilogy*, for although these works had now been published, Robertson, ever the perfectionist, still pored over them with an eagle eye, catching and correcting any "leftover" errors—slow work for him to be sure. At home, he was always composing, though not at the intense pace of years past. And ever the teacher, he also spent one afternoon at home each week giving theory lessons to a group of women anxious to learn from this master-composer.

After more than seventy years of composing, and now established as "one of the top few American composers," one may wonder what skills was he now passing on to others? What ideas concerning music and composing had he crystallized? One reporter wrote about and described him as follows:

> . . . a methodical, adroit man, his three-button suit buttoned, his speech true and lucid, his presence proper and ever cognizant; . . . glib only after he formulates his thoughts and never faulting —perhaps the quintessence of neoclassic man.

When asked to evaluate his own music, Robertson did become reluctant:

> The true artist is never fully aware of the substance of his work. To make positive declarations here would be to enforce limitations on the product.

But then he added:

> I will say one thing about my music. I have always tried to write it honestly and in the best fashion I know. By being honest I mean that it happens naturally, but it is never naive or innocent in that sense.
> Rather it comes from a mind highly disciplined, solidly grounded in the masterful thinking of the past.

Actually at the base of any good music there are the elements of facility and excellence. It is only from here that the creative process happens naturally.

I have tried to speak the same language as the people. And that is difficult in an age of multiplicity.

Next, quoting Pierre Boulez, renowned French composer and then conductor of the New York Philharmonic, Robertson continued:

We are living in a blotter society which absorbs everything. Of course, it's preferable to the nineteenth century, which condemned everything new, but in our present abundance of artistic viewpoints, there are many which only seem new the first time and then degenerate into experimental facility.

Speaking for himself, he inserted:

That's something I've never done . . . nor will ever do [i.e., compose only to follow some experimental fad].

Once again citing Boulez and recalling his own experiences, Robertson continued:

Today the same composer can be booed in his lifetime by one audience because he is too advanced and by another because he is behind the times.

Ever holding to his favorite definition from Longinus that the greatest masterpiece is "that which appeals to the greatest variety of taste over the longest period of time," he simply stated:

Knowing this, I have tried to write music that will do the same.

As a composer, Robertson realized the importance of performers, for, as he explained, all music is really brought to life by its interpreter, who continually "re-creates" [the piece] for everyone. In this vein he often stated, " A composer should write just the right amount—not too much and not too little." He then explained:

The composer should create enough structure for the performing artists to . . . grasp and use. However, he must not create too much structure or else he will limit severely how much . . . involvement, . . . personal style and [other] characteristics that the performing artist can . . . [bring] to produce a creative, rather than a mechanical performance.

He further elaborated elsewhere:

> No matter the composition, the gifted interpreter can unearth nuances and undercurrents perhaps never before realized—for all concerned. . . . The performer is the catalyst who makes the work work for an audience . . . and all good works have the capacity for re-creation. In all good lasting works there are avenues for the performer and conductor to give exposure to their [own] insight and vision. That is why they [good works] last.

Leroy Robertson had long ago experienced and come to understand that rather cryptic Picasso statement, which he often quoted:

> First one finds; then one seeks.[1]

* * * * *

As to his ongoing composing projects, it was *Pegeen* that continued to capture most of his attention. Though this opera would remain unfinished on paper, there is no doubt that in Robertson's mind, it was essentially finished. The libretto was completely written, and he had the entire work outlined and even timed down to the last minute. As to the notated music, the vocal-piano score of the first two acts and much of the third did get put on paper.

As has been mentioned, although Synge's play is, all in all, a rough satire, Robertson chose to turn *Pegeen* into a love story with a happy ending. Albeit written by a man in his seventies, very ill and virtually blind, the passion and love expressed in the music remain those of a heart forever young.

About two-thirds into Act Three, there comes a "Betrothal Song" to be sung by the hero and heroine, Christy and Pegeen. Sadly, after this eloquent number, except for brief sketches here and there, we find less and less notated music. Both in the rest of the score and throughout Robertson's notations in his edition of Synge's text, he did sketch the musical motifs and forms he had planned

---

[1]Robertson often attributed this statement to Goethe, but it actually came to the composer's attention via a letter written by Jean Cocteau to the author. Cocteau credits the remark to Picasso.

(Fugue, Double Fugue, Waltz, etc.), but between these sketches, the pages left empty and waiting for the composer's actual notes gradually increase. Finally, only blank manuscript sheets remain.

But interestingly enough, while *Pegeen* was to be left unfinished, there is evidence that Robertson still had even more and larger works germinating within. On one of those empty, unnumbered pages near the end of the *Pegeen* score, we find a sketch—very rapidly notated— of a whirling, developing triplet theme entitled "Gypsy Dance," *Rasputin*. And indeed, for quite some time he had been envisioning another music drama, this one to be a large Grand Opera based on that charismatic mystic who had held such power over the last Tzarina of Russia. Also, on a separate piece of manuscript paper, tucked alongside variants of his text to the "Betrothal Song," we find other quickly notated sketches labeled: *Symphony*: "Theme I, Theme II"; and *Clarinet Quintet*. Thus, even as his physical strength was steadily ebbing, for him new dreams and works lay yet ahead.

Then, one Thursday morning, in mid-July 1971, Leroy Robertson arose, dressed, and prepared to take the bus downtown and go to his office as usual. But this day, he simply could not muster the strength to leave the house and walk to the bus stop. As the hours passed, and the scheduled time for each bus came and went, he repeatedly decided "to wait and catch the next one." For the first time in his life, Leroy Robertson could not get himself to work. Finally, in late afternoon Naomi phoned Leroy's physician, who advised him to get to the hospital. After tests revealed that his heart condition—a result of the diabetes—had grown worse, he was admitted directly into the Intensive Care Unit. No one knew what to expect.

Every morning before 6:00 A.M., Naomi journeyed crosstown to the hospital to care for her husband, who had quickly become too weak and tired even to feed himself. As the busy nurses left each tray of food, it was Naomi who patiently and gently helped him eat. For days, he was moved back and forth in the ICU from a very small room where he lay alone to a larger one shared with two other men. During one of these short jaunts, he mustered enough of his old humor to joke, "I hope the hospital isn't charging me for transportation."

Somehow, word of Robertson's illness reached Abravanel, who was then spending the summer as director of the Music Academy of the West in Santa Barbara. Alarmed, and wishing to bring some cheer and encouragement to his longtime friend, the Maestro insisted on getting a direct telephone line hooked to Robertson's ICU bedside, an almost impossible feat to accomplish at that time. Abravanel at once greeted Robertson with the exciting news that his *Oratorio from the Book of Mormon* had already been scheduled for Utah Symphony performances the following spring. Robertson no doubt was glad, but much too ill to generate much enthusiastic reaction.

His family—brothers, sisters, children, and always, Naomi—went to the hospital every day, but their visits were restricted to a few minutes each waking hour. However, late every evening, two special visitors were allowed to see him for a moment: his loyal student, Crawford Gates, who was in Salt Lake conducting nightly performances of his musical *Promised Valley*; and son Jim, who was himself playing in the orchestra for these performances. Around midnight, after each show, they both stopped in to see their friend and bid him "Good Night."

Came July 24, Utah's State Holiday, and as Naomi made a late afternoon visit, she smiled to her beloved, "Well, here is your 'Old Faithful.'" Leroy replied, "You'll never be 'old' to me," and then softly he sang to her in his high tenor voice:

> Believe me, if all those endearing young charms
> Which I gaze on so fondly today,
> Were to change by tomorrow, and fleet in my arms,
> Like fairy gifts, fading away,
> Thou would'st still be adored as this moment thou art,
> Let thy loveliness fade as it will;
> And around the dear ruin, each wish of my heart
> Would entwine itself verdantly still.

Gently she kissed him.

Early next morning—it was at first light on a Sunday—the telephone jangled everyone awake in the White House on 1400 East. The hospital was summoning Naomi and her children to come at once, and in anguish, they rushed crosstown, not daring to believe the end was near.

Leroy Robertson died before his loved ones could reach him. His great heart, so tired and broken during those last years, finally just stopped.

But, as he had lain dying, the bright summer sun had also been rising from behind the high Wasatch Range, its rays striking first the rims of the imposing Oquirrh Mountains on the west—for in the high mountain valleys of Utah, daylight always creeps in from west to east. Soon the entire Valley of the Great Salt Lake was glowing in a golden, golden light. To his stunned, grief-burdened family, it seemed to signal that a very special soul was being welcomed into heaven.

EPILOGUE

LEROY Robertson, a man with the greatest of hearts who ironically died of heart failure; a visionary who embodied both imaginative idealism and unsentimental practicality; a determined soul of uncompromising integrity and great humanity—what was his legacy? Why is he remembered?

As to his tightly knit family—his brothers and sisters, his children and their children—they all may well tell their own stories, each one being fascinating and unique.

As to his students—too numerous to name and scattered across the globe—they also bear his mark, each in a different way. But be they musicians—teachers, performers, composers—or be they in other professions, they all felt and were impressed by this teacher's high standards, his love for great music and his belief in what it offers the human spirit. And they, in turn, have helped and are yet helping others.

As to his music, its popularity waxes and wanes with the passing years. But, without fanfare, it steadily persists. The *Quintet*, the *String Quartet*, *Trilogy*, the *Oratorio*, the *Passacaglia*, and his many other compositions—works that he affectionately called his "brain-children"—have reached audiences on every continent. Heard at different times and in different places, some, to be sure, have had more performances than others. But the depth and freshness of each one will touch any listener.

More than two decades after the composer's death, there was a funeral in Fountain Green for a close Robertson relative. As Prelude and Postlude music, the organist played nothing but hymns by Leroy, and, as requested, two of his daughters performed another of his pieces as a special number during the services. The people of this beloved home town had taken his music to their hearts.

Truly it has always lived amongst them. Born in the Rocky Mountains, expressing the beauties of high peaks and vast deserts, it speaks of Fountain Green, of Utah, of the Intermountain West. Having travelled north, south, east, and west, over diverse, sundry lands and across wide, wide oceans, the music of Leroy Robertson lives on also for the world to hear and know.

APPENDICES

Appendix A

NAOMI NELSON

NAOMI Nelson was born December 18, 1900, in Milton, Morgan County, Utah, where she spent her childhood and youth.[1] Like Leroy, she had a pioneer heritage. Her Danish father, Waldemar Theodore Nelson, walked across the plains from Iowa to Utah as a seven-year-old boy leading his little sister by the hand and allowed to ride in the old wagon only when the going was particularly difficult, or if he was sick.[2] At age fourteen, he worked on the last lap of the transcontinental railroad, and was present at the driving of the Golden Spike that linked the West and East Coasts. Later, he ran a dry farm. Naomi's mother, Karen Marie Jensen Nelson, was among the first white children to be born in Morgan County. A premature baby, Karen Marie, or "Mary," as she was called, weighed but two pounds at birth, an infant so small that her parents tenderly placed her in a wool-lined shoe and gently bathed her in a two-quart cup. She and Waldemar grew up in Milton. When Waldemar's first wife, Caroline, died in childbirth, leaving him with a newborn baby boy and a little two-year-old girl, he began to court young Mary, who had been Caroline's best friend and whom the dying Caroline had asked to care for her babes. Mary finally responded to Waldemar's entreaties, and when she was but eighteen years old, she married him. They eventually became the parents of thirteen children, and

---

[1] Renee R. Whitesides, "Family Record Sheets."

[2] Naomi Nelson Robertson (henceforth NNR), as recounted to the author.

together, reared a family of twelve: six boys and six girls, of whom Naomi was the youngest girl.[3]

A charming child, she quickly became the center of the family's interest and her father's true pride and delight, for she was the only one of his children to learn and remember how to speak his native Danish.[4] With her winning disposition, she soon was popular not only with her family and immediate friends, but also with the boys of the nearby communities. She was a bright student, and after eight years of grade school in Milton and three years of high school in Morgan—where she placed first in the county scholastic exams, as did all of her brothers and sisters—she continued her education, first at Weber Normal College in Ogden, then in Logan at the Utah State Agricultural College, popularly called the "AC."[5]

However, she had to interrupt her studies twice to earn enough money to help pay for her schooling. After just one year at Weber, she obtained a Teaching Certificate, and was immediately hired to teach in the new Elementary School at Peterson (a small Morgan County community). Here, in one room, she taught third, fourth, and fifth grades, having a grand total of twenty-six pupils under her care. The next year she was able to begin her studies at the AC, where she remained two years before dropping out, once again to teach, this time in the grade school at Uintah (a small community at the mouth of Weber Canyon). She proved to be a good teacher, always much liked by her students.[6]

After a year at Uintah, she returned to the AC, and graduated in June 1924, with a degree in Home Economics, and a contract in hand to teach in Utah County.

---

[3]Three of their children died in infancy. Mary mothered Waldemar's two children from his first marriage as if they were her own.

[4]NNR, as recounted to the author.

[5]NNR, interview. While in Ogden, Naomi lived at the home of her eldest sister, Zetta (Rozetta) Nelson Wilson; in Logan she lived at the homes of two other sisters, Mabel Nelson Fry and Linda Nelson Benson.

[6]This paragraph, plus the information following, is from NNR, interview.

She thought she was going to Lehi High School, a place she had at least heard of because of its good basketball team. However, one week before school was to start, she received a letter informing her that she had been transferred to Pleasant Grove, a town and school whose name she did not even know. She managed to arrive one day ahead of schedule, just in time for the Teachers Institute where she met Leroy Robertson.

Appendix B

TRILOGY TAX CASE

THERE was a spin-off from the *Trilogy* award that made this symphony almost as renowned in the legal profession as it became in the music world. From the outset, Robertson was not sure how much of the $25,000 would go for taxes. When J. Reuben Clark, Jr., opined that the award was a gift rather than earned income and advised Robertson to "get a good lawyer,"[1] the Utahn decided to seek legal counsel about the tax situation. While in Detroit, he conversed with a prominent attorney, who, after informally discussing the particulars with several tax experts, encouraged Robertson to pursue the matter.[2]

Therefore, upon his return to Utah, Robertson found a competent young attorney, Sam Blackham, who agreed to take the case free of charge if they lost. Robertson paid the tax under protest, then filed suit to recover the overpayment. He did not object to paying some income tax, but argued that since the *Trilogy* had been written in 1938-1939, and not specifically for the Symphony of the Americas Contest, the $25,000 should be taxed at the 1938-1939 rates—if at all—rather than at the 1947 rates, a difference amounting to more the $6,000.[3]

The case did not come to trial until July 1950. It was held in Salt

---

[1] J. Reuben Clark, Jr., 'Remarks,' in "Program of Tribute in Honor of LeRoy J. Robertson," Harold R. Clark, ed., typescript (Provo, Utah: Brigham Young University, November 25, 1947), p. 34.

[2] Karl M. Richards, Attorney for Automobile Manufacturers Association, letter to LJR, December 15, 1947.

[3] *The Salt Lake Tribune*, July 2, 1950.

Lake Federal Court, Judge Willis Ritter presiding.[4] Robertson won this decision, but lost on appeal to the Circuit Court of Appeals in Denver.[5] Feeling that he was in the right, Robertson stubbornly took the case to the United States Supreme Court, which gave it a hearing in April 1952.[6] Robertson lost in a five-four decision, with a strong minority opinion written by Justice Williams O. Douglas.

Though Robertson lost, this case and his arguments became standard references for subsequent trials, with law students routinely studying the case. Eventually his position prevailed.

---

[4]*Ibid.*

[5]Attorney Sam Blackham, letter to LJR, July 12, 1951.

[6]This became Case No. 388, October Term, 1951: Robertson v. United States. See Charles E. Cropley, Clerk [of the] Supreme Court of the United States, letters to Sam Blackham, January 3 and 5, 1952; and Sam Blackham, letter to LJR, describing his arguments before the Supreme Court, April 9, 1952.

Appendix C
1965 LETTER FROM ROBERTSON
TO THE LDS GENERAL AUTHORITIES

THOUGH many of Leroy Robertson's efforts in behalf of Church music left intangible marks, one petition to the Church General Authorities did have a very practical result. In 1965, upon leaving the Music Department of the University of Utah, he wrote to one of the GMC advisors from the Quorum of the Twelve:

> On July 1st, 1965 I will retire from the University of Utah. At this time it would be a great help to me if I could be employed by the Church at a salary of $100.00 a month to supplement my social security and modest retirement income. Since the position as Chairman of the General Music Committee is a professional one, the brethren who have held it in the past have been salaried.
> . . .
> There is a great deal of work to be done in expanding the music education program, preparing and selecting repertoire and co-ordinating and improving the performance programs of the various organizations of the Church. As I see it this requires professional supervision for the best results.
> Thanking you for your consideration of this letter, I am . . .[1]

---

[1]LJR, letter to Harold B. Lee, May 19, 1965. The previous GMC Chairmen, Apostle Melvin J. Ballard and Tracy Y. Cannon, had been salaried, but not only for their service as GMC Chairmen. Brother Cannon, for example, was also director of the McCune School of Music, while Elder Ballard fulfilled the duties of an Apostle. Robertson was thus the first to have the GMC chairmanship *per se* become a salaried position. Having lost any benefits he may have accrued during his twenty-three years at BYU, and with less than twenty years of service at the University of Utah, Robertson did indeed have a small retirement income during his last years.

The General Authorities granted this request, and henceforth, Robertson did receive that modest monthly stipend.[2] Thereby, he laid the groundwork for the future appointment of a full-time salaried GMC Chairman.[3]

---

[2]See LDS receipt of payment, July 1971.

[3]With the reconstitution of the GMC, Dr. Michael Moody became its full-time chairman in 1974. The GMC now consists of twelve regular members, plus other *ad hoc* members as needed. M. Moody, phone interview with the author, August 24, 1993.

Appendix D

THE LEROY ROBERTSON COLLECTION
AT THE UNIVERSITY OF UTAH

THROUGHOUT his life, Leroy Robertson carefully cared for his scores, manuscripts, and other pertinent documents, eventually storing them in file cabinets in his Music Department office at the University of Utah. However, upon his definitive departure from the Music Department, he decided to find a more permanent home for this material.

Therefore, in late 1966, he met with University of Utah Director of Libraries, Ralph D. Thomson, to discuss a proposal similar to that made so many years previous regarding the Leichtentritt Collection, i.e., in return for a modest sum to be paid Robertson over a few years, the library would posthumously acquire all his papers.[1] These papers would include the composer's scores (original and published), correspondence, photographs, recordings, and certain Leichtentritt materials still in Robertson's possession.[2]

An agreement was reached in 1967, whereby the composer was to receive stipulated payments over a short period of time, and the aforementioned materials would be shipped to the library when indicated.

Immediately upon Robertson's death in July 1971, the library took control of these papers, which went to the Special Collections

---

[1] Ralph D. Thomson, Director of Libraries, letter to LJR, December 28, 1966.

[2] See University of Utah Purchase Order No. 85420, signed by University of Utah Purchasing Agent, William L. Christensen, June 21, 1967.

Department of the Marriott Library. The monumental task of sorting and classifying all this diverse material fell upon Robertson's daughter, Karen R. Post, and librarian Della L. Dye. The Robertson Collection consists of thirty-five boxes that cover some nineteen linear feet of shelf space.[3]

Since Leroy Robertson's death, his survivors have continued to contribute additional manuscripts and recordings.

Two separate registers for the Robertson Collection have been published:

> *Register of the Papers of LeRoy J. Robertson* (Salt Lake City: Special Collections Department, University of Utah Libraries, 1972; rev. 1980).

> *Register of the Annotated Bibliography of the Compositions of LeRoy J. Robertson* (Salt Lake City: Special Collections Department, University of Utah Libraries, 1985).

---

[3]See *Register of the Papers of LeRoy J. Robertson* (Salt Lake City: Special Collections Department, University of Utah Libraries, 1972; rev. 1980), p. iv.

SELECTED BIBLIOGRAPHY

Conversations and Tape-recorded Interviews with Author

The present location of all tape-recorded interviews, recordings, and unpublished material can be found in the endnotes of the companion manuscript.

Abravanel, Maurice. Interviews, Salt Lake City, October 5, 1981, October 15, 1981, and late October 1981.

Anderson, Macel Robertson. Interview, Salt Lake City, December 1, 1980.

Barrus, LaMar. Interview, Rexburg, Idaho, September 28, 1981.

Cundick, Robert. Interview, Salt Lake City, July 5, 1980.

Durham, Lowell M. Interviews, Salt Lake City, May 22, 1980, May 29, 1980, and June 5, 1980.

Folland, Harold. Interview, Salt Lake City, May 23, 1980.

Folland, Helen. Interview, Salt Lake City, May 23, 1980.

Foulger, Josephine, Tabernacle Choir Historian. Phone conversations, June 15, 1993, and March 27, 1995.

Gifford, Mary, et al., LDS Church Historian's Office. Phone conversations, Salt Lake City, ca. 1985-1996.

Jones, McClelland (Kelly). Interview, Salt Lake City, July 8, 1980.

Keeler, J. J. Interview, Provo, Utah, July 8, 1983.

Moody, Michael, chairman of LDS General Music Committee (hereafter GMC). Phone conversations, Salt Lake City, 1990-1995.

Robertson, Doyle E. Interview, Salt Lake City, September 11, 1987.

Robertson, Joseph A. Interview, Salt Lake City, November 10, 1981.

Robertson, Naomi Nelson. Interview, Salt Lake City, Fall of 1980.

Robertson, Wanda. Interview, Salt Lake City, December 1980.

Sardoni, Lawrence. Interview, Provo, Utah, July 6, 1983.
Schreiner, Alexander. Interview, Salt Lake City, May 19, 1980.
Watts, Ardean. Interview, Salt Lake City, June 19, 1980.
Weight, Newell. Interview, Salt Lake City, early May 1980.
Whitesides, Stephen E. Phone conversations, Salt Lake City, 1955-1995.

Recordings with Commentary by Leroy Robertson and Announcer

Detroit Symphony Broadcast, ABC Network, Detroit, December 14, 1947.
Philadelphia Orchestra Broadcast, Philadelphia, April 1, 1960.

Transcripts of Credits Earned by Leroy Robertson

Brigham Young University, Provo, Utah, 1912-1914; 1925-1951.
New England Conservatory, Boston, 1920-1921; 1922-1923.
Pleasant Grove High School, Pleasant Grove, Utah, 1912-1914.
USC Admission Credit Summary Form, Los Angeles, April 7, 1947; and similar forms stamped "Supplementary," March 3, 1948, and February 27, 1951.
USC records, sent to Robertson from registrar's office, Los Angeles, 1936-1954.

Manuscripts

Adams, Melissa J. Caldwell. Diary, n.p., n.d.
_____. "A short skech [*sic*] of my mother Barzilla Guyman Caldwell," n.p., n.d.
Christiansen, Ballard. "The Talented Country Boy," Salt Lake City, ca. 1960.
Clark, Harold R., ed. "Program of Tribute in Honor of LeRoy J. Robertson," Brigham Young University, Provo, Utah, November 25, 1947.
Dalton, David. "How Education Can Help Music in the Church,"

address to BYU student chapter of Music Educators National Conference, Provo, Utah, February 15, 1966.

Despain, Melissa Adams, and Vilate Adams West. "Sketch of William Henry Adams," Pleasant Grove, Utah, n.d.

Koch, Uzella Caldwell. "Biography of Matthew Caldwell," n.p., n.d.

Larson, Mrs. John Farr (Ann Clayson). "Notes from Diary," n.p., 1933-1936.

Petersen, Marian. "LeRoy J. Robertson, Dean of Mormon Composers," Kansas City, Missouri, 1986. This is the most comprehensive biography of Leroy Robertson written prior to the present publication.

Post, Karen Robertson, comp. "Scrapbook about the Leroy Robertson Foundation," Salt Lake City, 1970-1971.

Robertson, James Leroy (Jim). "Family Tribute," Salt Lake City, July 28, 1971.

Robertson, Leroy. "Analysis of Schoenberg's 'Klavierstuck, op. 33,'" Los Angeles, ca. 1936.

_____. "Analysis of the *Trilogy*," Salt Lake City, n.d.

_____. "Biographical Notes," Provo, Utah, 1948.

_____. "Blessed the Bread. . . ." (original pencil corrections of text by Chrisite Lund Coles and melodic line quickly sketched), Salt Lake City, ca. 1968.

_____. "BYU Symphony Orchestra Touring Schedule, March 3-13, 1946," Provo, Utah, February 1946.

_____. "Brief Vita Sheet," Salt Lake City, ca. 1955.

_____. "Chronology," n.p., n.d.

_____. "Class Notes of Lectures given by Samuel W. Cole, Public School Music Notebook, New England Conservatory," Boston, 1922-1923.

_____. "Notes of Lectures given by Dr. Struble, Literary Criticism Class, USC," Los Angeles, October 1946—January 1947.

_____. "Corrections" (handdrawn in published *Trilogy* score), Salt Lake City, 1970-1971.

_____. Correspondence, 1910-1971. Complete details of the voluminous correspondence can be found in the endnotes of the companion manuscript.

_____. "Creativity in Music . . . Other Thoughts on Creativity," Salt Lake City, n.d.

_____. "Criteria for Selection of Band Music" (notes for First Annual Band Symposium, USU), Logan, Utah, June 1966.

_____. "Early Book of Compositions and Sketches," Fountain Green and Pleasant Grove, Utah; en route to Boston; and Boston, 1916-1920.

_____. "Early Notebooks, I, II, and III," Fountain Green, Utah, and Salt Lake City, 1918-1920.

_____. Financial Records, 1920-1971, which include American Express Traveler Cheque Record, 1920; checkbook stubs, 1922-1970; contracts, receipts, and record of payments, 1920-1970, and royalty statements from various publishers, recording companies, and ASCAP.

_____. "Harmonic Analyses," in F. Mendelssohn, *Songs Without Words for Pianoforte* (Schirmer's Library of Musical Classics, 58 [New York: G. Schirmer, 1893]), n.p., April 10, 1918.

_____. "Highlights in the Life of a Master Composer," Salt Lake City, March 1953. A reconstruction of public remarks made by Robertson to the Sons of Utah Pioneers, March 4, 1953.

_____. "Instrumental Combinations and their Relation to Music." M.A. thesis, Brigham Young University, 1932.

_____. "Musical Examples for Use in the Appreciation of Music," (examples taken from *The 'Appreciation' Pianoforte Album*, T. W. Swette and D. G. Mason, eds. [New York, 1907]), Fountain Green, Utah, 1919.

_____. "Music in an Age of Multiplicity" (Schoenberg Public Lecture given at UCLA), Los Angeles, November 18, 1953.

_____. "Notes and Musical Sketches for *Pegeen*," in John Millington Synge, *The Playboy of the Western World*, as found in *The College Survey of English Literature*, Vol. 2, B. J. Whiting et al., eds. (New York: Harcourt, Brace and Company, 1942), Salt Lake City, n.d.

_____. "Notes and Sketches," in E. A. Robinson, *King Jasper, a Poem* (New York: The Macmillan Company, 1935), Salt Lake City, n.d.

_____. "Notes from Class Lectures of Chadwick (Orchestration) and A. E. Foote (Piano Pedagogy), NEC," Boston, October 2, 1920–March 24, 1921.

_____. "Notes from Schoenberg Lectures in Advanced Composition, USC," Los Angeles, June 22, 1936 through rest of summer term.

_____. "Notes in Bach Chorale Studies prepared for Ernest Bloch," San Francisco, 1929.

_____. "Notes of Comments by Ernest Bloch," in LJR sketches of the *Quintet in A Minor*, San Francisco, 1929, or Roveredo-Capriasca, Switzerland, 1932.

_____. "Notes of First European Session with Ernest Bloch," Roveredo Capriasca, Switzerland, July 3, 1932.

_____. "P. A. Christensen," Salt Lake City, February 20, 1961.

_____. *Pegeen, A Folk Opera* ... (unfinished score), Salt Lake City, n.d. Attached thereto is a separate sheet with an outline indicating Robertson's plan of the music and basic action of characters.

_____. "Program Notes for the *Concerto for Violin and Orchestra*," Salt Lake City, ca. 1961.

_____. "The Psychology of Music" (notes prepared for BYU Psychology Class taught by M. Wilford Poulson), Provo, Utah, April 25, 1932.

_____. "Report on Compositions, 1960-1961," Salt Lake City, ca. 1962.

_____. "Report to Harriette Johnson" (editor of *Billboard Music Yearbook*), Provo, Utah, September 1943.

_____. "Report to *Pan Pipes*, 1961-1962," Salt Lake City, January 1963.

_____. "Sketchbook of Original Melodies," Salt Lake City, ca. 1950.

_____. Sketches of original melodies, on sundry scraps of paper, Provo, Utah, and Salt Lake City, 1930-1971.

_____. "Song of Praise" and "Song of Prayer" (manuscript copies pasted over pages of the *MIA Music Supplement, 1967-68*), Salt Lake City, 1968.

_____. "The Theory of Music" (remarks aired over Radio KOVO), Provo, Utah, November 13, 1940.

_____. "Vita Sheet," Salt Lake City, ca. 1962.

Robertson, Naomi Nelson. "Memories of Our Marriage, 1925-1948," Salt Lake City, ca. 1978.

Robertson, Wanda. "Leroy Jasper Robertson" (written for *The History of Fountain Green*, Jesse Oldroyd, ed.), Salt Lake City, ca. 1981.

Roth, Feri. "How Many Are in Your Quartet? Memoirs of a Musician," Los Angeles, ca. 1967.

Schoenberg, Arnold. "Letter to Registrar, USC," Los Angeles, January 31, 1947.

Wheelwright, T. Pearse. "Thistle Root" (script for Utah Universities on the Air, KSL radio broadcast), Salt Lake City, November 14, 1947.

Whitesides, Renee Robertson. "Family Record Sheets," Kaysville, Utah, ca. 1978-1982.

LDS General Music Committee (GMC) Materials

The General Music Committee. *Concerning Music in the Church of Jesus Christ of Latter-day Saints*. Reprinted and updated. Salt Lake City: The General Music Committee, 1968.

Robertson, Leroy. "Agendas for GMC Meetings," Salt Lake City, 1962-1969.

_____. "Correspondence" which includes letters from LDS General Authorities to LJR; letters and reports from LJR to LDS General Authorities; letters from Robertson to Music Regional Representatives, and notes from GMC members to LJR, Salt Lake City, 1962-1969.

_____. "Hymns in Translation" (report to GMC), Salt Lake City, n.d.

_____. "Memo" (about pipe organs in LDS Church), Salt Lake City, n.d., but after meeting with Mark Garff, August 15, 1967.

_____. "Notes" (penciled in on "Program for Music Session of Regional Conferences, 1968"), Salt Lake City, late 1967.

_____. "Regional Meetings, January 13—May 11, 1968" (report to GMC and LDS General Authorities), Salt Lake City, summer 1968.

_____. "Reports to GMC," Salt Lake City, 1964-1969.

Robertson, Leroy, *et al.* "GMC Bulletins," Salt Lake City, 1967-1969.

_____. "GMC Communique," Salt Lake City, 1968.

_____. "Correspondence" which includes letters from LDS General Authorities to GMC; letters and reports from GMC to LDS General Authorities, and reports to GMC from Music Regional Representatives, Salt Lake City, 1962-1969.

_____. "GMC Handouts," Salt Lake City, 1962-1969.

_____. "List of recommended but little used hymns found in the LDS [1948/1950] hymnbook," Salt Lake City, n.d., but after 1962.

_____. "Material to be used in stake priesthood leadership meetings, 1969," Salt Lake City, 1968.

_____. "GMC Outlines," Salt Lake City, 1962-1969.

_____. "GMC Outlines for Stake Seminar Programs," Salt Lake City, ca. 1965.

_____. "Program for Music Sessions of Regional Conferences, 1969," Salt Lake City, 1968.

_____. "Program for Music Sessions of Regional Conferences, Regional Meetings—1969 Objectives," Salt Lake City, 1968.

_____. "Proposals of GMC pertaining to music leadership training programs," Salt Lake City, n.d.

Woodward, Ralph. "Preliminary recommended anthem list," Provo, Utah, n.d., but after 1962.

Printed Matter

Ballif, Moana. "*Trilogy*, A Great Symphony of Our Times." *Utah* 10 (January 1948): 22-25, 32-34.

Bennett, S. W. *Program Notes for [Robertson] Concerto for Violin and Orchestra.* New York: Vanguard Records, 1962.

Concert Programs, 1916-1996. Complete details of these countless concert programs can be found in the endnotes of the companion manuscript.

Davidson, Karen Lynn. *Our Latter-day Hymns: the Stories and Messages*. Salt Lake City: Deseret Book Co., 1988.

Durham, Lowell M. *Abravanel!* Salt Lake City: University of Utah Press, 1989.

_____. "On Mormon Music and Musicians." *Dialogue: A Journal of Mormon Thought* 3 (Summer 1968): 19-40.

Dye, Della L., and Karen Robertson Post. *Register of the Papers of Leroy J. Robertson*. Salt Lake City: Special Collections Department, University of Utah Libraries, 1972. Updated in 1980 by Marian Robertson Wilson.

"The Era Asks about Latter-day Saint Hymns" (interview with Leroy Robertson). *The Improvement Era* 70 (February 1967): 16-20.

Harrison, Conrad B. *Five Thousand Concerts*. Salt Lake City: Utah Symphony Society, 1986.

Hymns of the Church of Jesus Christ of Latter-day Saints. Salt Lake City: Deseret Book Co., 1985.

Hymns—The Church of Jesus Christ of Latter-day Saints. Salt Lake City: Deseret Book Co., 1948 and 1950.

Kremenliev, Boris. "Prominent Musicians of the West: Leroy Robertson." *Music of the West Magazine* 7 (January 1952): 6.

Krueger, Karl. *American Arts Orchestra*. New York: American Arts Orchestra Society, 1950.

_____. *Instrumental Music in 20th-century America*. New York: The Society for the Preservation of the American Musical Heritage (henceforth SPAMH), 1961.

_____. *Music in America*. New York: New Records, 1950.

_____. *Music in America*. New York: SPAMH, 1965.

Latter-day Saint Hymns. Salt Lake City: Deseret Book Co., 1927.

LeeMaster, Vernon J., et al. *Punch and Judy Syllabus*. Salt Lake City: Salt Lake City Board of Education, 1960.

Lundstrom, Harold. "Culture." In *Deseret, 1776-1976: A Bicentennial Illustrated History of Utah*, ed. W. B. Smart and H. A. Smith, 171-84. Salt Lake City: Deseret News Publishing Co., 1975.

MIA [Mutual Improvement Association] Music Supplement, 1965-1966. Salt Lake City: Church of Jesus Christ of Latter-day Saints, 1965.

Meredith, Madeline, ed. *Biographies of the Class of 1923 of the New England Conservatory, prepared for the Fiftieth Anniversary Celebration.* Boston, 1973.

Newbold, Vern F. "Leroy J. Robertson—A Sheepherder Turned Composer." *National Wool Grower* 69, no. 5 (May 1979):14-17.

One Hundred Years, 1830-1930, Centennial Celebration of the Organization of the Church of Jesus Christ of Latter-day Saints, Beginning April 6, 1930. Salt Lake City: Church of Jesus Christ of Latter-day Saints, 1930.

Press releases, local, national, and international, 1920-1995. Complete details of these countless of press releases can be found in the endnotes of the companion manuscript.

Robertson, Leroy. "Autobiography." *The New England Conservatory of Music Bulletin* 24, no. 4 (December 1947): 11-13.

_____. "Creativity in Music." In *Expanding Awareness of Creative Potentials Worldwide: Seventh World Conference on Gifted and Talented Children*, ed. Calvin W. Taylor, 124-29. Salt Lake City: Brain Talent-Powers Press, 1990.

_____. "Music Compositions Suitable for the LDS Worship Service." *Notes L.D.S.C.A. [Latter-day Saint Composers Association]* 2 (July 1971): 8-9.

_____. "Symphony from the Mountians, My Life and Musical Philosophy." *Musical Digest* 20 (January 1948): 8-9, 33.

Sing With Me, LDS Children's Songbook. Salt Lake City: Deseret Book Co., 1969.

Smith, Oliver R. "From Sagebrush to Symphony, Leroy J. Robertson—A Study in Achievement." *The Improvement Era* 51 (January 1948): 18-19, 62-63.

Spaeth, Sigmund, *et al. Annual Bulletin, National Association for American Composers and Conductors.* New York: National Association for American Composers and Conductors, 1943-1944.

Wilson, Marian Robertson. *Register of the Annotated Bibliography of the Compositions of Leroy J. Robertson.* Salt Lake City: Special Collections Department, University of Utah Libraries, 1985.

Index